The Fourth Oldie *Annual*

Edited by
Richard Ingrams

Quartet Books

This compilation first published by Quartet Books and Oldie Publications Ltd

Copyright © 1999 Oldie Publications Ltd

Text copyright © 1999 Oldie Publications Ltd

Illustrations copyright © Oldie Publications Ltd

The moral right of the authors and illustrators has been asserted.

Oldie Publications Ltd, 45/46 Poland Street, London W1V 4AU.

The publishers would like to thank the respective copyright owners for permission to include material in this volume.

A CIP Catalogue record for this book is available from The British Library.

Printed and bound in Great Britain at C P D (Wales) Ltd, Ebbw Vale.

ISBN 0 7043 8131 1

Cover illustration by Bob Wilson.

ACKNOWLEDGEMENTS

Thanks to all the authors, writers and cartoonists whose work appears in this book.

Thanks also to Marcus Turner, Cathy Knox, Eleanor Hill, Alex Price, Ben Tisdall and Sarah Vesey.

Introduction

SOME ARE BORN OLD, some achieve oldness, some have old age thrust upon them. But you don't have to be old to relish *The Oldie*. It appeals to everyone, wise old teenagers and skittish irrepressible men and women in their sixties and seventies who relish writing which is funny, irreverent, unusual, eccentric and grounded in good sense. It has more laughs in its cartoons than the *New Yorker* and such stars as Beryl Bainbridge, Miles Kington and Ruth Rendell. This collection contains the very best of *The Oldie*'s writing over the last two years.

Edited by Richard Ingrams, who made *Private Eye* an irreplaceable National Institution, *The Oldie* is the perfect antidote to an overdose of youth culture, or endless columns about the sex lives, trouble with partners, panic about the school holidays, what to do with Granny or, at their most desperate, the difficulty of writing a column, which fill up the blank spaces in the newspapers. *The Oldie* is the magazine for perceptive and amused grown-ups of any age.

JOHN MORTIMER

'I didn't understand a word of that. Could you dumb it back up a bit?'

Contents

'We spoil that dog.'

H.M.P DORCHESTER

WE'RE IN THE NICEST PRISONS GUIDE

Confessions of an oldie lag

Jailbird **Wilfred De'Ath** *on life inside at 60*

I was sent to prison for the first time in 1990 at the age of 53. Since then I have been inside half a dozen times, normally on remand, but once as a convicted prisoner in HMP Exeter. (I have also done porridge in Oxford and Winchester.) My offence has always been the same: obtaining services by deception, which in my case means staying at a hotel and not paying the bill.

As an oldie, I have generally been well treated by staff and other inmates. This is no less to do with my age than the fact that prisons are, contrary to myth, extremely polite places. Everyone treats everyone else with great respect because, basically, they

are rather frightened of you. After all, until you choose to tell them, they don't know what you are in for. It might be for murder or it might be for not paying your TV licence. When I reveal that I am in for fraud, my cellmates look rather disappointed. Possibly they were hoping to be banged up with a serial sex-killer or something. (In that case, I would ask to be put under Rule 43 for my own protection.)

The one time I was not well treated in jail was on admission to HMP Exeter in 1993 when I stupidly told the landing tea-orderly, who by long prison tradition allots cells to new arrivals, that I was an 'intellectual' and wanted a cell by myself. This was a fatal mistake, since every kind of education is regarded with derision in prison. Word spread like wildfire and people came from all over the jail to spit upon me. The 'tea-boat' orderly, a drugs smuggler who was reaching the end of a hefty stretch, literally spat into my cell every time he passed it (twice a day, delivering tea) until he left. Later, 'on the out', I ran into him in a pub and he was perfectly civil, having no need to maintain the machismo contempt for intellectuals. For one awful moment I thought he was going to buy me a drink.

I should add that I got very fed up with being spat upon twice a day and, at one point, made a rather feeble complaint to an officer. He hid behind my cell door, watched the spittle fly through the air, and then proposed to do absolutely nothing about it: 'You get that type in prison,' was his laconic, unhelpful comment.

As a generalisation, I would say that prison officers are even more degraded – and certainly use worse language – than the men they are paid to look after. Some of the younger ones are not too bad, having been trained in more humane methods, but I genuinely believe that the older ones go home and lock up their wives in the kitchen. There was a certain Mr Hunt (I expect you can imagine his nickname) who gave me a particularly bad time because I declined to shave every day (I have a very light beard). Growing a beard in prison is a serious offence because it means you must be planning to escape in disguise.

There are a number of myths about prison life and I should like to explode a few of them. The first is that time passes slowly. It doesn't. The structure of the regime (lunch

11

at 11, supper at 4, locked up for the night at 5 or 6) means that each day is a short one, so that a week passes very quickly indeed. This is true even of a relatively long sentence. Before you know it, you are back 'on the out' again and wondering how to turn an honest penny.

The second myth is that prison food is bad. It isn't. A cellmate of mine once called it 'airline food' and I think that is a good description, though, admittedly, it is not an airline I should wish to fly with. Some of the meals are not bad. Breakfast is particularly appetising if you can stomach it after a noisy night: cornflakes (porridge in winter), bacon and egg, and as much tea, toast, butter and marmalade as you can manage. I never had a good meal in prison, but I never had a really bad one.

Third myth: they lock you up for 23 hours a day. Not true, except in very dire emergencies. You are normally allowed out about five or six hours a day and you can get plenty of exercise – either just walking along the landings or in the yard. (As chaplain's orderly in Exeter, I was allowed the run of the whole prison, including the Rule 43s – sex offenders – and I was never confined to my cell.)

Fourth myth: prisons are hopelessly overcrowded and you are 'banged up' two, three and four to a cell. Again, not true in my experience. In fact, I have only ever had three cellmates at various times: one a young tearaway who regularly beat me at chess; one a pathetic alcoholic; the third an aggressive Scotsman, in for 'unlawful wounding', who was quite a nice chap when you got to know him. Most of the time, I have been given a cell to myself, doubtless because I am (dread word) an 'intellectual' and an oldie at that. I am a great user of prison libraries, which are excellent (as you can order books from the outside). I average 15 books a week while behind bars.

Biggest myth of all: prisons are understaffed. They are not, despite the zeal of the prison officers' union to propagate this

I stupidly told the landing tea-orderly that I was an 'intellectual' and wanted a cell by myself. This was a fatal mistake, since every kind of education is regarded with derision in prison

belief. I counted 17 officers around the hotplate at breakfast at HMP Winchester last time I was there, though, admittedly, it was wintertime. They are all on about £25,000 a year.

I am frequently asked by less literate prisoners to help them write sexy letters home to their wives and girlfriends (no easy task) and, more importantly, for those on remand, to help them prepare their pleas in mitigation for when they go to court. A very young, charming armed robber (first offence) asked me what I thought he might get. Judging it by a similar case I knew, I rashly said 'probation'. He got seven-and-a-half years. I guess he was unlucky with the judge. I was rather

concerned that he might kill me, but he was very pleasant and philosophical when he came back from court.

Perhaps I have given the impression that I don't mind being in prison. That would, to some extent, be true (the worst part about being caught up in the criminal justice system is having to hang around magistrates' courts – truly depressing places), although I don't think I could handle a very long sentence. The most I have done is four months, 'a shit and a shave', as they say.

British prisons are a curious mixture of public school, the army and a lunatic asylum – the latter ingredient in particular. Most of the people held in them are pathetic and inadequate and should never have been sent there.

I expect to go back soon (HMP Dorchester this time) and, while it would not be true to say that I am looking forward to it, I really don't mind very much. I feel quite safe in prison. And one's creditors cannot get at one.

Miles Kington

Country pursuits

March 1st, the day of the Countryside March, was obviously a good day to be in the country as everyone else was in London marching, so my wife and I decided to stay in the wilds of Wiltshire and enjoy the peace and quiet. I had actually toyed with the idea of going to London for the walk, but I couldn't settle on a good slogan for my placard. One message I had experimented with was: 'ALTHOUGH I AM WORRIED BY SOME ASPECTS OF FOX-HUNTING, I DO FEEL THAT THE COUNTRYSIDE IS GETTING A RAW DEAL ON THE WHOLE', but my wife felt it was too wishy-washy, so instead I tried 'I HATE LONDON' and 'VEGETARIANS FOR FOX-HUNTING' and 'LOOKING FOR A REALLY NICE COUNTRY B&B? JUST STOP ME AND ASK FOR DETAILS!' but still none of them really seemed snappy enough.

So instead we went for a walk in the country, just the two of us, no, the three of us, because we have recently acquired a spaniel, the idea being that it will give our ten-year-old son something to look after and be responsible for. Madness, of course: we now have a dog and a son to look after, both of whom conspire against us. But the son doesn't like walking nearly as much as the dog does, so we left him behind and took the dog. At this time of year you can leave him off the lead quite a lot, because most of the cows and sheep are elsewhere (please note how much like a countryman I am trying to sound) and the fields are empty, except for other people with half-trained dogs, but you learn to keep your eyes open for sheep in case your dog has to be put on the lead at a moment's notice.

Well, we had a good walk, from Iford Manor to Farleigh Hungerford Castle across the fields and back along the bridle path, with the banks beginning to be full of primroses and the last of the snowdrops drooping and dying (still trying to sound like a countryman, you notice). We finally got back to the car and were driving home along the A36 when we noticed a farmer rounding up sheep in a field with the aid of a single dog. You don't get much free entertainment in the country, so we stopped to watch, and indeed it was very impressive the way the single dog rounded up all the 60-odd sheep and herded them up the ramp into the big lorry backing onto the field....

All except one. One sheep, bigger or braver or brasher than the rest, squeezed past the van and out into the lane, where it ran away, down towards us.

'Better stop it,' I said to my wife, and we stood threateningly with arms stretched wide to drive it back. It took absolutely no notice and ran straight past us onto the main road, where it started running down the A36 towards Bath.

'Better get after it,' I said to the wife, and jumped into the car, leaving her behind, to follow it.

The sheep had clearly never been on a main road before because it trotted straight down the white line in the middle, which might have been fatal, had not all the cars in both directions clearly been driven by country dwellers who respectfully slowed down to about 5mph. Within a minute there was a mighty tail-back in both directions, as nobody seemed willing to overtake the sheep.

This might have grown into a snarl-up big enough to make the local radio bulletins had not the sheep decided to dive into a hedge on the left just before the turn-off to Hinton Charterhouse. It seemed quite happy behind the hedge, so I turned round to report back to the farmer, but he was already running up the road behind me, followed by my wife.

Reader, have you ever helped a farmer catch a sheep which is attempting to make a new life for itself between a hedge and a fence? Here are some tips. Use a little gentleness, and a lot of force. Wear gloves, otherwise your hands will be lacerated on the hedge, as mine were. Bring a belt to put round the sheep's neck, otherwise it won't come with you. When you find it between your knees, put your arms round its neck and hang on for dear life. When the farmer says, 'I don't know how I'm going to get it back to the field', say, 'You can put it into the back of my car if you like' and when he accepts your kind offer, do remember to get your frisky new spaniel out of the back of your car first, and ask your wife to look after it. And when you try to get the sheep in the back of the car, make sure the farmer lifts the other end, because they're bloody heavy things, and they don't half struggle.

So, if you were driving down the A36 between Bath and Warminster on Sunday March 1st, and you saw a slow-moving five-door Saab with the back door open, and a farmer sitting in the boot with a sheep in his lap, looking like a country version of the Duke and Queen going down the Mall in their coach, that was me in the front, chauffeuring, hands scratched to pieces but feeling strangely satisfied.

Yes, I reckon I did my bit for the countryside on March 1st.

BEWARE OF THE BREATH

The Economist

Winifred Foley *on Madame Thrifty,*
the French version

She was a Parisian widow in her fifties, a neat little figure with the sharp, beady eyes of a mouse and its quick darting movements; a model for Beatrix Potter.

She had the scrounger instincts of a rodent, and her two ruling passions were frugality and her little grandson: she practised the first for the sake of the second. Her only child, Marcel, had come to England, got a job as a grill chef in a West End hotel and married a frail, almost useless, cockney wife, who – surprisingly – bore him a beautiful baby boy, Pierre, now the object of their adoration and ambition.

Pierre must have a good education and a secure future, not attainable on Marcel's humble wages, a good percentage of which went on the rent of a ground-floor flat behind a jeweller's shop in a dingy Paddington side street. Rigid economy had to be practised so that Pierre could be enrolled as a pupil at the Lycée in South Kensington. Luckily, this did not involve a school uniform, so his grandmère used to raid the dustbins that belonged to the flats around and stuff any discarded clothing and other useful objects into the capacious bags she carried. After sorting the garments into piles, she would unpick them, cut out all the usable pieces, wash and press them, and make them up into clothes for Pierre. Smart little two-piece suits were made from old trousers, the jackets lined with cotton or silk cut from ragged blouses and jumpers. Hand-knitted garments were unpicked and the wool washed, dried and re-knitted into socks, gloves, pullovers, hats, etc. Unusable scraps were bagged up, to make a few coppers from the rag-and-bone shop.

The hot water needed for so much laundering cost nothing, thanks to a little iron stove in the kitchen which burnt anything and heated up the boiler. Grandmère had an old pram in which she collected cardboard, old shoes and boots, scrap wood cadged or picked up where house alterations were in progress, and the odd knob of coal dropped from a coal cart.

The nearby market was another of grandmère's favourite haunts. She was there as soon as the stallholders dismantled their barrows, and left before the street cleaners arrived. Her hands were as sharp and quick as a lizard's tongue, picking out partly rotten fruit and vegetables which had been thrown on the ground. The rotten residue from her gleanings went into the compost bucket. This she used to enrich the soil they brought home after taking Pierre to the park. The narrow piece of courtyard that went with the flat was filled with a motley collection of containers in which grandmère grew her herbs – sage, mint, chives and thyme – and even tomatoes and runner beans, garnishes for her rescued vegetables and the slices of steak, ham, bacon and lamb which Marcel brought home, wrapped around his ankles in the special socks, with strong elasticated tops, which grandmère knitted from her scrounged woollies. Every Saturday she put in a few hours serving at the busy fish stall, and took the earnings in fish – at cost price of course.

Sometimes she walked as far as Marble Arch, eyes down for anything of value that might have been dropped – including, on one occasion, a ten-shilling note. She then went to a basement café called the Restful Tray at Marble Arch. The free toilet and washroom was at street level and, after refreshing herself, grandmère went down the carpeted stairs to the huge self-service cafeteria. After collecting a tray, two cups, a saucer and plate, she left the queue and found an empty space at a table. As soon as a customer left she collected up the left-over milk and sugar, as well as partly used pats of butter, untouched biscuits and sometimes whole bread rolls. It took her some time to fill her two cups with milk, find a teapot or two with the contents still warm in the bottom. Londoners are blasé about the eccentrics in their midst, and the overworked table-cleaning staff ignored her. Invigorated by her free repast, grandmère had the strength to carry her bags of pickings home and not waste coppers on bus fares. To work for someone else was unthinkable. She was proud of being a self-employed entrepreneur in the waste recycling business. It paid off. Pierre's expensive education got him a good job in the Foreign Office. Mission accomplished, grandmère – much to the relief of her daughter-in-law – took herself and her frugal habits back to her beloved Paris.

East
of Islington

In a departure from her usual column, **Sam Taylor** *writes about her beloved dog, Poopy, who was fatally run over on Christmas Eve*

POOPY DIDN'T OPEN her Christmas stocking this year. It still sits at the back of her food cupboard, waiting for me finally to get up the courage to dispose of it, a last reminder of her precious little life. On Christmas Eve we had travelled to Dungeness for the festivities, accompanied by Willy and his walker. It was midafternoon when we arrived. We didn't have enough fuel for the holiday period and the weather was filthy. We needed desperately to go to the shops, or at least we felt at the time that we needed desperately to go to the shops. The dogs, recently released from the constraints of the city, were off running after rabbits, glad to be back, surrounded by exciting smells with the freedom to explore. We were anxious to get the last of our chores done. Poopy and Willy weren't answering our calls. Finally we made the decision to nip to the shops – they often roamed out for a couple of hours; we'd left them before, and so we jumped in the car and went. It was a decision I will regret for the rest of my life.

It was teatime by the time we returned, and it was raining. Willy turned up, but no Poopy. It just wasn't like her. I searched everywhere, screaming her name, willing her to come bounding into view. As it got darker I became convinced she had been hurt and was lying somewhere. I phoned the police – nothing. The mounting anxiety was overwhelming. Finally a call came. She had been hit by a car nearly five miles away and had been dead on arrival at the vet's. He said she hadn't suffered. I realise now that she had returned to the house, seen that we weren't there and, because she often worried, darted off down the track in search of us. We must have passed her on the way back. We, like the driver of the car that hit her, didn't see her because of the rain.

Poopy came to me after I rescued her from a home where she was forced to live in a kitchen, without ever being taken to the park. We lived happily together for four years and my life now feels empty without her. I buried her in the garden at Dungeness so that she can still chase the rabbits and asked God to look after her and find her a good home. He took my close friend's mother at Christmas, too. I pray he puts them together.

R.I.P. DEAR Poopy

Colin & Colette Clark

Colin and Colette Clark, twin son and daughter of Sir Kenneth Clark, and brother and sister of Alan, in conversation with **Naim Attallah**. *Portrait by* **Jane Bown**

Colin, your memoir, Younger Brother, Younger Son, *recounts your life in relation to the two men in whose shadow you have lived: your father, the art historian Sir Kenneth Clark, and your brother, Alan Clark, MP. Would any other approach have been possible?*

I think I could have done the autobiography more amusingly if I hadn't had to relate it to those two famous men. But the only way my publisher would consider taking on the book was if I took that approach. Because of this, I felt slightly overshadowed by them even as I was writing.

Colette, if you were writing your autobiography, would it be on the same basis?

Not at all. Maybe I would have been influenced by my father, but not remotely by my elder brother. Colin would, of course, come into it a great deal – I adored him and he adored me, in fact we were almost the same person for a while – but I don't feel overshadowed by him.

Colin, it would be strange, or uncommonly virtuous, for someone to live in the shadow of others and not mind at all.

It would, but I do mind, and I always did. It gives me a lot of pleasure to read in the *Sunday Times* that my book was not one which either Alan or my father could ever have written. It gives me great satisfaction when I'm compared favourably to Alan.

You say that a younger brother and a younger son can be free. In what does this freedom consist, would you say?

I don't feel I have to stick to the same conventions as they did. Although my brother likes to pretend he's a renegade writer and politician and generally a rebel, he definitely feels that he wants to continue in the same line as my father. He desperately wants to be Lord Clark, for example. I didn't feel the same constraint; I felt I could go to America without really looking back at all, and for almost 20 years I really forgot about my brother and my father.

Would you say that being the son of a famous father and having Alan as a brother has advantages?

There are definitely advantages in being the son of a famous man, because then people are much more prepared to talk to you and listen to you and read what you've written. I don't think there are many advantages in being the brother of Alan, but of course it's fun. He's an amazing character and I greatly enjoy his company – although two hours is the absolute maximum I can stand, and even that can be pretty terrifying. I've not yet seen any material advantages.

Colette, you and Colin shared those early years together as twins – is that something that stays with you forever?

We're totally dissimilar twins, and not only in appearance, but we're terribly close as people, even though we don't have the same attitudes to life at all. It is incredibly important to me to have Colin, and we meet each other virtually every day.

Colin says that your mother was not close to you. It's difficult to imagine a mother giving affection to one twin and withholding it from the other.

Yes, but she adored Colin and thought I was evil, and when Colin tried to protect me she would be even angrier with me. Poor Colin had to spend his entire life defending me, and protecting me from her.

Colin, at the age of seven, you were both sent away to boarding schools. One imagines most twins would be devastated by a sudden separation after years of being together.

I missed Colette very much, but I didn't miss the comforts of home life. I was glad to get away from Alan and I was glad to get away from my parents because life with them could be pretty tempestuous.

I was interested in what you wrote about Arthur, the gardener's son, whose family was so poor that on Christmas Day his parents filled his stocking with potatoes. Did it not occur to you that perhaps Arthur's father was underpaid by your father?

No, it never occurred to me, but I did feel sorry for him. My parents only ever thought about getting the right cook or the right maid, and when it came to paying, I don't even remember them thinking about it very much. They were completely divorced from that particular aspect of things.

What are your views on the English class system?

It's one of my pet hates. I see absolutely no reason at all why some people should be considered above others just because they have inherited some land. I would even go so far as to say that, once the Queen has moved on, I think the British monarchy should be abolished.

You say in your book that in order to work

in films you had to be yourself, but that you separated yourself from the background which shaped you and which included people of power and influence. Was it as simple as you imply?

The great thing I had when I went into the film business was a sort of self-confidence with important people. I was not overawed by Laurence Olivier or by Marilyn Monroe – with whom I worked on T*he Prince and the Showgirl* – or by any of the people I worked with. I felt I could just say anything to them, and they tended to respond to that confidence.

To what extent were your family connections useful to you?

Family influence got me an introduction to Olivier, but it certainly didn't get me my job on the film – that was my own ingenuity – and the fact that I got on very well with Olivier and Vivien Leigh was nothing to do with my father. In fact Olivier really didn't like my father and my father didn't like Olivier. And to have worked for three years with the Oliviers was a much better start for someone working in showbusiness than being the son of Sir Kenneth Clark. But certainly when I went to New York and started making a film about artists, the fact that I could ring them up and say I was the son of Sir Kenneth Clark was a huge help.

Colette, did you benefit from your background?

Yes, in the sense that I also met many distinguished people. I wanted to go into the world of ballet and opera, and through my parents I met people like Frederick Ashton, Margot Fonteyn and so on, and later they became less my parents' friends and more mine.

What was your ambition as a young girl?

I expect my ambition was to get married, but I never have.

> **People often ask why my father left everything to Alan, and the answer is very simple: it's because Alan told him to leave everything to Alan**

Why have you never married?

I don't know. I was thinking about it only recently. I believe it must have been in some way predestined. When I was very young, 17 or something, I was already falling in love non-stop, but I remember clearly saying to my father, 'You know, papa, I don't think I'm ever going to get married.' It just came to me like that, but papa said, 'Don't you, dear? That would be very chic.' Of course he thought I would be married by the time I was 21.

You have a son in his early thirties. Being a single mother 30 years ago must have been extremely difficult, to say the least. How did you cope, and what was the reaction of your parents?

My parents behaved very well. Their Bohemian side was their best side; they weren't conventional at all, and so they were very supportive, but they were also quite shocked and told everybody in hushed tones. There was a great debate about whether to call me Mrs, and they spoke to the bank manager and told him I had to have Mrs on all my bank letters. In those days quite a number of my friends had servants and they all called me Mrs Clark – indeed they still do.

Why didn't you marry the father of the child?

He was already married. It was a tremendous trauma at the time because I was very much in love with him, and have been ever since. It was a conscious decision: well, if I can't have the father, I'm jolly well going to have the son. And my son turned out to be the most wonderful person, an absolutely golden character from the beginning.

Colin, you suggest that Colette's admiration for your father was unqualified by any need to escape from his shadow and that as a result she has led a very successful life. Do you mean material or emotional success?

Material success has nothing to do with it – Colette has led a modest and careful life and never sought material success. I mean intellectual success. She has continued to regard as important people whom my parents thought of as important. She thinks in terms of art and literature and ballet and opera and music, and those were the things my father was involved in.

Colette, do you see your twin brother as a success?

He hasn't been as successful as he should have been because he has never stuck at anything long enough. I think he was scared in ways I was not. It's much harder for a boy to have a famous father than it is for a girl. Of course, Alan pretends not to be bothered by it, but he is, more than Colin in fact. Alan is always inventing himself, and he also seems to invent my father. I mean he talks of a great landowner, shooting, fishing, hunting – he seems to forget who our father was.

Colin: Alan and I were both told implicitly by our mother and father that we could never, ever match up to our father. The idea that I might presume to talk to him about art wasn't considered even possible, but actually around the time my father was making his television programme *Civilisation* I knew much more about modern art than he did. I'd made films with great artists like Warhol and Lichtenstein, and he didn't really understand those characters, but we could never have discussed it. Alan and I had to find things that were not directly comparable to anything my father was doing. Even when Alan became an MP my mother considered it preposterous for him to hold that position, and my father's attitude was the same.

Colin, Sir Kenneth's infidelities caused your mother much suffering, but you speak of your own affairs much more light-heartedly, as though no harm was done. Do you actually believe this?

Well, people were hurt, but my infidelities were always, or mostly, outside marriage. And now I've been married for 15 years, and I wouldn't dream of being unfaithful to my wife, not for a split second. I am 100 per cent in love with my wife, just as much as I was when I first set eyes on her, and that's a real joy. If she came into the room now I wouldn't be able to take my eyes off her.

Even though your mother had a problem with alcohol and became a drug addict, you still say of your father's affairs: 'Well, who could blame him?' Why did you exonerate your father completely?

What I said was, who could blame him for enjoying the company of a beautiful and intelligent lady? That's slightly different.

But he did more than enjoy…

Yes, with some he did have affairs. It's difficult to say which came first, my mother becoming neurotic or my father having affairs. I tend to think they happened pretty much at the same time. As she became more neurotic, he began to discover he was very attractive to the ladies. And as he began to be attracted by them, and she caught him, she became more neurotic.

Rumour has it that your mother also had affairs.

I think she probably did. They were both very childlike when they got married. Father didn't have any knowledge of the world, he'd just been a sort of scholar and an aesthete, and my mother came from a big family in Ireland, and didn't really know about anything much.

You and Alan share your father's love of women. Do you believe you inherited the

promiscuity gene, or were you searching for a love denied in childhood?

Definitely the former. When I had affairs, I was never searching for love, I was searching for someone to love, someone to worship and adore, a perfect sexual partner. I had lovely sexual relationships with women, but I was not in love with them.

Colette, did you disapprove of your brothers' behaviour?

No, I'm afraid not. I disapprove of Alan as a person, but not of his sex life especially.

Colin, to the outsider it seems very puzzling that Alan inherited the whole of your mother's estate, and then your father's. This must surely have been wounding to you, though you offer no reproach. What are your feelings about it now?

People often ask why my father left everything to Alan, and the answer is very simple: it's because Alan told him to leave everything to Alan. He visited my father all the time when he was old and said, 'I'm the eldest son – you've got to leave everything to me,' and so my father, who was very obedient in a strange way, did just what he was told. I was living in America, and Colette is far too modest.

Colette: It was typical of Alan, typical.

Colin: On the other hand, it was a little bit of a surprise that my mother left everything to Alan, and nothing to either of us.

Colette: She wrote the most beautiful letters to us and devoted half her will to saying that Sammie, my son, must be treated in exactly the same way as her other grandchildren, as if he were legitimate, but in fact she didn't leave him anything.

Colin: Alan always steals a march over everybody. Don't ask us how he does it; he just does it. He's a conman and a genius. He's so persuasive, and he can see what other people are thinking – that's his great talent.

Colette: He's up to any trick. He doesn't give up.

A story of adultery and revenge in colonial Africa by **Donald MacIntosh**

Last orders for the Morleys

The White Man's Grave was for bachelors. Of that, I was convinced. Its drenching humidity and febrile swamps played havoc with delicate constitutions, so, apart from a few leathery old missionaries and the odd roving eccentric like Mary Kingsley, most white women of that colonial era steered well clear of the place.

However, gradual improvements in the field of medicine saw a consequent increase in the number of married couples arriving on 'the Coast' to see out the last years of the Empire. But it remained an uneasy association: lack of proper schooling facilities meant that, as children grew up, wives had to spend an ever-increasing proportion of each tour back home in the United Kingdom, leaving their husbands behind to fend for themselves as best they might.

It was not an ideal situation, but most couples consoled themselves with the thought that the financial rewards compensated for the separations. On the debit side, it was a situation that created obvious problems even in those more disciplined times.

The husband feeling the pinch of a long parting was expected to grin and bear it. In practice, either he got rid of his surplus energy on the tennis and squash courts when the day's toil was over, or he drank himself into an alcoholic stupor before bedtime.

Only the most foolhardy would have dared take unto himself a mistress. Such libertinage, while considered almost *de rigueur* in the French colonies, would have been regarded as highly improper by the British administration, especially if the lady in question happened to be an indigène. Being suspected of 'going native' was the surest way of finding yourself on the first boat home.

The Morleys had never had to face this dilemma. Those best acquainted with them knew that the sanctity of this particular union could never be disrupted by sexual desire for each other, far less for anyone outside the constraints of their marital vows. They were just too upper-crust. An archetypal colonial from the crown of his ridiculous topee to the soles of his calfskin mosquito boots, George Morley had been posted to our delightful little town in the hinterland as bank manager many years previously and he had no wish ever to leave it. Here, he was king.

More correctly, here, he was prince consort. His wife was the undisputed monarch. An unabashed snob who dominated every social function for miles around, Penelope Morley terrified everyone, including her husband.

Her absences from the Coast were mercifully frequent and prolonged. One would have thought that her husband would have been glad to see the back of her, but, in truth, he looked a lost and lonely figure without her. He spent a lot more time than usual in the European Club on those occasions, drinking steadily and telling interminable stories about banking to anyone within earshot. Most felt sorry for him, but rarely sorry enough to invite him to dinner. It always seemed such a waste of an evening to have to entertain such a thundering bore.

I suppose that none of us would have become privy to the last chapter of the Morley saga had not Ben the Bar confided in me. Ben was the senior steward at the European Club, and he was liked and respected by everyone. Everyone, that is, except the Morleys. During his spell as chairman of the Club some years previously, George Morley had been involved in a campaign to have Ben sacked for some trifling misdemeanour. Ben had survived, but one of his numerous brothers also employed as a barman had not. Although he was smart enough to realise that Penelope had instigated the campaign, Ben was a Tiv, and Tivs never forget a grievance. Years after everyone else had forgotten the incident, Ben's habitual joviality would evaporate noticeably whenever the Morleys entered the Club premises.

I had been away from the area for some time, and on my return I called at the Club. Ben the Bar looked inordinately pleased

Penelope Morley was the undisputed monarch. An unabashed snob who dominated every social function for miles around

with life, so I asked him if he would care to share his good news.

'The Morleys have gone!' he informed me.

'Gone!' I exclaimed, startled. 'Gone where?'

'Home to England. For good!' he replied smugly.

It was early in the evening and I was, as yet, the only customer. I bought him a beer and settled down to listen to his story.

Penelope's last act before departing on vacation had been to have one of her more vitriolic contretemps with their two domestic staff, her long-suffering cook and houseboy. When Morley returned from the metropolis after seeing his wife off, it had been to an empty house. Tired of her tyranny, the servants had fled. Morley had hired as houseboy the first lad to come to him with a decent reference.

His choice of cook was less conventional. George Morley had succumbed at last to the temptations of the Coast.

Comfort, for that was her name, took charge of the house. She was an excellent cook and she produced wild and exotic dishes from his kitchen that Penelope had probably never even heard of. She was a pretty little thing, too, and she taught him wild and exotic things in bed that Penelope had most certainly never heard of.

There was an effervescence about her that seemed to brighten the darkest corners of his gloomy old house. She and the new houseboy had hit it off instantly. They sang as they attended their domestic chores and the sound of their singing followed Morley down the verandah steps each morning. As he drove sedately through the town to work, it was a fact that his thoughts were invariably focused less upon the banking problems of the forthcoming day than upon the happy turbulence that had so engaged him in the Morley four-poster during much of the preceding night. George Morley, in other words, had never known such contentment in his life.

The bombshell that was to blow his Elysium apart caught him quite unprepared. It came via a cable from his Lagos office. Penelope had arrived on the Coast and was on her way by hired car to see him. Someone had blown the gaff on him.

George Morley had never been regarded as a man of action. Even to his few

R.G.

admirers, words such as 'phlegm' and 'inertia' came most readily to mind when describing him. Not, it has to be recorded, in this instance. Now, he was transmogrified. He left his office like a ferreted rabbit. Seconds later he was streaking for home with that frantic urgency best exhibited by erring husbands the world over when attempting to extricate themselves from similarly unpleasant predicaments. He made it by a whisker. Comfort and her accoutrements had just been shovelled out of the back door when Penelope arrived at the front, travel-stained and bristling with suspicion. She had received an anonymous letter to the effect that he had been misbehaving, she informed him, and she had decided to pay him an unscheduled visit.

It was a tricky moment, but Morley had covered his tracks well. Not a trace of his mistress remained and, as he had kept her existence a secret from the outside world, none could betray him. A modest sweetener secured the houseboy's silence and the crisis was averted. Dreary normality returned to the Morley household.

Then Penelope had one of her predictable rows with the houseboy. It was, as usual, about something trivial – the incorrect folding of napkins or some such nonsense – but it could hardly have happened at a less opportune moment: the touring

Comfort taught him wild and exotic things in bed that his wife Penelope had never heard of

British ambassador and his lady were among the many interested spectators. As her tantrum reached its crescendo, the houseboy stalked out, pausing at the door to fire the fatal broadside: 'Old woman, you are no bloody gentleman. This was a greatly happiness house in your absence when the black Mrs Morley was here.'

'And that,' concluded Ben, 'is why the Morleys have now retired to England after long and faithful service on the Coast.'

I gazed pensively at him. 'I wonder who could have sent that letter to Mrs Morley?'

Ben's expression was that of a man quite untroubled by his conscience. 'The mills of God grind slowly, sir,' he intoned softly.

'Ben,' I said, 'you're a cunning, vindictive old rascal.'

'Yes, sir,' he replied imperturbably. 'That's what my youngest brother tells me. He claims that it runs in the family.'

'Your brother?'

'Yes, sir. Mr Morley's houseboy.'

The silence that followed was broken only by the steady CHUNK… CHUNK… CHUNK… of the ceiling fan. Ben's eyes were dreamy as he lifted his beer mug. 'My little sister keeps emphasising the value of strong family bonds. You must meet her, sir. She is a good cook and she is very pretty.'

I MUST BE one of the few men alive to have helped Evelyn Waugh into the bath. In 1949 he came up to St Andrews as the guest of the University Literary Society and of the Roman Catholic Society. He had agreed to address their joint meeting on the subject of Christian influences on the fiction of G K Chesterton, Graham Greene and Ronald Knox. He had similarly lectured, as a penance, at various American universities.

Waugh's crowded programme dictated a date in mid-January. The secretaries of the two societies could not book him for a different month without jeopardising his acceptance of the invitation, though they were aware that Rusack's Hotel, the Grand and the Royal would all be shut. Waugh had insisted that a large, comfortable bedroom with private bath be retained for him, and that the accommodation should command an interesting view.

The secretary of the Literary Society reserved an attractive bedroom at Mason's Golf Hotel over the Valley of Sin, the famous approach to the 18th green of the Old Course. The windows looked out over the North Sea and the coastal shipping into Dundee; but, alas, there were no private bathrooms.

Waugh's insistence on a private bathroom presented the president of the Catholic Society with a problem which he solved by persuading me to enlist a suitable 'tub team', while he canvassed a sympathetic Fife castle-owner for the loan of a comfortable hip-bath.

To make up the tub team, I chose a future inspector in military history at Sandhurst, a prospective novelist, a recently demobilised Gunner officer and a kindly Roman Catholic geologist. The five of us dressed in clean white flannels and floppy hats. We awaited Waugh on the hotel landing, unaware that he detested cricket. The housekeeper had found us each two large, gleaming, copper ewers to

'Well done,' said Waugh. 'You have brought me some private soap. I never use public soap – all those skin diseases'

Evelyn Waugh

carry the hot water from a tap on the same floor as the Waugh bedroom.

On arrival at Mason's, Waugh was preceded up the narrow staircase by a bossy Scottish porter whose day job was caddying. Waugh was silent and unmistakable. Pink-faced, he was wearing a tweed suit, a deerstalker and a deprecatory expression. We, the bathing team, were ready for him with our towels and sponges, and meticulously called him 'Sir'.

Waugh did nothing to disguise his habitual asperity until I gave him some mollifying dry sherry. 'Very good manzanilla,' he remarked on tasting it, 'bring me another glass in an hour.' Meanwhile, the future Sandhurst instructor had carefully placed the hip-bath by the hissing gas fire and was floating a celluloid duck in it, which Waugh regarded sternly, without comment. The novelist-to-be, opening Waugh's modest overnight case, deferentially enquired: 'Dinner jacket or tails, Sir?'

'You'll find a dark suit under the dressing-gown,' Waugh icily replied. He covered himself with the gown while preparing, obstructively, to enter the hip-bath, led by the Gunner officer and myself.

He visibly thawed, however, as he lowered himself into the hot water. At the arrival of the geologist, who was thoughtfully unwrapping a bar of Lifebuoy, Waugh became almost genial. 'Well done,' he said. 'You have brought me some private soap. I never use public soap – all those skin diseases...'

When Waugh was dry and dressed, and we had removed and drained the hip-bath, he drank his second glass of Tio Pepe and told us to order a cab.

During his lecture he said a few patronising words about the university of St Andrews but spoke warmly, though briefly, of Chesterton, Greene and Knox. He devoted most of his time to *Brideshead Revisited*, which was then enjoying enormous sales. Afterwards, a young lecturer in the English department remarked that he had greatly enjoyed *Put Out More Flags*.

He asked Waugh a question about Basil Seal. Waugh replied that, frankly, he had forgotten writing the novel and that he had never read it. Mercilessly put down, the young lecturer left at the first available opportunity. Waugh's post-lecture conversation was less than sparkling. We felt he was keeping his observations for sophisticated friends, rather than giving them to undergraduates.

David Freeman

Driving in Europe lost much of its thrill when internal borders ceased to exist. Continental lorry driving, once the preserve of adventurers and bigamists, now seems terribly tame. Never rich enough to practice bigamy, it was a misplaced sense of adventure that led me to become a *routier* on the Côte d'Azur at a time when crossing a border still promised a whiff of drama.

One of my jollier border experiences was thanks to a company named Tooth Removals. If the significance of its logo was lost on the eponymous founder of the company, it did not escape the attention of other truckers. Tooth operated from a part of Fulham much favoured by drunken ex-mercenaries and minor public schoolboys who had gone off the rails. He was permanently in a rage – hardly surprising when you consider the human resources he chose to employ. Many of his drivers were Australian, and most seemed to have something in their past that they wanted to hide. More than one of them had been taken away in handcuffs by the police. They all fiddled their fuel chits. Some even sold batteries and spare tyres from Tooth's lorries, claiming that light-fingered Frenchmen had stolen them while they were asleep.

One of my jobs was to promote public awareness of the company. Tooth paid me extra to drive one of the few serviceable lorries at his command up and down the Croisette in Cannes as a kind of mobile billboard. Once, during the Film Festival, I handed out Tooth Removals flyers to a clutch of bare-breasted starlets, one of whom was positively offended. 'Zere is nossing wrong wiz my teeth,' she hissed, and covered her breasts for good measure, in case I should try to remove them instead. This practice is now known as 'Brand Building'. In reality, public perception of Tooth's brand stemmed from the seemingly unending series of catastrophes that befell his drivers. One succeeded in destroying most of Lady Rothermere's furniture when he repaired to a drinking den without checking that the handbrake was on. The lorry rolled down a steep incline and crashed into a conservatory where her possessions were neatly assembled and waiting to be wrapped. This did the driver little good. He was already in Tooth's bad

books, having destroyed another lorry (and its load) the week before. The lorry had been 12ft high, until he took it at 60 miles an hour under a bridge in Beaulieu that was only 10ft. The result was a rather fetching convertible with matchwood trim.

Working for Tooth was agreeable on the whole. I lived in Antibes, parked next door to Graham Greene, through whose door women would come and go at all hours of the day and night. I slept in my lorry; Angus, a Scottish driver whose truck had been destroyed in yet another mishap, slept underneath it, face up, under the exhaust pipe. Angus would often wake me as he banged his head on the chassis, after crawling back from a session in a local 'boite'. In the mornings he would not wake up until I started the engine.

Bored with Cannes, Nice and Juan les Pins, I decided it was time to spearhead a marketing drive in the Alps. This proved more interesting, especially when I wedged Tooth's lorry between a couple of them and had to be removed by *pompiers* with cranes and cutters. After that I did my best to stay out of trouble, with varying degrees of success. One Saturday afternoon, driving up the coast road from Nice towards Menton and Ventimiglia, I found myself even drunker and more carefree than usual, having lunched in Cagnes-sur-Mer on pastis 'Tomate' and rough wine from the Var. On rounding a bend in the road, I was absolutely delighted to be confronted with 38 pairs of Spandex cycling shorts. They contained 38 female bottoms of a variety of shapes and sizes. They were all pedalling standing up, wiggling in an unself-conscious, French, kind of way. It was at this point that the pastis took a hold, and before you could say 'Alan Clark', I had stopped the lorry and offered them all a lift. 'To hell with Tooth!' I raved, 'and to hell with Removals!' Their leader was a handsome girl in her twenties, moist and somewhat out of breath. My mind was made up. I would seduce as many of them as possible before Monday.

'Bonjour, Mademoiselle!' I slurred in finest 'plume de ma tante' French. 'Je roule vide… would you and your friends like to… get in the back?' Suddenly, I was Leslie Phillips. They unanimously agreed to climb into the yawning cavity of Tooth's loadspace. On closer inspection, I noticed

that some of the girls were decidedly muscular. Several were heroically hirsute and had Zapata moustaches. But I was undeterred. I loaded 36 girls in the back and made small talk with two in the front as we headed for the Italian border. Where were they from?

'From Beaulieu, Monsieur,' the leader replied. And did they all belong to a cycling club? 'Mais oui, d'accord, Monsieur,' their leader replied. 'We are the Lesbian Cycling Club of Alpes Maritimes!'

This came as something of a blow. They were on their way to their annual 'Weekend in the Saddle', an international gathering for Dykes on Bikes from all over Europe. Strapping girls from Greece, Bulgaria, Germany and Poland were toiling away in

The Sapphic Cyclists of Beaulieu

Christopher Hamilton *confesses to a failed attempt to drive a lorry-load of lesbians into Italy. Illustrations by* **Geoff Waterhouse**

25

East
of Islington

Sam Taylor *begins the unexpectedly difficult task of giving a home to a dog*

sweaty Spandex as we spoke, heading our way. That evening, she explained, a sleepy and unsuspecting Ventimiglia would find itself the throbbing crux of the lesbike world. So entranced was I by all of this that I omitted to turn off down the loop road for vehicles not destined for the Italian Republic. In those days it was illegal to cross from one European state into another in an empty lorry without special paperwork. This oversight would spell trouble.

A sullen Neapolitan customs officer slouched over to my lorry and raised his hand. 'Dogomenda… Documenti!' he said.

'I'm terribly sorry, officer, but I missed the turning. I have no documents. Can I go back into France?'

'Impossible! This is a commercial vehicle! You must have documents! What is in the back of your lorry?'

'Well,' I said, 'actually… I don't think you are going to believe this…'

'Tell me.'

'OK… 38 French lesbians.'

'Trent-otto lesbiche francese? I see.' He waved at a colleague. 'Gianni! Come over here. We have a comedian here. Uno comico. Now signore, tell my colleague what you told me. What is in the back of your lorry?'

'Thirty-eight French lesbians.'

They pulled in their pasta guts, unbuttoned their holsters and sneered. 'Open up!'

No sooner had I thrown open the back doors than the two Italians yelped in stereo falsetto. My cargo was even hotter and sweatier than before, for the party had begun, all over my packing blankets.

'Get them out of here!! Non vogliamo piu' lesbiche in Italia!! Turn the lorry round!! Immediatamente!! You must leave Italy!! Subito!!'

Doors were slammed shut, whistles were blown, conflicting orders given, barriers raised and lowered, holsters buttoned and unbuttoned as I climbed back into my cab. But the girls were not to be so easily deterred. A young lieutenant sidled up to me and together we watched as the Sapphic cyclists disembarked from the lorry, mounted up and, swiftly overwhelming the two senior customs officers, set off for Ventimiglia at speed.

'Incredible!' the lieutenant grinned. 'Whose idea was this?'

'Mr Tooth's,' I replied, a trifle disingenuously, and gave him a card. 'He wishes to raise his profile all the way to Versiglia…'

I HAVE DECIDED to give another dog a home. Not a dog to replace Poopy – no dog could replace Poopy – but I am a dog person and it feels strange not having a dog around, so I have decided to give another dog a home. There are lots of dogs needing homes. I know this because there are lots of ads in lots of newspapers featuring lonesome-looking pooches under banners explaining how a dog is for life not just for Christmas/Easter/birthday/takeaway curry.

I go to Rescue Homes' HQ, where I am vetted, interviewed and quizzed about my income, status and the class of my degree. Finally, I am visited at the home that I am trying to give to a dog. No easy task, but I pass. Armed with my suitability certificate, I am free to contact the mass of rescue homes scattered throughout the south of England. I could probably go to rescue centres in the north too but, as I have only a 2CV, I have to be realistic.

To narrow things down a little I have decided on getting a female, under the age of five, preferably a terrier, although not a West Highland White for fear of constant Poopy reminders that would cause work-inhibiting depression (see income clause above). I am given a great deal of advice: why don't you get a puppy? Puppies are lovely, get a puppy etc. etc., but my mind is made up. I want to give a dog a home

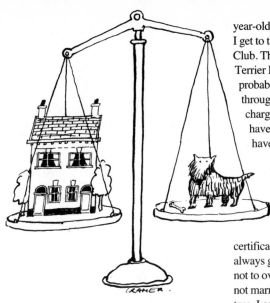

and so a rescue dog it is. I am given more advice: what about a Jack Russell? Too snappy. Staffordshire bull terrier? Too butch. Yorkshire terrier? Too weedy. And so on.

Finally, after much deliberation amongst friends, family, the man who arrives to cut back the trees and the plumber from my sister's church, I am left with the impression that the new dog for me is a cairn terrier. Smallish, although not weedy, plucky, but not snappy, bold, but not butch. The cairn, by popular consent, represents what I need in a dog.

I alert the various rescue centres to my decision and wait by the phone. 'Hello, Miss Taylor, this is Tina from the Twilight Rescue Home, are you still looking for a dog?' I am, I am, I excitedly reply, urging her to reveal the details immediately. 'Well, we've got a King Charles spaniel with separation anxiety and a passion for chewing the sofa, would you be interested?' I am keen not to appear too picky, but a cairn it is not. Not even a terrier. Still, I should show willing. 'Umm, is it a girl?' 'Oh no, he's a nice bouncing boy,' beams Tina down the telephone. I explain that I was really looking to give a home to a girl. 'You could always get him castrated, then you'd probably never know the difference.' I agree that she has a point but decline politely, explaining that I'd rather hold out for the real female thing.

Weeks go past, with offers of a bull mastiff, a three-legged boxer and two ten-year-old Westies (one of whom dies before I get to the centre). I contact the Kennel Club. They suggest the Cairn and Small Terrier Rescue Centre – after all, they probably have what I'm looking for. I get through to Deirdre, the matriarch in charge of the metal cages. Yes, they have cairns that need homes, they even have female ones.

'Are you married?' demands Deirdre. 'Well, no,' I say. 'But I might get married. I've got a boyfriend, and anyway I work from home and I've always had dogs and I've got my suitability certificate and I have a nice garden and I always go to the park and I'm very careful not to over-treat...' I trail off. 'But you're not married, are you?' insists Deirdre. It's true, I can't deny it. I'm not married. Deirdre brings the conversation to an abrupt end, suggesting that I ring her again in a couple of weeks and she will consider my application.

Two weeks pass. I brace myself for another telephone conversation with Deirdre. Finally I make the call. 'I've thought about it,' says Deirdre. 'And I've decided that your lifestyle isn't suitable.' I am stunned. 'What do you mean?' I gasp. I find myself pleading with her: I am a dog lover par excellence, I work from home, I've been vetted, I've read all the books… 'I'm afraid our dogs prefer to live with normal middle-aged married couples who live in semi-detached houses,' Deirdre pronounces. I plead with her. I've got a 60ft garden with an extensive collection of chews and balls. But no, it's a semi or nothing for Deirdre's dogs. Crushed, I replace the receiver.

I pen a letter to the Kennel Club, demanding to know why it is that cairn terriers, described in their literature as bold and plucky, would want to live only in semi-detached houses. What about bungalows or garden maisonettes or even detached houses? Giving a dog a home is more difficult than I thought. They can be very choosy. I don't remember anyone saying that nine out of ten cairn terriers prefer semi-detached houses and it's never cropped up on *Animal Hospital*.

The phone rings. 'Hello, is that Miss Taylor?' enquires the polite woman on the end of the phone. 'Yes,' I sniffle from under my semi-detached crisis. 'This is the co-ordinator for Cairn Rescue, I understand you want to give a dog a home.' I gather all my strength before admitting that I have a bit of a problem: I don't have a semi-detached home. 'Oh, you've been talking to Deirdre, haven't you?' she asks. 'Yes,' I reply. 'Well, I'm afraid,' she continues, 'that Deirdre was removed from the organisation some time ago, but she set up a breakaway splinter group. Unfortunately, she still manages to intercept some of our enquiries. It really is quite tiresome.' I am stunned. It's mad out there in dog world. 'So what do I need?' I mutter, after she explains that it's really OK that I don't have a semi. 'You need to fill in the forms and we'll see if you're suitable.'

'From what I've heard, this queue is definitely the queue to be seen queuing in.'

27

A vintage palate

*His Uncle Sidney, art school, and a former editor were the formative influences for **Mike Molloy** in his pursuit of fine wines. And there's nothing like the taste of money... Illustrations by **Larry***

M y Uncle Sidney was the first wine drinker I ever knew; an indulgence that was held in deep suspicion by the other members of my mother's family. He also ate spaghetti; not the real stuff – that came in cans – but strange bundles of what looked like hay, which he boiled, and mixed with a concoction of mincemeat and tinned tomatoes.

Uncle Sidney picked up both habits in Italy during the Second World War after he'd resigned from active duty. His resignation came about after his battalion had fought through North Africa, the invasion of Sicily and the beginning of the Italian Campaign. He had been wounded twice and then buried alive for two days when shellfire brought part of a building down on him. After the battle of Monte Cassino only four members of his original company were still in the line and Uncle Sidney's nerves jangled so much that a cat coughing would cause him to twang like a tuning-fork. So he and his fellow survivors went to see the colonel and told him they'd had enough; done their bit, paid their dues, etc.

Incredibly, the colonel, instead of having them shot as a less enlightened man would have done, agreed. He wangled them all cushy jobs out of the line and Uncle Sidney found himself looking after a swimming pool near Naples and billeted with an Italian family who taught him their ways.

Demobbed into post-war Britain, Sidney so missed the Latin home comforts he had grown to love that he would make regular trips to Soho for his supplies of Chianti and raw spaghetti. One hot summer day, he invited me to join him under the apple tree in his garden where he ate his Italian meals – another habit that was viewed by our relatives as dangerously eccentric and possibly injurious to one's health. It was there that he gave me my first sip of wine. It tasted awful. I had expected the dark purplish liquid to be as sugary as hot-house grapes, instead it was a mouth-puckering disappointment – the spaghetti was pretty dreadful as well.

My next encounter with wine was at art school, where we tyro Bohemians learnt that our heroes, the Impressionists, were known to have quaffed large quantities of the rougher peasant vintages.

Sadly, the pubs of Ealing were unable to supply the stuff we desperately craved in those unsophisticated days during the late Fifties.

Then, one November evening, we located an off-licence that stocked a new line in Spanish sauterne and triumphantly brought a bottle back to the warren of bedsitting rooms we inhabited close to the Uxbridge Road. Eagerly we scrabbled at the tin foil around the

cork until an authoritative voice rang out. 'Stop,' ordered the arbiter of fashion among our set. 'Wine should be served at room temperature.' Taking the bottle, he placed it on top of an iron stove that emanated enough heat to melt the core of a nuclear reactor. When the bottle was removed, small quantities of the hot brew were poured out for each of us.

Well, it was sweeter than Uncle Sidney's Chianti, but, in its own way, just as vile. 'What is the magic?' I asked myself. Wine drinking seemed to be about as exciting as sucking an old penny or quaffing boiled sweets diluted in tap water. In later years social pressures demanded I learn a little about the usual rituals. Reds

with beef, whites with fish – that sort of thing.

Time passed and eventually I found myself editing a newspaper in Fleet Street. By then a revolution had taken place. Wine drinking had become popular in Britain. Supermarkets, even pubs, now stocked it for the burgeoning army of connoisseurs; but it still tasted to me like Uncle Sidney's Chianti.

Of course, I learnt to inhale the bouquet and sigh in imitation of my more knowledgeable friends. It wasn't that I doubted the pleasure they gained from a fine wine, it was just that I was unable to appreciate the subtleties for myself, a similar phenomenon to the one I experience when I am confronted by the music of Andrew

Lloyd Webber or the paintings of Salvador Dali.

My lack of appreciation would come home most forcibly when entertaining Sir Larry Lamb, founding editor of the *Sun*. A man of robust views on the great vintages, Sir Larry once destroyed the aplomb of the sommelier at a famous restaurant by asking: 'Do you call this a fine bottle of wine?'

'But, yes, sir,' the waiter replied smoothly.

'Well, I wouldn't wash my fucking car with it,' Sir Larry replied.

When I was the host at our lunches I always deferred to Sir Larry, who would then take up the list and after a long and careful scrutiny say: 'Would you like a bargain or an experience?'

Who could opt for the bargain in those circumstances? And so bottles would be produced from the darker recesses of the cellar and presented with reverent care. Sir Larry would sip, swill and give the nod of approval and I would close my eyes in mock appreciation, pretending I was equally transported.

I thought it would always be so, then one day my old friend Patric Walker changed my point of view. We were returning to his flat in Mayfair for a nightcap after supper and found the stairwell littered with packing cases.

'Oh, damn,' Patric said. 'This shouldn't have been delivered here.'

'What is it?' I asked.

'Part of my pension,' he answered. For a moment I imagined the boxes were packed with banknotes, then he prised open a case and took out two bottles. Once inside the flat, he opened them and, putting them aside to breathe, made some coffee while he told me a story.

In his younger and more impressionable days he had been taken up by a member of one of Europe's great families. Their fabled wealth included banks, estates, mighty industries – and vineyards. Patric had been the last autumn romance for the old man and together they'd made a grand tour of the continent. Shortly after that, the old boy expired, leaving Patric all his possessions. Not just

a few treasured mementoes – the lot: castles, paintings, antique jewellery and most of a town in southern Germany.

Patric had the will presented to him by a team of Dickensian solicitors at the Inner Temple. When the last item was read out, there was a slight pause and the senior legal gentleman said:

'You do realise you won't be able to keep any of this?'

'Of course,' Patric replied lightly.

A smile like the crack on a Greek vase appeared on the solicitor's face. 'Ah, Mr Walker,' he said in warmer tones, 'I'm delighted you're going to be sensible. Now let me tell you what the family are prepared to offer you.'

Half an hour later Patric walked out into the sunshine with an inflation-proof income and a lifetime's supply of wine – to be delivered every month from the family's shippers.

'Is it good stuff?' I asked.

Patric shrugged. 'In those days I knew less about wine than you do, dear. When the first summer deliveries started I had a party and a chum of mine made sangria with it. We'd used about five or six cases when an old Brigadier in the Guards started sipping his glass with a curious expression. Then he said: 'Can I have a look at the bottle this came from?' We showed him one of the empties and he screamed: 'Stop, don't open any more!'

'Why?' I asked.

Patric passed me one of the bottles from the table next to him. I glanced at the label. Even I had heard of the legendary vintage.

'One hundred and seventy pounds a bottle,' Patric said. 'Three times that in a good restaurant and probably five times that in a few years.'

He poured two glasses. It tasted extraordinary. All the extravagant claims I had heard others make over the years were suddenly revealed to me. It did taste of elusive fruits, oak barrels, honeysuckle, old leather and pipe tobacco. But then again, maybe it was just the taste of money.

Dick Barton

The voice ordering a pint of real ale in his local pub is as steely and forceful today as when he thrilled the nation 50 years ago. In the saloon bar of the Cross Keys, in the heart of the Welsh village where he lives in genteel semi-retirement, Noel Johnson lifts his personal tankard to the 'great old days' when he starred as the daring hero of the BBC's nightly escapist radio serial.

'He started it all. James Bond, *The Sweeney*, *The Professionals*, you name it. Dick Barton was in there first. That's why he made history.'

Noel Johnson, who has just celebrated his 80th birthday, was the original Dick Barton in the slam-bang-wallop series. He is still an erect figure with a military bearing, level grey-green eyes and an air of cool authority. 'People have always said my voice is my calling card, and that I sound like a hero.' The lined face splits into a grin of nostalgia. 'That's fine with me. People form pictures in their minds from radio, and that's the way it should be.'

Between 1946 and 1951 a generation of youngsters abandoned their homework every night at 6.45pm and sat enthralled with their parents to catch up with the latest 15-minute cliff-hanging instalment. Heralded by the thundering Devil's Gallop, and assisted by his faithful henchmen Jock (Alex McCrindle) and Snowey (John Mann), two-fisted Dick Barton would wade into a variety of villains and send them packing.

The ace sleuth was an ex-commando described as 'reliable, patriotic, cheerful in adversity and unswerving in his opposition to enemies of Britain'. Those enemies ranged from a German with a ray gun more powerful than a nuclear bomb to a French count with a plot to flood the world with synthetic diamonds.

The serial – before the BBC axed it, to cries of outrage, in favour of *The Archers* – was all-action, and never lost its rip-roaring pace. As producer Neil Tuson recalled: 'We got more action into one 15-minute episode than Neighbours does in a week!'

At his peak, Noel Johnson was receiving 2,000 fan letters a day. When he left the cast in 1949, more than 500 people applied for the job. 'I was 29 when I was offered the part. I thought: this will do wonders for my career, and make me a bit of money, too,' says Noel. He was paid the princely sum of £18 a week, and when the BBC realised the series was a runaway success, the money was generously increased to £20.

When Noel left the series he faced almost ten years with virtually no acting roles: 'I was typed as Dick Barton, and that was that. I even got letters hiring me for detective work. That was the extraordinary power of the show, and the medium itself.'

He recalls: 'Barton never swore. He was never allowed to have any affair that might hint at a whiff of sleaze. The violence was restricted to "clean socks on the jaw".'

He grins wryly at the shackles he was forced to wear. 'The fact is that Barton became almost impossible to play. In the beginning he smoked and drank, and had a girlfriend. When it became apparent that he had an army of young listeners, the BBC was anxious to avoid anything that might be a bad example.

'So the girlfriend disappeared, and Barton never smoked or drank again. Any young women in the serial would have to be villainesses. He was almost too good to be true. But the public loved him.'

Johnson himself has smoked since he was 18, likes a drink and always enjoyed the company of women. He found his halo a little hard to keep polished. 'But I have no regrets. I look back on Dick Barton as someone who changed my whole life. So I think I owe him one.'

Noel realised early on that Dick Barton would never make him a movie star. 'Some things just don't work when they try to transfer them to TV, films or stage. You see someone on the screen who doesn't look remotely like the image you've built up – and bang! That's the end of it.' A trio of movies, from Hammer Films, all flopped at the box-office.

'The art is in the writing – it's what people see in their head. In the same way, when you're acting for radio you are playing to that microphone in front of you, not to an audience or even to

other actors. You are saying: "My dear girl, I love you so much!" – to a microphone. And you've got to sound as though you mean it.'

In the days before tape, Dick Barton was recorded on discs, with the actors smacking their fists into their hands in the fight scenes and doing many of the sound effects themselves.

'In my day leading men always spoke properly,' declares Noel in his crisp tones. 'Then the anti-hero came along, and the dialogue got blurred. That's why I hardly go to the cinema any more.'

Noel Johnson appeared on TV recently in an episode of *Frost*. 'Someone said to me: "I hope I'm not going to embarrass you, but only David Jason and yourself are completely understandable." '

Surprisingly, the actor who became the idol and fantasy role model for millions never had formal training. 'Either you can act, or you can't. I hope my voice is distinctive. I try to keep it clear. But I just used it as the script in front of me demanded. As far as I'm concerned,' says the original Dick Barton, reaching for his pint, 'I'm pleased to say that my voice paid the bills and kept me alive!'

William Hall

Death of an 'Oldie' reader

He loved The Oldie; he hated funerals. When Royce Salt died, his widow **Caroline Salt** *was determined to have the most dignified, plain ceremony possible*

Yesterday I changed my wedding rings from my left to my right hand, because I have now been a widow for six weeks. I wear two wedding rings – my mother's and my own. I can envisage some future great-great-great-great-grandchild – for they will be passed down to my daughter, and then her daughter, and so on – with her wedding finger weighed down like a Masai woman's neck.

My parents were clearly far more erudite, for their ring is inscribed *Ne cede male – sed contra* (roughly translated as 'be good'), whereas mine only has our nicknames – 'Bun', as my grandfather said I looked like a pasty bun, with currants for eyes, and 'Bim', from Lewis Carroll's 'Come to my arms, my Beamish boy' – and the date of our marriage, 30.3.57. Perhaps we are unusual as a family: most of the friends I have asked have no message inside their rings, and jewellers say it is rare for young couples nowadays to ask for any engraving in the wedding rings that both husbands and wives so often wear.

I moved my rings because I have said my final goodbye to my life as a wife. The grandchildren, who are very young, have already forgotten who 'Papa' was; the dog

'I'm afraid you're an incurable romantic, Mr Keats.'

no longer sits expectantly by his chair; the pensions have been sorted out; the bank accounts and house put into my sole name; and the funeral – that ultimate commitment – is over. Royce hated going to funerals so much that I was determined that his body would not be attended by the usual ceremonies. The family wanted a Christian burial, for he was a good man and a practising Catholic, but I did not want a large gathering of relations and friends, some of whom he had not seen for years: the 'funeral baked meats' syndrome afterwards could easily degenerate into a rather awkward party, with a lot of comparative strangers struggling to make conversation, generally about their holidays and rarely about the dear departed. All I wanted was to say a quiet and very sad farewell.

When a friend and I went to register his death at the hospital where he died, we were given a Coroner's Report, which is necessary after a death by accident or – as in his case – within a short time after an operation. We saw on the form that a funeral director had been assigned, but we insisted that all I wanted was a priest, the body, the dog and me; and, as he had expressed a wish to be cremated, the agreement of the local crematorium.

At first, the registrar did not believe that what I wanted could be done, but she got more and more interested as the obstacles were overcome. Yes, the mortuary would keep my darling's corpse until a date had been arranged, and would not charge for storage; yes, they would give us a blue hospital body-bag for use as his shroud; and, yes, they would place him in the back of our camping van and I could drive him to the crematorium. The statutory fee for the cremation was £235 (and, astoundingly, no VAT is payable), but here a snag arose; the manager of the crematorium insisted that a body-bag was not acceptable – the bearers did not want to feel the shape of the body as they carried him – and that a wooden coffin was obligatory. He eventually conceded that chipboard would do, and as my friend had been quite good at woodwork at school, we considered going to a hardware store and buying the necessary bits of wood and nails – after all, it did not have to be perfect; it was only going to be burned. His name would have to be written on the box, but this could be done with a felt-tip pen.

After all these arrangements had been made, our daughter asked if I would compromise. She knew Paula Rainey Crofts, who owns Heaven on Earth in Kingsdown in Bristol, an international award-winner for improving the quality of death and dying. Would I meet Paula and see if we could work out a dignified, plain funeral, attended by only the immediate family? It would not be too expensive, and everyone would share the cost.

I liked Paula, and she understood exactly what we wanted. Because she is a registered funeral director (although 'alternative'), the crematorium manager agreed to accept Royce's body in a cardboard coffin – dark brown, plain, nice-looking and costing only £85, including the linings. They had their own funeral car – not a dismal, black hearse, but a silver Escort – and our sons and son-in-law could be the bearers. Simple, and just what we wanted. Our daughter bought five yellow roses – one from each of his children and one from me, in memory of the rose Royce pinched for me from a garden in Chelsea the first time we went out together.

Along with the Monsignor from Clifton Cathedral, we were due to arrive with the dog at the crematorium at 9.50am and – just as at our wedding 40 years before – we were late. The trouble was that on the night before the funeral we decided to sort out Daddy's clothes, which I had put up in the loft when he went into hospital four weeks before. Trying on his dinner jacket, his British Warm, his old suits, shoes, blazer

'What was his name again?'

and Panama hat, his sons were, like me, in tears. It was so horrible that we decided we had to get out of the house and recover in the local pub, always quiet on a Sunday night. Unfortunately, the entire bar had been taken over by a large party, complete with a stripper, initially dressed as a policewoman. Shaken and full of morbid thoughts, we sat and stared as layers of her clothing were removed to loud cheers. It was far too late to eat, and – tired, distraught and dreading the morning – we fell into our beds and did not wake until half-past nine. We had 20 minutes to get dressed – we had decided on informal dress, but that did not mean nightclothes – grab the readings, the dog and the tape of our favourite tune, and get to the crematorium.

When I had arrived at the large and hideous family church in my white wedding dress all those years before, the organist had been playing 'Jerusalem'; and now that the coffin was waiting for the bearers, the organist was, once again, thundering out 'Jerusalem' and I was, again, walking – late and fast – up an aisle towards my love, though this time he could not turn towards me and smile lovingly.

Paula had arranged everything perfectly, although she was looking a little wan, the result of a burial at sea the day before: she had strained her back while heaving her client into the boat.

Our funeral was a magical ceremony. His oldest son read a song that had been written for him when he retired from teaching French and running the CCF; his middle son tried to recite his favourite poem, Gerard Manley Hopkins's 'As Kingfishers Catch Fire', but broke down in tears and had to be joined by me; Monsignor gave a short talk about Royce's life, saying that as he had obviously been such a good, kind and generous-spirited man, he would not have to stop at amber but would go straight through green to heaven. We placed our yellow roses on his coffin and left the church while the tape played 'Two Sleepy People', to which we had so often danced, not just at parties, but alone together at home.

A funeral is a part of our pattern of life, and commemorates a temporary parting. Our mortal life together is over; that is why my rings are now on the other hand, as I realise finally that I am a widow.

Easy does it, all aboard a Goanese ferry

Mortimer on the Goa

John Mortimer *meets ageing hippies and is disowned by his children on holiday in India*

It was sunset, a few days before Christmas, and we were sitting on the wide verandah of a cool house, built by a Portuguese landowner, now owned by our friends Denis Forman and his wife Moni. The sun was setting over the paddy-field, rare birds were settling down for the night, when a cart came trundling down the road, drawn by two white oxen with proud horns and sagging chins, driven by a boy wearing nothing but a loincloth. And then, capering in the twilight, came eight or ten figures, some in saris, some in grotesque Father Christmas masks with white beards, some carrying sticks with lanterns, singing at the tops of their voices 'Rudolph the Red-Nosed Reindeer'. They crossed the garden and pranced up the steps to the house. They gave us 'God Rest Ye, Merry Gentlemen' and we gave them money and Indian champagne.

It was just one of the religious festivals of north Goa, where Epiphany is celebrated by three boys wearing brocaded silk and crowns, who ride to a hilltop on white horses; where the Bandeira festival is marked by returned emigrant workers marching through

The author and an apt resort for oldies

the village firing pea-shooters; and Shiva's wedding is celebrated by the drinking of a mixture of milk, sugar and ground cannabis leaves. It's the country conquered by Portugal for the Catholic Church, where glistening white churches, like baroque wedding cakes, stand next to brightly coloured Hindu temples. Goa's first Bishop was a Franciscan friar, it suffered under the Inquisition, and now the church, about half a mile from Denis and Moni's house, calls the faithful to mass at dawn, not by a gentle bell but with taped music of the sort which can be described as Hollywood devout, played at an ear-splitting volume for an hour between six and seven. It fills the landscape like thunder, wakens the exotic birds and sends the children scurrying for the school bus with their ears ringing – and I, sitting on the terrace trying to write, find myself concentrating entirely on 'Mary's Boy Child', 'A Winter Wonderland', 'White Christmas' and a no longer appropriate rendering of 'Silent Night'.

We were a large party setting out from England, where religion manages to pass almost unnoticed. Bill, my father-in-law, and I, both in wheelchairs (by far the most comfortable way to travel), he because of a replaced knee and I from a failure to see steps and judge distances, my wife as commander-in-chief, our daughter Emily, who exhibits signs of uncontrolled terror as soon as she hears the distant sound of an aeroplane, and Rosie our younger daughter all flew to India.

At 2am we were among the crowds in the baggage arrival at Bombay airport, having waited more than two hours for our suit-cases. Emily, her fear mercifully blocked out by tranquillisers, was asleep, draped elegantly over a trolley. I was reading the small Oxford India-paper edition of Trollope's novel *The Prime Minister* and my wheelchair pusher said, 'That is right, you go on reading your Bible, sir. And pray that the luggage will not be delayed very much longer.' God must have mistaken Trollope for the Bible because he sent our luggage and a mini-bus to take us to a hotel where we could spend four hours until we had to set out for Goa.

Emily and Rosie woke up, watched television and rang room service.

Then came the Indian Airlines flight, which, with no smoking, no alcohol and slightly dubious vegetarian curry, is like an operation without an anaesthetic. But at Goa airport Denis was waiting, smiling and endlessly hospitable. Having found room in his head, which already contains all the Beethoven symphonies, the Mozart piano concertos, most operas and the accumulated wisdom of a man who was responsible for the best years of British television at Granada, for a detailed map of north Goa, he had worked out a number of trips in the land of Christmas and Shiva which turned out to have an unforgettable magic about it.

Driving in Goa is enormously exciting. Stuck behind a bus, a bursting-at-the-seams taxi, or a lorry full of goats, the driver twists the wheel and is out on the wrong side of the road with another bus, or taxi, or a loose water buffalo charging towards us. Death is missed always, if not by a particularly wide margin. It's a pity if your attention is diverted from the roadside notices, some of which contain dire warnings such as those contained under the general heading 'GOOD NEWS BIBLE'. One such commands:

DO NOT COMMIT MURDER / DO NOT COMMIT ADULTERY / DO NOT COMMIT RAPE / DO NOT COMMIT ABORTION / DO NOT COMMIT DIVORCE / DO NOT TAKE ADVANTAGE OF WORKERS / DO NOT ROB SOMEONE ELSE'S HOME/SON/DAUGHTER / DO NOT ACCUSE ANYONE FALSELY IN THE COURT OF LAW JUDGES ARE VERY BUSY THERE IS A TIME FOR SOWING/REAPING GOD TO MANKIND. WHO CARES WHO!

The notice at the end of the road pointing to the old farts' retirement spot says, 'Home for the beautiful aged'. Bill and I read it with satisfaction and felt inclined to book in.

The hippy era may be over and all those head-bands, beads and Afghan waistcoats that set off to find the Holy Bagwash, or danced to the full moon on the beaches of Goa, have no doubt become accountants or computer programmers. But there are still ageing hippies on huge motorbikes among the straying oxen. Some of the motorbikes bump down the paths of a mini-jungle towards a clearing where the 'German Bakery' welcomes hippies in exile. A wandering elephant has 'Welcome to Goa' written on its vast rump. There's an *As You Like It* feeling about the place, with bright scarves and shawls hanging from the trees instead of Orlando's love poetry, and fresh fruit juice and vegetarian samosas instead of ale and venison. But melancholy old Jacques, pierced and long-haired, sits on his own and similarly dressed German or Scandinavian lovers hold hands in silence.

There's a noisier, dirtier, more strident hippy beach at Arambol, with sands crowded with fishing boats, wooden shacks and tourist bars. In search of genuine, up-to-date hippies, I found two young men, stripped to the waist, skirted in bright sarongs, with shoulder-length hair, nose rings and numerous tattoos. I asked them how long they had been living the free, careless, lotus life of Arambol.

'Just a week,' said one. 'Actually we're window cleaners from High Wycombe on a package tour. But it's great fun here, isn't it?'

A fierce undertow dragged off my Marks & Spencer shorts. My children disowned me and left the beach

'Wonderful,' I said. 'Where are you staying?'

'In a shack on the beach. We're hoping to find some girls to shack up with us. We've asked about 200 so far and we hope to get lucky before we have to go back to High Wycombe.'

Notices on the beach at Arambol threaten '10 years rigorous imprisonment' to those found taking drugs, a threat probably as effective as health warnings on cigarette packets. Denis took us to Holywood beach, a huge, empty stretch of golden sand where the palm trees grow down to the breakers of the Arabian Sea. On Holywood the shacks are closed down, having orders for the High Court of Bombay pinned to their walls shutting them pending trial. Some might have been used for drug-dealing. We called at one shack and a carpet, table and chairs were pulled out of some recess. The carpet was spread on the sand and bottles of cold Kingfisher beer appeared on the table. We were about to drink gratefully when a police patrol was seen approaching. Like the magic meal in *The Tempest*, the tables, chairs, carpet and Kingfisher disappeared and the police were engaged in friendly conversation with the shack's owners. We stood gazing casually at a group of children on the edge of the water who ran away, screaming with laughter, at the sight of flying fish. Then the police patrol moved on down Holywood and, by another blessed stroke of magic, the Kingfisher and the carpet returned.

Moni Forman was previously married to James Cameron, legendary journalist and magnificent reporter. It's odd that no one becomes famous as a foreign correspondent any more, snatching stories from the jaws of death. Well-known journalists stay at home, writing columns with their pictures at the top about their diets, their illnesses, their orgasms or their favourite bands. Anyway, Moni was married to a famous journalist and is now married to the famous Denis and, having great authority and beauty, can deal with all the crises in the house, such as the telephone or the electricity vanishing in a magic Goanese manner, or the fact that one of the staff, told not to bring drink into the house, keeps a bottle of Feni, a potent local tipple, outside the back door for illegitimate refreshment.

On one beach where we went for lunch, nuns in fluttering white habits congregated on the edge of the water like seagulls and schoolgirls in blue uniforms paddled. An old man, another wheelchair rider, was pushed to the water's edge and an umbrella was put up over him; but umbrellas are not allowed and it had to be put down again. I ignored the red flag and plunged into the sea, where I was immediately knocked over by a huge wave and a fierce undertow dragged off my Marks & Spencer's shorts. I tried to remember stories of drowned writers and felt sure that Shelley never lost his Marks & Spencer's shorts in the undertow. My children disowned me and left the beach. Finally I and my shorts were rescued by the old man's wheelchair attendant – another proof, if proof is needed, of the value of that form of transport.

'Ramshackle Mapusa,' says the Rough Guide to Goa, 'is the state's third largest town. Other than to shop, the only reason you may want to visit Mapusa is to arrange onward transport.'

We didn't want to arrange onward transport and I didn't want to shop. The others vanished into the ramshackle town, which seemed to contain at least half a million inhabitants jammed together, with acres of fish, miles of meat, hectares of vegetables,

On the bench: Mortimer and Forman

old iron, second-hand clothing, small statues of the Buddha and religious pictures for sale. Off they went and I was left alone in a sweltering car park, sitting on a stool and trying to write a story about life in the Thames Valley.

Later Denis came to rescue me. He took me to a chemist's shop where he bought a small bottle of artificial sweetener, not because he particularly wanted it but so that he could borrow the chemist's padded bench, which the obliging shopkeeper brought out and stood on the pavement for us to sit on. So we sat, among the jostling crowds, the hooting cars and gasping motorbikes, the swift, evasive bicycles and pecking chickens, the lost tourists and wandering oxen, and chatted of this and that as the others tried to find a payphone, or a lavatory, or bought saris, shirts and Buddhas carved out of fishbone.

Later still, we were joined by a youngish Goanese man who was on holiday from Australia, where he programmed computers. I was grateful for the company and the bench and resolved to leave the story until next morning when I would get up before Bing Crosby, singing: 'At the end of the day / I will kneel and pray, / Thank you Lord / For my work and play.'

But what I remember most are the rusty ferry boats, chugging across the broad, sluggish, khaki-coloured river, past mangrove swamps, towards a Portuguese fort on a high cliff, put there for a defence against the British, or the Dutch, or the army of the Hindu Maratha from central India. There were old vans on the ferry, and bicycles, and a tall, hawk-faced hippy dressed in yellow with his motorbike (later we saw him on the beach with two beautiful women and a baby). There was an old woman with a jewel fastened to her forehead with Sellotape, and a boy carefully wrapped betel in a palm leaf to chew. An Australian girl in a long white dress with a rucksack stood at the rail, impeccably clean on the rusty boat, on the oily river beside which the turtles were nesting. It was a moment to remember in the early darkness of an English February, when the talk is all about the sex lives of pallid politicians in suits.

Detour round my father

Artist, adulterer, foreign correspondent, pilot – Dick Wyndham made a great Bohemian, but a lousy father, says **Joan Wyndham**

Dick Wyndham, my father, was brought up at Clouds, in Dorset, one of the great Victorian country houses of the day. The walls were hung with Pre-Raphaelites, the floors carpeted by William Morris. His family loved to entertain the 'Souls', a group of poets, painters and politicians, devoted to the Arts and their own egos. The whole house vibrated with good talk, intellectual games and music from the Great Hall, where Isadora Duncan loved to dance.

But my father was just a normal, grubby little boy, known to his family as Dirty Dick.

In 1914, when war broke out, he became the scruffiest soldier in the Royal Rifle Corps. His buttons were always undone, and the art of puttee-winding totally foxed him. Sometimes he would appear on parade in his bedroom slippers. Nevertheless, he made a good officer and was awarded the MC.

He later developed a passion for sketching, and spent a few weeks on his own in Venice, drawing the old *palazzi*. One day he was introduced to the Vorticist painter Wyndham Lewis. At the word 'Clouds', Lewis's ears pricked up. He started to give Dick lessons. Dick drew holding the pencil in one hand, and his nose in the other (Venetian cesspools were notorious). Soon he was Lewis's patron, paying him monthly sums of money in return for lessons. If the money was ever late, he'd get a rude letter: 'Where's my fucking stipend?' But when Dick lost his money in the Wall Street Crash, Lewis became a vicious enemy. Poking fun at what he called 'Champagne Bohemians' in his book *The Apes of God*, Lewis caricatured Dick as 'the Authentic Ape, the World's Prize Ape'. He described him in gruesome detail: conceited, foolish, a clumsy mover and a great farter, he lives in a glass vacuum in which his own image is reflected from every wall.

Dick was posted as ADC to Field Marshal Sir John French, who had with him his mistress (my grandmother, Wendy Bennett), to whom Dick sent notes addressed to 'Darling Wendy', signed 'Peter Pan'. One shudders to think how much time he spent in Never Never Land while commanding the British Expeditionary Force.

Wendy's daughter, Iris, was with her – my beautiful, innocent mother, with her flat chest, long feet and striking violet eyes. Dick fell for her instantly, and asked her to marry him. They were both virgins, with nothing between them but a chaste kiss behind the conservatory. The day before the wedding, Iris asked her mother for a few tips. Surely this once-famous beauty and 'grande horizontale' must know a thing or two. 'Tell me, Mummy, what should I do to please a man?'

'Always wear lots of scent, and never let him see you clean your teeth,' came the reply. Armed with these counsels, she married, resplendent in satin and pearls, and suffered a horrendous first night. Both virgins, they practically tore each other to pieces, and had to go to a doctor the next day to learn how 'it' was done.

Their first months at Clouds were pleasant enough. Dick took to racing and succeeded in killing three horses under him in one season. But he longed for a son and heir, and when I popped out he seemed to lose all interest in his marriage. Admittedly, I was not a particularly delightful child, judging from my mother's entry in her 'Baby's Progress' book: 'Joan bites her nails, dribbles incessantly, is clumsy, obstinate and contrary, has terrible yelling fits, and fidgets all the time, cracking her joints, picking her nose and making sizzling noises.' No wonder he soon fled to London to console himself with the company of more mature women. The last straw came when Iris caught him kissing the Marchioness of Queensberry behind the Christmas tree. She divorced him, and moved with me to London, where she soon acquired a female companion who converted her to Catholicism. I was dunked in the baptismal font, yelling my head off and trying to bite the priest.

My poor mother, now forbidden to remarry, consoled herself in bed with a bar of Bournville, a glass of milk and a detective novel. Once asleep, there were wonderful dreams – she was on a desert island, watching Dick, bronzed and stripped to the waist, wading through the Blue Lagoon to ravish her under the palms.

One night, after a few sherries, my mother told me that my father was now a famous painter. After that I looked longingly at

Joan Wyndham

every long-haired bearded layabout in cords and sandals that prowled the Fulham Road.

Two years later I was staying with my grandfather in the country when a big open-topped Rolls roared up to the gates, and out came a tall, gangling figure who stared at me in puzzlement. Suddenly, he realised that I was his daughter, and we hugged and kissed. I had to call him 'Daddy Dick', not Daddy, as this sounded more exciting and less odiously parental. In the evening there were charades, for Dick loved dressing up.

As I got older, Dick began to take a vague sort of interest in me, and invited me one night to a party given by his friend Cyril Connolly. It was full of clever, bitchy people – like being thrown into a bowl of piranhas. Dick vanished and I was terrified, but luckily Arthur Koestler befriended me. Watching Dick stumbling off myopically, in search of fresh talent, he laughed unkindly. 'We have a saying: you can always tell when a pretty girl comes into the room, because Dick takes his glasses off.'

As we left, Dick said in a voice of bewilderment, 'Do you know, some of my friends seem to think you are rather prettah.' This cheered me up no end.

In return, I took him on a pub crawl of all the sleaziest hangouts: the Fitzroy, the Burglars' Rest and the Wheatsheaf. We met lots of louche characters, all wanting either to pinch my bottom or borrow money. 'I do hope you're not going to turn out like your Aunt Olivia!' My aunt, once a highly respectable member of society and champion show-jumper, eloped to Harlem with a black lesbian actress, strode around in her father's military cape and a tiara, and taught the locals to make bread sauce.

In the taxi on the way home something awful happened. Dick, who was now drunk, forgot who I was, and made his usual mental connection – taxi, girl, make pass. He began to kiss me passion-

Dick Wyndham

ately and tried to undo my shirt. Thank God we were nearly home. Afterwards I don't think he remembered anything about it.

Soon after this he got rid of Clouds, that albatross around his neck, and moved into Tickerage Mill, a much smaller and cosier house where he entertained such celebrities as Cyril Connolly, Stephen Spender, Tom Driberg and Constant Lambert, plus any girls he fancied. His cellar was famous, and so were his house parties – bathing, fireworks, fancy dress and croquet on the lawn at night by the light of cigars. Dinner was an elaborate affair, with at least six magnums of the finest claret. Connolly was Dick's greatest friend, and also his sternest critic. Dick's nails were always black,' he wrote, 'his fly-buttons undone, his teeth yellow and his chin unshaven. Nevertheless it was impossible to resist the charm and humour of this middle-aged schoolboy, this battered Bulldog Drummond, this Don Giovanni in rags.'

Dick then got a job as Foreign Correspondent in the Middle East for the *Sunday Times*, where he used his little Moth plane to hop from scoop to scoop. In London he was based at the Hyde Park Hotel. There he worked on his 'swindle sheets', his enormous bogus expenses. He always carried a shabby leather bag containing Valium, whisky, cigarettes and a battered black book containing short, cryptic notes – 'red tie, toothbrush moustache, very influential' or 'small breasts, tight bottom, free on Wednesdays'.

Some months later, back in the Middle East, he crashed in the mountains of Iran, and walked back for miles with frostbitten feet, living on sunflower seeds.

I was in the maternity ward, having just given birth to my second child, when a strange tall man lurched in on crutches. He was wearing a long, dirty sheepskin coat, and had bandages on his feet.

38

'Looking for my daughtah!' he said, gazing myopically around. He had obviously forgotten my name, but finally recognised me.

Proudly, I showed him my baby. 'Hideous, isn't it? They all are!' I was delighted he had managed to come, and hoped for a real family relationship in the future, but that was the last time I was to see him.

One sunny day in May I was reading the *Times* at breakfast when my heart stopped beating. 'Dick Wyndham died today on the northern outskirts of Jerusalem. Wearing Arab Legion uniform, he stood up to photograph the fighting between the Arabs and the Israelis. He was hit by a sniper's bullet, and died instantly.'

Ian Fleming's obituary followed. 'One of the great Bohemians of his age, moving arrogantly through the circles of his time with one foot in White's and the other in Bloomsbury – we saw in his insolent but gentle brilliance those qualities of "panache" and chivalry which are the inheritance of great Englishmen.'

Soon after, Connolly and Freddy Mayor – joint inheritors of Dick's famous cellar – were seen haring off to Tickerage, intent on bagging the best vintages. Alas, all that remained were three bottles of cheap plonk and two tins of sardines.

> **Out of a big open-topped Rolls stepped a tall, gangling figure who stared at me in puzzlement. Suddenly he realised I was his daughter**

A few days later, I was summoned to lunch by Cyril Connolly. I put on my smartest suit, but on the way to the station I was lured into tobogganing down Shooter's Hill with the post-boy. I arrived at L'Etoile looking like something the cat had brought in. Cyril took one look, and practically choked on his plover's egg. There was a box of papers to be gone through, 'But first, of course, we should go down to Tickerage and hide the whips.' Cyril saw my puzzled look. 'Good God, girl, didn't you know your father was one of England's most famous flagellists? Some of the women who came to Tickerage had to spend a lot of their time up trees!' I couldn't visualise my father as a sadist – perhaps it was just another form of the play-acting he loved.

The following week there was a very grand and very moving memorial service. I was the first to leave, and waited on the steps, convinced that I would soon be swept off to some boozy and nostalgic wake. Out they all poured, chattering and laughing, discussing where to go on to. 'Didi's? Bobo's? Oh, Didi's always has the best champagne.' No one spoke to me. Then out came my last hope, Connolly with his lovely girlfriend, Lys. Cyril turned his clever-ugly face away from me, but Lys managed, 'What a pretty hat.' 'Yes,' I said feebly, 'I made it myself.'

They swept off without saying goodbye, leaving me beached and in tears on the church steps. Finally, I pulled myself together and dried my eyes. 'Bugger them all,' I thought, making for the nearest pub, where I ordered a large whisky and drank a farewell toast to the father I tried so hard to love, but never really knew.

Noël Coward

I ONCE HAD words with Noël Coward. Well, I had several and he had one. I triumphed – or so I thought at the time.

It was in the 1940s, while he was on a fund-raising tour of South Africa. He did two nights in Kimberley, where they mine the myth that diamonds are forever.

I was a cub reporter, er, the only reporter on the *Diamond Fields Advertiser* and donned an ill-fitting hat as theatre critic for the night. I was, predictably, bowled over by Coward's performance and wrote at length and with enthusiasm to that effect. At the same time, I was unimpressed by his accompanist, Lionel Bowman, and said as much, but in fewer words.

The next morning my editor had an irate telephone call from Coward, doubtless with Bowman fuming at his elbow, demanding the most abject apology for my scandalous and utterly unwarranted references to his estimable fellow artist. I was summoned to meet Coward in his dressing room that very night. I jumped at this chance of meeting the great man face-to-face and duly presented myself for the dressing down.

He said: 'Well?'

I explained that, with the greatest respect, I could not possibly apologise for writing what I believed, rightly or wrongly, to be true. Bowman's support had been, in my humble view, woefully short of the standard set by his principal. There was a brief silence. Coward offered me  a whiskey and, without another word, returned to his application of make-up. That was that. It was only in my more mature years, as editor of the self-same provincial daily, that I came to realise why Coward was happy to let the matter rest where it did.

The reason was that we were all left ever so happy. I thought I had struck a resounding blow for press freedom. Bowman believed my guts had been reduced to garters. Coward ensured the show went on. It did. **Archie Atkinson**

After we'd finished with the pyramids and the sphinx, Imud, my guide, asked me if I could ride. A good question; he'd already seen me on a camel (well you have to, don't you, and it's more fun than *walking* between pyramids) and I suppose he wanted another bit of quiet entertainment.

On receiving a qualified assent, he drove me to a sort of shed on that scruffy street where Cairo ends as abruptly as a knife-cut, and the desert begins. There he introduced me to his Uncle Fouad, who rents out horses and camels for a living. Fouad was a rotund Bedouin of 50, with a smiling sun-darkened face and better English than his nephew, whose eccentric pronunciation had rendered our tour of the Egyptian Museum that morning more confusing than enlightening.

Fouad and I shared a glass of tea and a chat, and he asked me if I'd like to go riding in the desert at night. I said I hadn't ridden in some years and that perhaps a trial run by daylight might be a good idea.

So a nice little Arab pony was brought out, Fouad twisted a white head-scarf round my head against sun and dust, and I had a ride, after which he said I'd passed, and, if I liked, we could go riding that night. I could watch the *son et lumière* on the pyramids from the desert side, and we'd have a picnic. Sounded good… How much?

'*How much*? Let's not talk of money! Give what your heart tells you.' My heart told me $10 now (broad smiles) and, I thought, another $20 later. I returned to my hotel, the Cleopatra Palace (if that's Cleopatra's palace, I'm Nefertiti), had a shower and a rest, put on 'riding clothes' (some thick socks), and thought about what I might be letting myself in for.

Nothing to worry about. I'm old enough to be his mother. Never turn down an adventure. Besides, it's my last night in Egypt

> **There's a moment in camel-riding when the camel alarmingly vanishes. When it's time to dismount, he sinks, gurgling mutinously, to his knees and just isn't there any more**

and there's a full moon. Yes. Go for it.

I left Fouad's card on my bed just in case I didn't come back and took a taxi to the Mina Hotel, a very grand establishment where nobody looked anything like Fouad (or me either, come to that). Just as I was deciding it wasn't going to happen, he came swanning up the drive in his black robes with his fat tummy preceding him, and swept me off in a beat-up old car which he hadn't dared bring onto hotel premises.

The pony wasn't ready and the *son et lumière* was starting, so he led me to a recumbent camel and I perched on its soft, commodious saddle. Behind me the moon rose over the city. The camel grumbled and belched and shifted under me while the French commentary wafted over the darkening sands ('*La p'tite reine, couchante pour l'éternité…*').

The pony arrived and I mounted, with some help from a rock. There's dismayingly little of an Arab pony. Accustomed to quite a lot of horse in front of the saddle, I felt as if I were on an edge, but this didn't faze me after the camel ride that afternoon. There's a moment in camel-riding when the camel alarmingly vanishes. When it's time to dismount, he sinks, gurgling mutinously, to his knees and just isn't *there* any more – for a moment you are left at a one-in-two gradient still far from the ground, held in place entirely by the strength of your grip on the pommel.

Off we rode. Fouad on his camel, looking every inch a desert wanderer, and in his orbit a little satellite child on a donkey with a rolled-up carpet across its rump. I looked at the carpet, and an 'oh-oh' did cross my mind, but I banished it. Unthinkable, surely.

We rode for about 15 minutes straight into the Sahara, till the city passed from sight and we arrived at a point from which we could still see the pyramids peeping over the dunes. There we dismounted, and the carpet, a beautiful Persian one, was spread out on the sand. Cold beer was produced. While we were washing the dust out

of our throats, the little boy silently vanished into the night, taking with him horse, donkey and camel.

We watched the play of lights on the pyramids and listened to the music while the moon climbed the sky. It was really rather wonderful. Then Fouad spoke.

'Would you like to sit closer to me?'

I have heard that line before, though not for a number of years, and my previous 'oh-oh' suddenly didn't seem so unthinkable.

'I'm fine where I am, thank you. Pass the beer.'

Pause. Then, in a definitely lecherous tone: 'Aren't you afraid to be out alone in the desert with me?'

'Not in the very least.'

'Why not?' (rather peevishly).

'Because,' I said pleasantly, 'I know a gentleman when I meet one, in whatever part of the world.'

'And if I am not so gentleman, and I try to hug you and kiss you, will you kill me?'

There's a thought! How would I do it? No doubt he has one of those curved daggers in a sheath at his waist. Snatch it out as he pounces, scream loudly, plunge it in, the beautiful Persian rug soaked with blood, my honour saved…

'Kill you, Fouad? Possibly, but you're not going to, so I won't need to.'

'Why I'm not going to?'

'Well,' I said, 'for three reasons. One, you're a gentleman, as I said, whom I trust, or I wouldn't have dreamt of coming out here alone with you. Two, I am well aware of the Arabs' respect for age, and for women.' (This was an outrageous lie. It has not been my experience that Arabs have much respect for women, and the present situation bore out my impression that a lot of them will shag anything that moves.)

'And three,' I continued smoothly, 'I am wearing, as you may have noticed, my medallion on which is inscribed a prayer in Arabic to Allah. Allah is watching us and he will not allow you to show me the slightest disrespect.'

Since Fouad was swigging back the beer, I knew he couldn't be a very strict Muslim, but I thought this would carry the day if the other two points were weak.

Happily, I was right – or possibly the deciding factor was when I proved that I was older than he took me for. Luckily, the satellite child returned after what was

A desert seduction

*Allah looked kindly on **Lynne Reid Banks** when she placed her trust in Arab hospitality. Illustration by **Larry***

perhaps planned as an enabling interval, bringing pots of delicious hot food and pitta and more beer, and we feasted in the moonlight and watched the delicate play of lights on the pyramids while I described my happy marriage, my three grown sons, my hordes of (imaginary) grandchildren, though he seemed to have lost interest by then. Afterwards we remounted and rode for an hour through the desert. It was heavenly.

As we rode back he said plaintively, 'Your husband is how old?' I told him, over 70. 'And can he still, er, does he still…?'

'Fouad,' I said kindly, 'don't worry. You've got 20 good years ahead of you.'

It's great being old. One really does feel so safe.

I ought to add that the idyll ended on a somewhat sour note. When I handed over the $20 bill he let out a roar of disappoint-ment. 'But this is not enough!' he yelled.

'You said what my heart told me to give,' I said feebly. But to no avail: he sent a cohort back to the Cleopatra Palace with me to collect another $30. I couldn't help wondering if $20 would have been enough, if…

It would be rather fun to think that my ageing favours could be worth at least half a ride in the desert.

41

Clean Living

In today's classless society, it's not just the rich who have servants, and you don't have to have been born into service to end up in drudgery. **Zenga Longmore** *describes her experience as a modern British charlady.*
Illustration by **Peter Bailey**

FOR THOSE OF YOU who have only ever seen the glamorous side of cleaning, allow me to take you by the hand and guide you into the heady world of pinnies and bleach.

On paper, being a charlady appears to be the ideal profession. You do exactly the same thing as you occasionally do at home, only you get paid four pounds an hour for it. Cash in hand! Simple as falling off a mop bucket. And it involves neither qualifications nor tough interviews. The only uniform required is an apron and a pair of rubber gloves, and you get to travel – from one house to another.

But in real life…? The relationship between the modern servant and mistress is very confusing. On the one hand, we are all supposed to be equal and friendly to one another these days. Orders cannot be barked out, and first names must be used in a jocular manner. On the other hand, the mistress is ever wary of the cleaning lady – is she stealing or breaking things? Is she cleaning on top of the cupboards? Being relaxed with your cleaning lady is an art which transcends age, class and status.

Earlier this year, being short of a few bob, I decided to clean for my supper. Joining an agency seemed a bit too official. Questions are asked, forms have to be filled in. That would never do. So, taking the coward's way out, I looked in sweet-shop windows, and wrote down the numbers of two potential 'mistresses'. 'Jean wants cleaner', read one notice, with engaging simplicity. 'Busy Working Mum Seeks Help With Housework', said the other, with what I construed as sly intent. Ringing both numbers, I arranged appointments.

Jean lived in a condemned council estate near Neasden. It was one of those estates built 25 years ago by idealistic but potty architects. There were walkways and byways, underways and overways, smothered in graffiti and all manner of evil-smelling matter.

> **Her three-year-old son trotted after me like Mary's lamb, bleating out complaints. 'Why haven't you done under the sink, cleaner?'**

Groups of elderly men holding beer cans leant against concrete pillars, occasionally shouting friendly greetings to passers-by. 'Hey, Spice Girl!' I was addressed with a loud slur, 'Wanna meet Mr Big Spice?' I didn't, at that precise moment. I was late for my meeting with Jean, having become hideously lost in the underbelly of the decaying concrete maze.

The outside of Jean's flat, when at last I found it, was surrounded by split bin-liners and bundles of old rags.

Jean answered the door, accompanied by a giant, hippo-like rottweiler, who unrolled several yards of tongue, and panted asthmatically. She was short and very shaky, with large round blue eyes and a rather terrifying smoker's cough. On seeing me all dressed up in my interview suit, she embarked upon a laugh which finished with a hacking choke.

'I can see you ain't a cleaner, luv! What are you, an actress?'

'No, actually, I'm a freelance journalist.'

'You dun any cleaning before, luv?'

'Well, I clean my flat…' Then, something in Jean's innocent blue eyes drew out a rare bout of honesty, so I added, 'but not that often.'

'I like you, luv, I really do. Come and sit down.'

Jean led me slowly down a narrow corridor, doubling over every now and again to cough violently, then heaved herself into an easy-chair in her living room and lit a roll-up. Her domain, I saw to my delight, was very messy indeed. Dogs and cats sprawled over the furniture, leaving great clumps of fur in their wake. Unwashed teacups, clothes, ashtrays and cigarette butts littered the entire area of her front room. I smiled. Not only was there something for me to get my teeth into, so to speak, but I have a profound admiration for someone who is even messier than me. Quentin

Crisp, I gather, manages to achieve this great feat. It takes guts and great strength of personality.

'So, when can you start, luv?' asked Jean in a wobbly drawl.

'Now!' I replied, removing an apron and a pair of rubber gloves from my bag with heroic agility.

Half an hour later, the living room, the kitchen and the hallway sparkled and shone. I was able to achieve an uncanny brilliance in Jean's flat, creating a cleanliness unknown in my own dwelling, which rarely gets a smell of New Jif With Bioderms. Jean was suitably awed.

'Oh, Zenga luv, you're brilliant! You really are! I've made a pot of tea for you. Come and sit yourself down. What do you smoke? I got roll-ups, Rothmans, and B an' H [cough, cough, cough]. 'Ere, push Old Rowly out the way, an' 'ave a fag.'

For the next hour, we chatted about Jean's life, Jean's luvs, Jean's problems with the neighbours ('They smashed me baffroom winda, an' me bedroom winda, and they was only kids! Three years old, one of 'em was'), Jean's friends ('Oh, she's a right bitch, that one. I hate 'er so much. She's coming round soon, you might see 'er in a minute'), and Jean's illnesses, which far exceeded her luvs. She had very bad arthritis, and a disability which entitled her

to extra payments with which to hire a cleaner.

Tea over, I tackled the bedroom and bathroom with vigour. Half an hour later, Jean all but collapsed with glee and coughing.

'I'm not paying ya four pounds an hour,' she announced. Oh no! Was she about to pay me two pounds an hour, and cruelly dock the tea-break hour from my wages? 'I'm payin' ya six fifty an hour! You're brilliant, Zenga luv. Bleedin' marvellous!' I glowed with pride. Ah, praise! Cleaning, I thought, is a doddle. Most of the work appeared to entail smoking and drinking tea.

But I was soon to learn the more sinister side of charladying.

The busy working mum, whom I saw the next day, was one of those scrawny, neurotic women with a small son, a demanding job and a lazy husband. There were no offers of cups of tea as I stepped into her plush apartment. Instead, I was handed a lengthy list of my duties: clean behind the microwave; hoover behind, round, underneath, and on top of sofas; make sure you bleach and polish the entire toilet area – you get the gist. The busy working mum (BWM) followed me round the flat, anxiously pointing out missed spots of dust. Her flat was embarrassingly untidy, but, unlike Jean, BWM had left unmentionable items all over the place. There are two distinct types of messy, cosy messy, and health-hazard messy, and BWM's flat bordered upon the latter. Thank heavens, I thought, for rubber gloves, although I sometimes wondered whether a surgical mask should not also have been provided.

'Actually, I don't like you to use polish on that sideboard, it smudges. Could you do it again? Oh dear, Timmy's toys aren't neatly arranged, he likes them put into lines. Did you polish the hall tiles? Did you? Oh! Well, would you mind…' And so began five hours of unceasing drudgery.

Her three-year-old son also put his future tyrant skills into action. He trotted after me like Mary's lamb, bleating out complaints. 'Why haven't you done under the sink, cleaner?'

'Mummy! You told her to do under the sink, and she hasn't done it! Shall I tell her off?'

'No, Timmy, I'm sure she will clean under the sink in a minute.'

'OK. I'll watch her. No, she's just standing there, giving me a funny look.'

A mountain of creased shirts beckoned in the bedroom. 'If you have time, Zenga, after you've cleaned out the cupboards and re-polished the hall tiles, could you finish the ironing? I'm hopeless at ironing.'

'So am I!' I was just about to reply, before remembering I was being paid four pounds an hour and had become, strange to say, a professional ironer. The very thought plunged me into an agonising, existential angst.

BWM and her husband earn a lot of money, and have very small mortgage payments – not that I would dream of nosing around in their personal papers, heaven forbid! But occasionally a few of her very private letters fell open in my hands by mistake. My theory that the richer you become, the meaner you are, was proved correct. My other theory – that being a charlady is no job for a creature of my delicate sensibilities – was also vindicated. More and more people are employing cleaners to perform those bothersome tasks around the home. The servant class is expanding – but I have vowed that the only cleaning job I shall accept from now on will be on my local condemned council estate.

'Repetitive strain injury! No more scratchcards for you!'

Dictators I have known

*The BBC's **Brian Barron** looks back over 31 years of meeting some of the world's most unsavoury leaders*

The ancient Romans knew about dictators: they gave us the word itself, the concept of a Roman magistrate who was handed absolute power in times of crisis. But the 20th century has been the Age of Dictators. Mass murderers like Hitler, Stalin and Chairman Mao have been followed, in my time, by lesser fry, no less grotesque in terms of their grisly deeds. Most have been military men. Since the Sixties I have lost count of the number of coups I've covered in the Middle East, Africa and Asia. The usual background was post-colonial chaos and civil war. To seize power you only needed a few tanks, the right fellow-plotters and a willingness to kill.

In the roll call of dishonour were just about all ranks – from that self-promoted Field Marshal, Idi Amin, who had opponents fed to Nile crocodiles or brained with sledgehammers, to Master Sergeant Samuel Doe, whose first act was to have the entire cabinet he'd overthrown shot in front of us by a drunken firing squad, and General Lon Nol, the inept Cambodian strongman and CIA ally, who was closeted with his astrologers while the Khmer Rouge throttled the capital, Phnom Penh.

The currency of dictators is fear. Take General Park Chung Hee, one of the founders of industrialised, modern South Korea. An interview was scheduled in the Blue House, the presidential mansion. As we waited, I noticed an ashtray askew on a coffee table. It was wired up, containing a hidden microphone for the Korean CIA. In this police state, even the dictator was bugged. A few months later we were on holiday at a ski lodge in the Korean mountains. By chance General Park turned up for a private lunch with a dozen bodyguards in tow. Our paths came close as my family strolled across the lawn. As the President disappeared from sight, the head bodyguard rebuked two of his colleagues for inadvertently allowing us to walk close to his boss: he spat in their faces, kicked each very hard in the shins and, as they doubled over with pain, punched each of them in the head. A couple of years later, at a shoot-out during a security meeting, General Park was killed by the head of his Secret Service. Shortly after that he too was executed.

In the early Seventies I shared a helicopter with General Yahya Khan, the rambunctious dictator of West and East Pakistan. This was supposedly a morale-boosting flight over the flood waters of Bengal, where 600,000 people had drowned. On this and other flights that day the General was drunk, throwing beer cans out of the chopper. A couple of hours later he turned up to meet the world's media, gathered to record his reaction to the cyclone disaster. By then Yahya Khan was even worse for wear from alcohol. As he entered, the TV lights were switched on. 'Turn those bloody things out,' he bellowed. The media obliged. We all stood there in the blackness. A few months later East Pakistan seceded and became Bangladesh. Yahya Khan, having lost a war with India, quit in disgrace.

He was succeeded by the suave, Oxford-educated Zulfiqar Ali Bhutto, a civilian with ruthless instincts. Mr Bhutto was a deceptive charmer, personally dispensing bottles of Black Label to keep the Western media sweet in his Muslim state, but terrorising legitimate opponents. Eventually he was overthrown by General Zia ul Haq and sentenced to death after a dubious trial. I was finishing a documentary on the General during the final power play. Come to dinner, he said. Our host spent most of the meal analysing the MCC's batting problems. Over the saffron rice I asked him about Mr Bhutto, on death row a few hundred yards away. 'He deserves to die,' said the General. 'I have his file. It's appalling.' But surely, I countered, if you hang him you'll create a martyr – and a dynasty that could haunt Pakistan for centuries. 'No,' said the General, 'this is an evil person; I feel the hand of God on my shoulder.' A few months later Mr Bhutto, shrunken in weight, walked to the

Master Sergeant Samuel Doe's first act was to have the entire cabinet he'd overthrown shot in front of us by a drunken firing squad

hangman's noose; a few years later General Zia, all his closest advisers and the American ambassador died when their plane inexplicably fell from the sky. Assassination, I'm sure, but exactly how isn't clear.

Few of these strongmen seemed to learn from history. Meeting President Najibullah, the KGB-trained secret-police chief who'd become dictator of Afghanistan, I wondered why he didn't save his skin by fleeing to Moscow. Instead, he was holed up in his palace as the Mujahidin rocketed Kabul from the surrounding mountains. A few months later Najibullah was outside the palace, a battered corpse dangling from a noose on a lamp-post.

Master Sergeant Doe, one of the nastiest people I've shaken hands with, presided over the destruction of Liberia and, eventually, died indescribably at the hands of his enemies. At least the Romans forewarned their dictators, putting a slave in the chariot of the latest military conqueror parading in triumph to whisper constantly: 'Remember you are only a man.'

The elderly General Pinochet forgot this fact, thinking he had made himself immune from prosecution. It's true that the General gave unstinting Chilean intelligence and naval help to Britain in the Falklands war, especially when the Royal Navy was stretched almost to the limit in the South Atlantic. In fact, compared with most of the brutal bully-boys I've encountered, Pinochet is a man of accomplishment, having created the prosperous, stable Chile that stands out today in a turbulent continent. But in the heart of Santiago lie the mass graves of some of the 3,000 people his soldiers and supporters killed. That too is part of the Pinochet record, and it seems right that the old man himself is asked to explain it.

Adapted from Radio 4's From Our Own Correspondent.

Press

John
Sweeney

I saw Andrew Neil boogieing at the BBC disco on the last night of the Tory party conference. 'The BBC is so sexy,' he confided, breathlessly

THERE'S NO SURER SIGN that the country is going to the dogs than that all the yoof want to be journalists. A friend of my old history teacher, countless clever and witty sixth-formers, even nasty people who make too much money in the City, all want to be hacks. Why not become a dentist? Rotting teeth are more fun than working in the House of Commons lobby. Pulling carious molars is more satisfying than trying to explain reality to the average newsdesk. Dentistry is also more financially rewarding. Bear in mind that the very best journalists are sick and twisted human beings.

The most successful journalists of the modern age, in terms of fame and wealth, are the Andrews, Morton and Neil. One was a former royal rat-pack reporter on the *Daily Star* who told the story of Diana's miserable marriage; the other a habitué of Tramp nightclub who printed the story in the *Sunday Times*. Morton is a cunning and smooth opportunist; Neil the same, but also a man of formidable energy. (I saw him boogieing at the BBC disco on the last night of the Tory party conference. 'The BBC is so sexy,' he confided, breathlessly.)

If you or any member of your family are still determined to become a hack, there are ten rules of thumb on how to make it into the Street of Shame.

1. Never work for the *Daily Mail*.

2. Read improving books – at least the three below. Everyone should read George Orwell's *Homage to Catalonia*. Orwell tells the story of the Stalinist terror on the Republican side during the Spanish Civil War in beautifully clear English. The book predicted the fate of Eastern Europe and defined the hollow villainy of Soviet communism years ahead of its time: a superb piece of journalism. In *A Moment of War*, the late poet Laurie Lee covers the same story and period with a lyrical power. His evocations of smells, his descriptions of the horrible reality of war – the still-warm beret of a comrade executed by firing squad in an underground jail – are models of how to use the language to describe a scene. Anthony Delano and Peter Thompson's *Slip-Up* is about the failure of Scotland Yard to bring back Ronnie Biggs to justice and is a glorious read which gives you something of the flavour of Fleet Street, the heroic cock-ups, the absurd competition, above all our pure, unadulterated love of story-telling.

Read these three, then try to tell a story of your own in something approximating their honesty and power. Don't get too depressed when you fail.

3. Don't do a media studies course. No one in a newspaper office will be impressed. If you want to go to university, read History or English or Religious Education. *The Song of Solomon* is still the sexiest read in English literature.

4. Don't bother writing general-interest tosh. Anyone can do that. Make yourself a world expert on something horribly obscure: pyroclastic flows, disgusting tropical diseases, the appalling treatment of British prisoners of war by the Treasury. Get to know your subject, find a human-interest angle and then flog it to death, offering it to all and sundry, though always make sure that you know your market. Let's look at three examples. Your intro should be:

a) 'The pyroclastic flow shot down the slopes of the volcano at 100 mph, incinerating Fred the farmer...'

b) 'Daphne Tharg went on a holiday of a lifetime up the Amazon, little suspecting that she would catch a bug that would eat up her face…'

c) 'Len did his bit for his country when Hitler was knocking at the door. Now he is old and poor and no one gives a damn…'

5. Don't tell lies in print.

6. Make a point. 'The Government should act to stop the illegal recycling of charred pornography from toxic chemical waste incinerators by workmen who know the cold spots of the furnace…' 'Mr Snotty the children's entertainer, in reciting Dostoevsky in the original Russian to a gang of eight-year-olds, is poor value for money…' 'Either Councillor Moron does not know how to add up or he has been fiddling his expenses.'

7. Never give up. If ten newspapers refuse to run your stuff, try ten magazines.

8. Get hold of secret documents. However uninteresting they are, some thickhead on a newsdesk will get excited. Go through rubbish bins. A friend sourced the first ten minutes of a BBC *Panorama* by going through 17 bin-bags left outside the Iraqi arms-buying office in London shortly after Saddam invaded Kuwait. He found the document linking the Iraqis to a Swiss engineering firm in the 17th bag.

9. Write with nobility.

10. No newspaper ever said no to a well-told human-interest story with a beginning, a middle and an end.

Mr Camp

WANDER THROUGH the side streets of Putney or Clapham on a Sunday afternoon, as far south even as New Malden or Tooting Bec, loiter awhile by any house where a bunch of balloons tied to a door handle advertises a children's party, and if it is a fine day and the windows are open, you can be pretty sure of hearing the voice – sonorous but somehow softly confiding – of Mr Camp. 'That's right. Young lady down the front in the pretty dress. That's *right…* and when Sid looks in the box, what do you think he finds there? Well, I never did. I n-e-v-e-r did. Who would have thought it? Did someone say "silly sausage"? Well, and I thought you were such a *polite* lot of boys and girls, I really did. Did Sid say something? Did he? What did he say? He's shaking his head. He's asking if there's a young lady whose birthday it is…'

Mr Camp – 'Melvyn Camp and Slippery Sid' to allow him his professional title – is a children's entertainer. As such, with his props – several boxes with false bottoms, a top hat and a woollen snake made of three green scarves knitted together – he is a fixture of London's infant-party circuit from Richmond Park to Lavender Hill. Smartie Artie, Mr Mysto, Captain Bong and the other denizens of this queer landscape, its gossip circulated at the school gate, its trends governed by the whims of five-year-olds, are as nothing compared to the roaming leviathan of Mr Camp. The profession isn't what it was, of course, there are too many in on it, and the circuit is full of amateurs who think that an ability to amuse your own children means that you can amuse other people's, but Mr Camp, 20 years in the game now, is one of the acknowledged ornaments. On a good day – a Saturday towards Christmas, say, if the addresses aren't too far apart – he can fit in three shows and, allowing for the mileage on the Rover and the cost of 60 party bags, come away with £400.

There is not very much to Mr Camp's technique – a combination of relentless patter, patience and a schoolmasterly fixation with sitting with your hands folded across your knees – but it is hugely effective, and he can keep a roomful of five-year-olds silent for the best part of two hours. 'All down to confidence,' he will sometimes gamely suggest to any parent who takes the trouble to enquire. 'Let up for a sec – you know, stop the chat – and you've lost it.' Observing Mr Camp charm an audience of four-year-old girls, consequently, is rather like watching a row of rabbits luxuriate beneath the remorseless gaze of a boa constrictor.

In appearance, Mr Camp is small, late middle-aged to elderly, purposeful and fey. Red-faced, a few hanks of silvery-grey hair spread thinly over the crown of his head, he has the look of a zestful yet innocuous pixie – one less interested in mischief-making with the goblins than in having tea together beneath the fairy ring. Mr Camp's history is as penetrable as his magic boxes: the

'I think they want us to leave.'

schoolboy interest in theatricals; the plate-spinning uncle who worked the halls during the fag-end of Variety; the concert parties of his National Service days in the RAF. Mr Camp didn't 'go professional', as he puts it, until his forties – before that he worked in gentlemen's outfitting – but his conversation is peppered with archaic bits of showbusiness gossip about 'Maxie' and 'Kenny' Williams.

Despite overwhelming evidence to the contrary – the damp handshake, the knotted foulard, the rather mincing demeanour – Mr Camp is not, in fact, homosexual. Privately, he leads a blameless domestic existence with his aged mother in a seaside flat in Hove. Social life is hard to come by, what with the perpetual London engagements, but there is a small circle of oldish gentlemen, retired voice-over merchants and out-of-work repertory actors, whose pleasure it is to inhabit the remoter fringes of 'the business'. In these circles, armed with a full wallet and the story of how he once saw Tommy Trinder backstage at the Worthing Hippodrome, Mr Camp cuts a far from negligible figure.

It is not quite certain what will happen to Mr Camp. Convention would predict a morose and solitary old age – Mother Camp dead, the Hove ensemble in decline, thrice-weekly visits to town an increasing strain. Yet Mr Camp is a shrewd customer in his way. The probability is that he will make a prudent late marriage – despite his faintly androgynous air, he is far from sexless – and transfer the mild narcissism of his professional routines onto the uncomplaining shoulders of a wife. Friends sometimes think it 'a crying shame' and 'a pity' that one who delights so conspicuously in the company of children should have none himself; Mr Camp would profoundly disagree. Twenty years of children's parties have left him with not the slightest desire to extend their atmosphere into his private life. Curiously enough, long-term exposure to the young has never been accompanied by any particular interest in them. Were you to suggest that being a professional children's entertainer is merely a higher form of childcare, Mr Camp would be deeply shocked. His career has many consolations and one of the greatest is the thought that this, however minor or rarefied a form, is still showbusiness. **D J Taylor**

IN 1951 SENATOR Fulbright invited me – together with several hundred others – to spend an academic year studying at a university in the United States. We were to imbibe the True American Way of Life, and take back the Good Word to a corrupt and decadent Europe.

The *Queen Mary* carried us to the Promised Land. The Statue of Liberty loomed through the mist, and in Manhattan we tasted dry martinis, Budweisers, whisky sours and toasted BLTs. For those from rationed, dried egg, gin-and-orange England, this was a land of plenty. Automobiles and girls bulged astonishingly – 'falsies', as we soon discovered.

That semester, the Harvard Drama Society had decided to mount W H Auden's *The Dog Beneath the Skin*, to be played – how else? – as an outrageous pantomime. As I was, like the author, a Britisher, I was invited to direct. I bought a green eyeshade. Rehearsals began. Soon we were chorusing:

Stand aside now: the play is beginning
In the village of which we have spoken;
called Pressan Ambo:
Here too corruption spreads its peculiar
and emphatic odours
and Life lurks, evil, out of its epoch.

On the first night, the producer, director and heroine, Miss Iris Crewe of Honeypot Hall, complete with falsies, waited at the train station to meet and greet the author, who had condescended to receive applause and homage. Not yet scarred with facial furrows, Wystan Auden was a shambling, unkempt figure, saying little, every inch a 'foreign' poet. During the drive to Cambridge, he intimated he was thirsty: wouldn't it be lovely to stop at a convenient saloon for a cocktail? We looked at our watches, but had to agree.

After two or three martinis, he livened up enormously. Cricket, he told us, was like bull-fighting – a question of style. He was reading William Faulkner for the first time, and liked *Intolerance*. New York was best in early morning because of its clarity. The only other tolerable city in the US was San Francisco.

'As you can see, we have a neighbour from hell.'

W H Auden

Christopher Fry's *The Lady's Not For Burning*, then playing successfully on Shaftesbury Avenue and Broadway, was beneath contempt. *The Rake's Progress*, on which he'd been working, was delicious, and Igor Stravinsky a darling. Down went the dry martinis, as wit and wisdom flowed. We struggled to bring the conversation (monologue) round to *The Dog Beneath the Skin*, which he had written with Christopher Isherwood some 15 years earlier. It became apparent that the great poet's recollection of his oeuvre was fragile.

'What's it about?' he asked us.

'It's a pilgrim's progress through Life and Society,' we told him.

'Ah, yes.'

'Alan and Sir Francis – who has been hiding in the dog's skin – reject authority, learn about life and, finally, go off together to be a unit in the army of the other side…'

'What other side?'

'We hoped you'd tell us.'

Auden visibly scratched his memory and downed another dry martini in a single swallow. Miss Iris Crewe, who'd kept very quiet, suddenly asked him:

'Are you a Commie, Mister Auden?'

He looked at her as one would an alien creature, but replied evenly:

'I have become agnostic: I am learning sacred formulae for combating demons. For reuniting the divine element in man with its proper sphere.'

We gulped our drinks in uncomfortable silence.

Unprompted, he expounded the sense of language necessary to a poet, and how that sense manifested itself. The notice 'Pleasure Vehicles Only', he found satisfying. We nodded but failed to understand. Soon it became apparent his eyes were closing. On his feet, slightly unsteady, our distinguished guest needed to be helped back into the Oldsmobile.

At the theatre, there was just time to welcome VIPs, including the British consul general – neat moustache, black tie – and his good lady in pink. What on earth would they make of the play? Particularly the louche scene in the Nineveh Hotel, in which a diner chooses the third chorus girl from the right, pinches her thigh and orders her stewed in white wine, fingernails served separately as a savoury. Like all first nights, it didn't go smoothly. Iris Crewe forgot her lines, and the dog moved too slowly in his heavy costume. The words of the chorus were indistinguishable. From the wings I could see the author slumbering happily throughout, but he awoke at the end, and clapped heartily. Otherwise, applause was perfunctory, puzzled and weak. There was booing. No one could understand what was the 'other side' in whose army the two heroes were going to fight. They'd walked off, hand in hand. Were they just good friends? Or something more? Something unmentionable?

As pre-arranged, there were several loud cries of 'Author!' For a while, nothing happened, then Auden got up and shambled on stage. The theatre fell quiet as he sang in a cracked Oxford voice to the tune of 'John Peel':

The sun has arisen and it shines
through the blind,
The lover must awaken and recall to mind,
Though the pillow be soft and the boy be kind,
Yet the man has to pay in the morning.

In the ensuing embarrassment, he wandered off; mercifully, the curtain fell. Later, at the first-night reception, he dozed throughout in an armchair. The consul general, his lady in pink and the other VIP guests departed immediately without so much as a thank you, so that cast and director were left to congratulate/commiserate together, aided by a generous supply of dry martini cocktails. In the morning, when we poured Auden onto the train, he finally muttered that Christopher or someone had written most of that crap, and we'd been crazy to bother with it.

Oliver Stanley

End of the pier, end of the line

Amy Mandeville *reports from Worthing, with illustrations by* **Martin Honeysett**

AT CHIPPER'S Nursing Home on Sompting Way, Lorna, a native of New Zealand with long black hair and the memory of a beautiful brown body, serves all the retirement needs for her eight residential gentlefolk, just like the sign on the door says. Her son, a 15-year-old schoolboy recently weaned off his aerosol paint-sniffing habit, will cheerfully get up from the sofa to change the channel on the television in the front room, should one of the gentlefolk misplace the remote control. Lorna's daughter, stricken with cerebral palsy and banned from Woolworths for knocking over the Pick 'n' Mix stand, will be kept out

of your way as much as possible.

This isn't weird. This is Worthing.

Worthing was once a rich, opulent and mildly perverse patch of southern England. Oscar Wilde visited often, writing *The Importance of Being Earnest* there before scuttling off to Paris. Anonymous Twenties movie stars are recalled by the residents of the Kingston Gorse estate a few miles west in East Preston, an area now blighted with sports journalists, rock stars' aged mothers and Richard Gere's rumoured summer home on Tamarisk Way.

Ask a native of Worthing where she lives and she will reply, 'Werving' –

though with 11 per cent of the population migrating every year, you might have a little trouble finding a local. No figures are available as to who these migrants are, but 43 per cent of the population is made up of people collecting their pensions. Almost half the people in the country over the age of 90 end up here, whether of their own volition or someone else's. The highest age density is between 65 and 79, though the 80-to-84 group still outstrips the zero to fours, suggesting that more people end up in Worthing than start out. And with 15 funeral homes and only eight day nurseries, it shows.

**People move here to find a better life for their children,
but drug use is higher than the national average**

People come to Worthing for the quiet. A quiet life and, in the case of the old, a still quieter death; an abandonment of adventure for those facing what we're often told with optimistic insincerity is the last great adventure. Lying in bed, jaundiced and with a nasty cough, is the rock-climbing and bungee-jumping of the aged.

In Worthing, Sunchaser and Lark invalid carriages turn in front of the post office, where the elderly collect their pensions every Wednesday. Old men in Teflon trousers (which wipe clean with a little dry tissue) are strapped into their wheelchairs. Small dogs are allowed into shops on their laps. Shopmobility wheelchair loans are very popular, as are the orange and white buses that carry residents from home to Sainsbury's and back again. Three mobile hairdressers advertise regularly in the local Friday Ads (where you can also find used tap shoes, budgies and bingo with a possibility for romance). Five chiropodists, four hearing-aid shops and eight nursing agencies providing home visits are listed in the phone book. The largest colostomy bag company in the country is located just outside Worthing, in Fiddleworth. A local firm sells two pairs of polyester trousers for £19.95 in the weekend sections of national newspapers. ('When it says "Cut Extra Loose" it means that there's room in them for your colostomy bags. One on each side. Like six-shooters,' explains the managing director.)

Montague Street provides ample seating every few yards, well stocked with old women rubbing tiny feet and tired ankles swollen from high blood pressure. A large square at the centre opens to the Marine Parade and the blue and brown of high and low tide. Regular buskers include an old man who sits outside Laura Ashley, across from McDonald's, with his accordion and his white rabbit (available for weddings and all other functions). A tattered man carries his upright piano on his back. A determined convert in a cardigan and tie witnesses loudly every Wednesday with his hand on the Bible and his eyes moving back and forth behind closed lids. Transplanted Cockney accents call out the sales of fresh flowers, and gypsy voices reply with their luckless dried ones.

It's not only the elderly who come down to Worthing. People bring their families from congested London, looking for a better life for their children – which has a certain irony as, except for cocaine and barbiturates, the rate of drug use among 14-year-olds is above the national average. 'It's not like there is anything else to do,' the boy from Chipper's Nursing Home commented. 'We can't even get Channel Five.'

Casey, who was once a data programmer for the Body Shop headquarters down the road in Littlehampton, is one of the local part-time drug-dealers. 'Just the soft stuff. You can't do it full-time, though. Too much competition, and with the target users being so young, you can't bring the prices up too high.' Casey admits that he has the advantage over the dealers in the larger cities because of Worthing's proximity to the ports of Shoreham and Portsmouth. Despite the easy availability of illegal substances, half of all drug-related deaths in the area are a result of sniffing legal household and personal hygiene products.

Recent publicity and stricter EU regulations have forced the local council to clean up the beaches. There are fewer complaints now about sanitary products and human waste settling on the shingle, and the bits of

wood and old tyres washing up during high tide smell mostly of themselves and of the salt rather than of sewage. But there's still a whiff of terrestrial rot, particularly when the wind blows in from the west.

The sewage outlets just outside nearby Rustington and Ferring dump smells that slither easily up the coast.

The water has the slightly slimy feel of all the Channel, and is warm from the extremes of tide first pushing the cold water up over warmish mud and shingle and then soaking up the sun in the corresponding shallows. Most residents don't realise this though, choosing to stay high on the beach near the pedestrian walkway in one of the complimentary striped beach chairs, or walking up the shallow ramp onto the pier, where they can rest on a hard bench on the windless side of the plexiglass divider. On a hot July afternoon, the elderly, in their winter coats and heavy shoes, line up on the benches between the decrepit ice-cream stand and the mini-amusement centre, warming their eyelids in the sun. Signs line the pier at 20-pace intervals, reminding them neither to jump nor dive from the railings; something which would be hard to forget, as the pier doesn't touch the water at low tide.

Worthing youths still leave the pier for the shingle, but only by using the ladders left along the sides. Under the pier drug use is popular and, thanks to the ladders, easy of access. The council paints the railings white to keep them clean and pretty.

The pier is most popular between 11 o'clock on a Saturday night and four on Sunday morning. Rutherford's nightclub rounds out the pier, its railings perfect puking distance above the sea. The young men are skinny, hesitant and shy, the young women skittish in short skirts and clunky black heels. In the morning they return to

their parents' westward homes by train, or to their own shared houses along the tracks. If they're from out of town, they might stay in one of the hotels lining Worthing's mile-long coastline. The hotels are almost always full on weekends, no matter the time of year, and have ramps at the front for handicapped access.

Most of the residential and rest homes are in the streets perpendicular to the hotel row of the seafront, the best ones stacked into the first half-mile before the streets meet the rail lines. Although listed as rest or residential homes, not all are for the elderly. Worthing has a high ratio of mentally retarded residents living in group homes and benefiting from the fortifying coastal air. This distinction is not, however, made in the phone book – but it is on the buildings, labelled in lettering so small that only a tired daughter-in-law could read it.

Within shouting distance of these homes is the Rivoli pub. The sign on the door reads, 'Bikers Welcome'. Many of these bikers come from nearby Littlehampton, a place thought by Worthing residents to be seedy and disreputable. A local psychologist, who wished to remain anonymous, confirmed this bias, stating that her primary patients are the victims of incest there. 'In Littlehampton,' she said, 'it's normal.'

At Chipper's Nursing Home they are mourning the death of Hilda, who had been with the family for a good few years. The congenial boy recovering from substance abuse, who will cheerfully get up to change the channel should the remote control be misplaced, was called from his GCSE exams to be told the news of her passing. He grows very attached to his mother's wards, and mourns for and with them in the front room of his mother's nursing home, where you are invited to bring your own furniture, pets or partners.

'When it says "Cut Extra Loose" it means that there's room in them for your colostomy bags. One on each side. Like six-shooters'

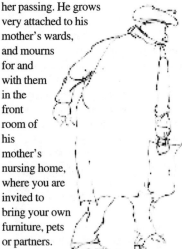

Lionel Begleiter

ON 10 APRIL 1948, 15 years old and the personification of inexperience, I started my new job as messenger boy and trainee at Zec Limited, the Baker Street commercial art studios founded by Philip Zec, the *Daily Mirror*'s political cartoonist.

It would be my job to sweep the floors, wash out and refill the artists' water jars, run for cigarettes, tobacco, Chelsea buns, rubber nails and buckets of steam, and to deliver parcels of artwork to stylish advertising agencies around the West End. My arrival *ipso facto* promoted the previous boy, who would now show me the ropes and then move on to the drawing board, leaving most of the drudgery to me.

He was a little older and bulkier than I. Olive-skinned beneath a mop of black curly hair, he had a bulbous nose, a thick, cocky, cockney accent, and an East Ender's swagger. He overawed me, the new boy from the north Surrey suburbs, full of innocence and yet instinctively aware of his street-wisdom which, I somehow knew, might be the saving of me if I could tap into it.

As the weeks went by he showed me how to go by bus and pocket the taxi fare. He revealed the whereabouts of J. Walter Thompson, Erwin Wasey or S.H. Benson, and he fired my youthful lust with his encyclopaedic knowledge of the minds and bodies of their receptionists. He made known the secret ways: the narrow, smelly connecting tunnels and alleys or the fast nip through Brown's Hotel from Albemarle Street to Bond Street. He pointed out the street girls in Lisle Street and Shepherd Market; showed me how to fiddle the Waygood-Otis pre-selector in the housing on the roof of our building to cause the lift to stop between floors so that we could rescue the office girls from the Sta-Blonde Laboratories; and I joined him, with an enormous sense of audacity, pouring Coca-

Cola over the barrow boy in the street below the studio after he'd sold us a bag of rotten cherries for sevenpence.

But in a serious vein, perhaps the most important thing he ever did for me was to kill an unquestioned prejudice inherited from my childhood.

One day, walking along New Oxford Street, wanting to show off my grownuppedness, I nudged him and pointed at a black-clad, Homburg-hatted figure and said: 'Look at that greasy old Jew.'

Lionel stopped me dead. 'Why did you say that?'

'I-I don't know,' I stammered, shocked

'Postcode?'

by the look of anger and hurt on his face.

'Don't you know that I'm a Jew?' he asked.

'No.'

'Look at my skin, my hair, my nose; listen to my voice – my name is Begleiter! What did you think I was?'

The plain fact was that, too young, too wet, I had no idea. 'Italian?' I hazarded, awkwardly.

He shrugged, palms upward, and looked to heaven. Then he laughed and put his arm around my shoulders. 'Think before you speak in future,' he warned.

My unthinking prejudice and his understanding forgiveness are lessons I have never forgotten.

Years later, when I had gone to live abroad, I read an article about the brilliant man who had written the musical *Oliver!* There was his photograph. I knew that face. It was Lionel Begleiter.

Excitedly, I wrote to him care of the London theatre which was staging the show. Although it was a long shot, I hoped the letter would find him, for I wanted simply to remind him of our days as messenger boy-commercial art trainees and to congratulate him on his success.

Some weeks later a mauve, slightly scented envelope arrived in my mailbox. It contained a mauve, slightly scented letter from his secretary.

'Mr Bart is unable to answer your letter as he is fully engaged in working on his new musical…'

I never did hear from him, in person. I wonder whether he ever read my letter? I believe his fortunes later fluctuated and I have no idea what happened to him. I'll not forget him, though. He was a good teacher.

Now that he's an oldie he might read this. It's a reminiscence by way of saying 'thank you'. **Don Donovan**

That was Willie, that was

Barry Cryer *finally gets a word in about his fellow* Old Fart *and comic genius Willie Rushton*

I can't remember where and when I first met Willie and neither could he. In the same way, I can't remember where and when I first met Raquel Welch, but that may be due to the fact that I never did. Willie always maintained that we must have met 'somewhere round the back of David Frost', and that was probably true.

Willie, was, of course, a founder member of *That Was the Week That Was*, not to mention *Private Eye* (so I won't). My wife and I went to witness the pilot programme of *TW3*. It ran some two and three-quarter hours, as I remember. Millicent Martin was going on holiday as soon as she'd sung her opening song and the folk tale had it that she was in Spain before the programme finished.

But back to Willie. We didn't meet that night, but I do remember enjoying this fleshy-faced, beardless youth, with his droll voice and an uncanny ability to become Harold Macmillan. It's surprising to recall the impact that had in those days – someone actually impersonating the Prime Minister. Peter Cook had already done his own hilarious demolition job on stage in *Beyond the Fringe*, but I think Willie was the first on television.

We finally worked together on a programme rather snappily titled *The New Stars and Garters*, an updated version of a pub-based show I had already worked on. Willie and his wife Dorgan were featured, but it didn't set the ratings on fire.

We became friends, but didn't work together on a regular basis until the birth of *I'm Sorry I Haven't a Clue* on Radio 4 in 1972. Tim Brooke Taylor, Graeme Garden and I were already on board, with chairman Humphrey Lyttelton, but after the departure of John Cleese, Bill Oddie and Jo Kendall, who didn't enjoy the ad lib free-for-all of it, Willie was invited to join, by common consent.

Talking of common consent, Willie would invariably go against any consensus of opinion. Once a decision, apparently acceptable to all,

The Two Old Farts

> '**Have you a smile about your person?**' carolled Willie

had been reached at any meeting, he would suddenly discover a reason why it should not be acted upon. This was more out of his innate sense of mischief than anything else, but it led to some spirited exchanges. When he died, I had this fantasy that someone said to him: 'I hear you died in December, Willie.' 'No, not me – where did you hear that?'

In 1990 we were invited by the Spinal Injuries Association to do an evening in the theatre. We asked Graeme Garden, a wonderful anarchic stand-up comedian/juggler Pierre Hollins, and the singer Christine Pilgrim to join us, with the stalwart Colin Sell at the piano. We did this for the first time at the City Varieties music hall in my home town of Leeds. Willie drew the raffle at the interval, with merry cries of 'Pink 32!' and the like, and I still remember a good burgher arriving on the stage to collect his prize – a small man of forbidding aspect. His face was a graven image and he didn't utter a word. 'Have you a smile about your person?' carolled Willie, and the man took his envelope and departed. Willie beamed at the audience. 'And now for the next miserable Yorkshire bastard,' he boomed.

We then did dates round the country and in 1991 Willie said to me, 'Let's see if there's any money in this.' His son, Toby, was about to present a student production of *The Duchess of Malfi*, or 'What's it all about, Malfi?', as Willie dubbed it, on the Edinburgh Fringe. He rang up the owner of the venue and asked if he would like a late-night show to follow the play. The reply was in the affirmative, so we journeyed up, bearing posters drawn by Willie. I still think his incredible talent as an artist, not just a cartoonist, has not been acknowledged. We arrived to be greeted by the news that we were sold out for the week. And so *Two Old Farts in the Night* was born. The title was Willie's idea – he said we couldn't be done under the Trades Descriptions Act. We subsequently toured until his death in 1996.

What can I say about him, that he wouldn't interrupt? One story. He sat one night at the top table at a dinner. The chairman of the company, whom I shall call Sir Charles – for that was his name – was talking loudly into Willie's left ear as he ate, with Willie murmuring, 'Good Lord!' and, 'I can imagine,' at suitable intervals. Finally the man said, in front of the whole table, 'You'd better be funny tonight, Mr Rushton, we're paying you a lot of money.' 'Well, most of it's for sitting with you,' responded Willie.

His ashes are buried by the boundary at the Oval. This has denied him the pleasure of the inscription he wanted on his gravestone. He saw the word 'Discontinued': 'That's what I want!' Discontinued? Him? Never. Cheers, Will.

Pin-ups
Katharine Whitehorn

1. Laurence Olivier
Only actor for whose autograph I ever begged at a stage door; only possible Heathcliff, Mr Darcy, Henry V.

2. Libby Purves
Best columnist going, whose writing could never be mistaken for unisex.

3. Sir George Godber
Great Sixties Chief Medical Officer, who knows that care does not mean Items of Treatment, *and* taught me to open a milk carton without getting drenched.

4. Michael Young
Ace social innovator – Consumers Association, Open University, College of Health: what next?

5. Penelope Fitzgerald
Her books are not only brilliant, but *short*.

6. Katharine Hepburn
Because that's the face I wish I had.

Miles Kington

Spectacularly inaccurate

There was a letter in the *Spectator* of March 7 this year (yes, I've got a bit behind with my magazine reading) from a Mr Robert Avery of London, taking its then editor to task for getting things wrong. Apparently Frank Johnson had said that it was Tsar Paul II who was assassinated in 1881 rather than the correct Alexander II. Johnson had apologised but had said that only one reader had objected anyway. Mr Avery was furious. He said he had spent half his time in the 1980s firing off letters of correction to editors and never got any acknowledgement. Now he contented himself with pointing out mistakes in the press to children and asking them: 'If this fact in the media is certifiably wrong, how many other facts do you think are wrong?'

Well, Mr Avery may be misguided in one way (in wasting a whole decade trying to make editors feel guilty and firing off pedantic letters), but he is right in another: it certainly is a fool's game trusting the press. We have all known that moment when we have read a piece in a paper on a subject we know a lot about, or about an event at which we were present, and have felt dawning on us the realisation that the writer of the article has not the faintest idea what he or she is talking about. We have then proceeded to question everything else in the press.

I can actually remember my first stirring of doubt. It came when Meade Lux Lewis died. Meade Lux Lewis was a great hero of mine, being one of the great boogie-woogie pianists, along with Albert Ammons, Pete Johnson and Jimmy Yancey. His *Times* obituary said that he had learnt the art of piano-playing from Jimmy Anthony. This I found puzzling, as there had never been a jazz pianist of that name. Finally I worked out that the obit had been dictated over the phone, and that the copytaker had misheard Jimmy Yancey as Jimmy Anthony, who had been duly created and credited by the *Times* as Meade Lux Lewis's teacher. And the *Times* had printed it without suspicion.

A small thing, but we all have our tiny turning points on the road to Damascus. In our own way, we also leave small traffic hazards on the Damascene road. I myself have been guilty of mistakes which have been enshrined in print, as when I was reviewing TV for the *Times* and wrote a notice, based on a press showing, of the first part of a Clare Francis documentary series on the sea. What was odd about that was that I wrote the review a week BEFORE the programme was shown on TV. What was even odder was that only one reader bothered to point out the mistake.

All right. So we know that the press is riddled with mistakes, caused by people sincerely getting things wrong, misunderstanding things, not having time to check things or even making them up. We all know this. What is extraordinary is that we still all go on implicitly believing everything we see, read and hear. Even hardworking people in the media, hard-bitten, hard-to-impress people in the media, swallow impossible things…

Example One, Shortly after the end of the Falklands War I pretended in 'Moreover', my *Times* column, that General Galtieri had found new employment writing a guest problem corner for me. One 'reader' wrote in to ask General Galtieri what Argentina would be prepared to give up in order to have the Malvinas back. 'Oh,' said the made-up General Galtieri airily, 'we would let you have [kidnapped racehorse] Shergar back.'

Two weeks later I got a phone call from the editor of the *Times*, complaining that the *Times* correspondent in Buenos Aires was getting death threats because of me.

'Because of ME?'

'Yes. Apparently some Italian news agency picked up your Galtieri story, didn't realise it was tongue-in-cheek, and put out a wire report saying that Argentina was now claiming to have kidnapped Shergar, which has gone down very badly in Buenos Aires…'

That was then. But it still happens. Example Two. Several weeks ago I wrote a piece in the *Independent* reporting the proceedings of a curious trial of a postman, who was accused of biting a dog. This postman, whom of course I had entirely fabricated, had decided to combat the threat of dangerous dogs by taking his own dog, called 'Profumo', with him on his rounds. At one house where there had never been a dog problem before, he found a new hound in residence. Unfortunately he had left Profumo outside the gate, so as the dog leapt on him, he did what Profumo would have done and sank his teeth in the hound's rear quarters. The owner was now suing the postman for assault…

All I wish to add to this is that several days later I received a fax from an editor in NBC's main TV news office in New York saying they had read the transcript of the trial about the dog and the postman and were desperate to know what happened next, as they thought it was a very interesting story.

I wish now, how I wish, that I had had the courage and patience to invent a continuation, but being short of time and guile, I faxed back the truth.

I have not heard from them since.

The joy of insects

Winifred Foley *on things that go buzz in the night.*
Illustration by **Peter Bailey**

Sixty-seven years ago, aged 16 years, I didn't know what a bugger was – although I was familiar with the word. I had never used a phone, so didn't know what phone bugging meant – I had also never seen a house bug. Brought up in a cottage in a mining village, I was only familiar with cockroaches.

Changing my job from a general domestic servant at a remote Welsh farmhouse, for five shillings per week, to a general domestic, at ten shillings weekly, for a large Jewish family in Aldgate, London, soon made me learn a lot about a variety of bugs. Leman Street, Aldgate, consisted of tall terraced houses, populated by Jewish tenants who had turned the top floors into clothing factories making dresses and sewing furs for the wholesale trade. The family I worked for made fur collars and cuffs for ladies' coats, much in vogue at the time. Four of their ten children had married and left home, and only the two youngest, still at school, were not employed in the family business. There was plenty for me to do, but luckily, my mistress gave me plenty to eat. I did all the washing for nine, including me, by the old-fashioned methods of scrubbing board and copper with a pennyworth of chloride of lime mixed into a huge tub of water to steep 'the whites' in before the final rinsing. Carpets were sprinkled with a mixture of damp tea leaves and salt before being brushed off with dustpan and hard brush. Factory windows apart, I cleaned all the others – inside and out – often sitting several floors up on the windowsills, legs inside (gives me the horrors when I think of it now). My winter scouring and polishing battled with some terrible pea-soup fogs.

Every Thursday evening I cleaned the huge copper samovar for use over the Shabbat period, and also the dozens of silver candlesticks lit at the same time. Milk drinks were prepared and cooked in the big kitchen and meat dishes on the scullery gas stove – for never the twain shall meet in an orthodox Jewish family. Time off for me was never mentioned, but I managed to get outside the house while running errands and now and again escorted the youngest child, 11-year-old Rosie, to the pictures. Bless her heart, she always let me choose the picture she wanted to see. They kept me in daydreams from one visit to the next. Winter had its drawbacks, but the big bugbear for me was the summer, when the insects, which had kept themselves to themselves behind the wallpaper and in the nooks and crannies of the ancient house, crawled out in their hundreds for their holidays. Many regarded the beds as luxury hotels – which meant that once a week I had to strip them, take the iron bedsteads to pieces and brush every point and surface with spirits of salt. It deterred them for a while, but there were plenty left to crawl up the walls. Rosie and I slept in single beds in the same room. When we spotted two bugs about parallel on the wall we would have halfpenny bets on which would reach the ceiling first. All too often I fell asleep before one got there.

After a year, I was allowed two weeks' holiday. Sitting with Dad, Mam and my three younger siblings at the table for the best homecoming meal Mam could muster, I was telling them about London, the quaint ways of my employers, and the bug races with Rosie. It was then Mam gave a little scream, ran upstairs, fetched my case down and tipped the contents on the little front lawn. The thought that I could have brought home a bug had sent her into a frenzy. Considering our cockroaches, I thought she was being a bit snobbish pest-wise.

I am writing this at ten minutes to three on the morning of 14 September, which is the copy deadline I have been given by *The Oldie*. Please don't feel sorry for me. It was three years ago that Richard Ingrams first asked me to write about being a grandmother. Three years ago I had four grandchildren; I now have five. Three of them visited me this afternoon. I was lying in bed, eating grapes and reading the Sunday papers. When I heard them come thundering up the stairs I hurriedly put my lipstick on and modestly pulled the sheets over my Knickerbox satin shorts 'n' camisole bed wear. After kisses all round, the seven-year-old gave me an excited account of the Spice Girls concert she'd attended in Sheffield the night before. 'They changed their clothes six times,' she said, admiringly, 'and Emma was the best.' Meanwhile, the three-year-old fell upon the bunch of grapes, ignoring her sister's stern warning that, 'If you eat the pips you'll *die*'. I noticed that when there were only stalks left in the bowl, the little one went to a mirror in the bedroom and studied herself closely. Was she searching for signs of imminent pip-induced death? Who knows? All three-year-olds are mad. It's pointless to speculate on what goes on inside their heads.

My husband gave the 11-year-old boy a balsa-wood aeroplane that he'd constructed the night before, and this techno-wiz of a child went into the garden and marvelled that something without batteries or remote control could fly and dip so elegantly, using only the low-tech breeze.

None of the children asked me why I was in bed in the afternoon. They are used to seeing me lying around. I have six sofas in the house and one hammock in the garden for that very purpose. I was reminded that my own grandmother always went to bed on Sunday afternoons. She took the *News of the World* and a half-pint of dark brown tea with her. It was probably the high spot of her hard working week.

She was called Lillian (my middle name) and she looked after my granddad, Jack, two grown-up children, two lodgers and various visiting grandchildren. She worked full-time and kept her small terraced house immaculately clean. There was a back-breaking routine of housework, starting at seven o'clock in the morning, when she would empty the urine from the pots under the beds into an enamel bucket, ending at eleven o'clock at night, when she would bank up the coal fire in the back room, in the hope that it would last until morning.

I was one of the first teenagers. We were invented so that our 'never had it so good' prosperity could be exploited by the teen-based industries that were springing up.

We were told by the American generation above us that teenagers were rebellious, moody and difficult. So we became those things, though not in the house, because it wasn't allowed. In the house you didn't answer back, and you did as you were told, though you wore an outrageous teenage uniform which shrieked rebellion.

My own grandma was soberly dressed at all times. Sometimes I shared a bed with her, and in the morning I watched through half-closed eyes as she dressed – large brassiere, directoire knickers, vest, corset, full-length petticoat, stockings, dress, cardigan, wrap-around apron and slippers.

Theories of relativity

Once she was one of Leicester's four beatnik teenagers, now she wears a long fleecy nightgown, pickles cucumber and indoctrinates little children: **Sue Townsend** *is a grandmother. Illustrations by* **Arthur Robins**

Just before she died I saw her bare legs for the first time. They had never been exposed to the sun. They were as purely white as the underside of a swan's neck. Her hair was steel grey and crimped into waves by the metal curlers she wore during sleep. There were no cosmetics of any kind in the bathroom.

In fact, there was no bathroom.

Her word was law. If she had told her grandchildren to throw themselves into the canal we would have done so immediately, without stopping to remove our shoes.

I went to meet her from work, late one Saturday afternoon. The sun was streaming through the high factory windows. The air was full of floating white fibres from the white cotton socks that she helped to make, eight hours a day, six days a week. At the time I

was enchanted. It seemed to me that my grandmother worked in a perpetual internal snowstorm.

Much to her alarm I turned down one of the roads marked 'beatnik' in the subdivision of the teenage highway which eventually opened up. 'Beatnik' incorporated most of the things I was interested in: jazz, cigarettes, Russian books, French films. There were very few beatniks in Leicester. I was one of four.

I bought the *Manchester Guardian* and read it secretly, with a dictionary to hand. I knew that one day I would be able to understand it.

I'm writing about my grandmother because, I think, I'm slowly turning into her. I've started to bake bread and cakes, and I steep cucumber slices in malt vinegar like she used to. When my

59

husband is away, I wear a long fleecy nightgown and bedsocks. After years of prevarication, I am now developing certain fixed opinions.

The turning point came when I was forced to take to my bed for six months in August of last year. Disc trouble and sciatica brought me down as violently as a rugby tackle. The pain was dreadful; it felt like a family of particularly sharp-toothed beavers was gnawing at my back and legs. Painkillers and tranquillisers became grandma's little helpers. These pills dull the wits and allow one to watch junk TV day and night. (Are the programme makers on the same pills, I wonder?)

On the few occasions when I left my bed, I was assisted by a stick. When my grandchildren saw me hobbling towards the lavatory, stick in hand, wearing a sensible nightgown and bedsocks, hair in need of a cut and dye, I think for the first time I became a *proper* grandma to them. And, when I briefly lost control of my bladder and bowels – incontinence is a dirty word, but double incontinence is even dirtier – I was entirely sympathetic to my two-year-old granddaughter's struggle with toilet training.

I've taken it upon myself to inform my grandchildren about the natural world. These children are entirely modern – skilful with the video, the computer, the microwave and the mobile phone. But they

None of the children asked me why I was in bed in the afternoon. They are used to seeing me lying around

are not totally seduced by technology. They are still full of wonderment that a dull-looking grey bean can transmogrify six weeks later into a beanstalk as tall as the house. And they are thrilled that they can actually eat the lettuces they have sown themselves.

Breadmaking is another satisfying activity (we like our food in this family). When we're pounding the dough we talk to each other and I take the opportunity to indoctrinate them with my beliefs: *kindness* is the most important thing in the world, and *good manners* are a form of kindness. *Socialism* is good. *Capitalism* is bad. I am a shameless propagandist. I also play music while we bake. I am currently obsessed with Bach's suites for cello, and the children seem to enjoy the sonorous sounds echoing around the kitchen.

I act as a buffer between their harassed, busy parents. If there is a dispute I am usually on the side of the child. I am haunted by the feeling that I didn't do the best I could have done for my own children. Though, in my own defence, I remember shouting up the stairs to them, 'Will you please stop *laughing*!' Being a grandmother is giving me another chance to love and be loved by children. Last week I took a row of previously despised pearls from their box, and fastened them round my neck. When I looked into the mirror I saw Lillian, my grandmother, looking back.

Olden Life

What was...
Hallé's Band?

IN 1946 I JOINED a symphony orchestra in Manchester, affectionately known to the citizens as Hallé's Band. This was Barbirolli's Hallé, and to modern orchestral musicians we Hallé-types would seem a rather odd lot. John Barbirolli had come home from the New York Symphony in 1943 to reform the Hallé, and found himself with half an orchestra of excellent professionals who had risked it and left the BBC Northern to join him. He then proceeded to find the other half in a biblical manner, pulling violinists out of the Kardomah Café, a lady trombonist from the Salvation Army, third-year students from music colleges. I joined as second oboe, fresh from the Royal Academy, enthusiastic and very green.

The Free Trade Hall had been bombed, so we rehearsed in a dusty old primary-school hall where trains clanked by at regular intervals, and we drank our much-needed coffee from thick mugs at a coffee stall out in the street. Barbirolli was extremely patient and kind with his motley crew, and once took me through Elgar's *Second Symphony* in his sitting-room, conducting with a pencil, so that I shouldn't get into difficulties during the concert.

Every Friday during the season, Hallé's Band journeyed to Sheffield in two Leyland buses. The first of these, containing the principals and most of the ladies, was known as the 'Posh' bus. The second was called the 'Boozers' ' bus. The brass mainly travelled in this, and while the Posh bus set off immediately after the concert to carry us to our virtuous beds, the Boozers' bus waited for horns, trumpets and trombones to finish their pints in peace. It was rumoured in the Posh bus that there was a lonely pub on the border between Yorkshire and Lancashire which stayed open all night, much to the approval of the Boozers.

We played all over the north, mostly in Methodist church halls. It was a bitter winter and, coal being rationed, there was very little heating. A second violin and I had both served in the WRNA, and we never hesitated to wear our Wren bell-bottoms under our long black dresses.

We were a mixed lot. There was kindly Stuart Knussen, the principal cellist and grandfather of Oliver Knussen, the composer and conductor; Joyce, one of the first

Hallé's Band and the 'Posh' bus in 1946. The author is fourth from the left

John Barbirolli

You know the rains are over when the bush cherries come into season. Slender stems of trees, barely three inches in diameter, suddenly sprout clusters of berries. They look more like clusters of green frogspawn in the permanent gloom of the tall trees, and even when they ripen to a gleaming scarlet hue, ready for eating, they don't look much like cherries.

Cherry season in November is my favourite time in the tropics, the equivalent of spring in the temperate zone. There is an excitement in the air, a stirring of life, a freshness and warmth after the chill and the wet and the numbing ennui of the rains. The storms may still boom over the pygmy forests of central Africa, but in the coastal forests of the White Man's Grave the skies are suddenly blue and cloudless. But from May to October, it rains and it rains. For six long months Mother Africa hardly ever closes the sluice gates.

It begins innocuously enough. The first rumbles come from over the sea far to the south, a faint low growling sound, inaudible to those who live deep in the forest and barely audible to those who live by the sea. It doesn't last long. The growling soon subsides to little more than a discontented muttering, fading into nothing as the storm takes itself off over the vast hot wastes of the Gulf of Guinea.

There is a lull for a couple of days, then it starts up again. A gun-metal grey wash of colour on the horizon widens almost imperceptibly, fitfully illuminated by the faint flickerings of an electric storm fretting over the water. The growling becomes progressively louder as the sapphire cloak of the sea is replaced by a mantle of sullen, liquid lead, and the dry, burning orb of the sun is transformed into a harsh, watery glare. There is an oppressiveness in the air, a brooding, suffocating heat. When the sudden breeze that presages the storm hits the land at last, it is almost with a sense of relief that the people of the Coast settle down to await the arrival of the rains.

The first storms are at their most dramatic in the forest interior. Clattering bursts of thunder shake the earth with their violence, and lightning flares and sears and splits the heavens in a continuous

woman timpanists; Paddy on the clarinet (who used to say, with good reason, 'My pianissimo is my forte'); and our own JB, as we called Barbirolli. He was affectionately regarded by nearly all the players, even if he did sometimes hurl the score onto the floor or glare at you with flashing eyes if you made a bad 'domino'. Charlie, a veteran harpist, was a tall old man with a face like an amiable crocodile and big old hands which sometimes got entangled in the harp strings, especially in the cadenza in Tchaikovsky's *Waltz of the Flowers*. JB had great respect for the older men and treated them with invariable courtesy, so all he did was chuckle a little.

When summer came round again at last, a small group of us set out on a short tour of the Lake District as an unofficial chamber orchestra. At the end of the tour we set off home again in a small bus. It was a pleasant evening and we stopped to refresh ourselves at several pubs. Carrying

on our way, we suddenly stopped in a narrow lane edged with thick hedges. Some of the men got out for the usual reasons. There was a longish pause and then some crashes. Someone seemed to be opening the boot, so we got out as well – to be greeted by delectable sounds. There, by a gate in the moonlight, watched by two cows, were Charlie and his harp and Paddy with his clarinet, playing Irish folk songs.

We were a very human collection of musicians, but with the inspiration and sheer hard work of John Barbirolli we achieved standards of performance that cheered and delighted our audiences in those distant, austere days. It is many years since I was a happy second oboe thrilling to Debussy, Delius and Elgar. But for all the long journeys and draughty halls, I have happy memories to last me a lifetime. I am proud that I was once in the Hallé Orchestra, which I shall always think of as Hallé's Band.   **Joan Swift**

Seething armies of ants devour anything in their paths and monster
worms emerge from the swamps. **Donald MacIntosh** *describes the rainy*
season in the White Man's Grave. Illustrated by **Paul Hogarth**

The rains came

brilliance of cold yellows and greens beyond the dark of the trees. These first storms bring with them a wind that flurries and swirls and shrieks through the forest in demonic rage and cause real damage. Great trees are incinerated by lightning bolts, others are uprooted and flung aside by the wind. On hillsides and exposed river banks, swathes are blasted through the forest, forming morasses of fallen trees and thorny vines.

But the ferocity of those early storms soon fades. As suddenly as they started, they stop. The forest settles down to the humdrum monotony of the rain season proper. The air is still and the rain comes down in a relentless torrent, so heavy that it is often impossible to see more than ten yards ahead.

Only foolishness or hunger makes anyone venture outside during these months. Main roads become little better than ploughed tracks, blocked by abandoned vehicles, and rivers become completely impassable. Water levels rise ten feet overnight, and rivers that had been as quiet as English chalk streams one day become roaring torrents the next.

The Owena in Nigeria is one such river. During the rain season it is transformed into a thundering, rolling brown flood that stops for nothing. After the Second World War, here and there along its course, bridges were built across the Owena to a standard design: abutments and piers were monoliths of stone and concrete, each pier being 15 feet long by five feet wide, and tall enough to ensure clearance above the river at its maximum rain season height. For double security, each pier was bolted into the bedrock of the river. Spanning the piers were great baulks of ironwood, three feet square, and, nailed to the tops of those beams with six-inch nails, the heavy plank decking and running strips required for the bridge surface. Until the season of 1957, I felt sure that nothing the elements could hurl at them could have inflicted the slightest damage.

That year produced the heaviest rains for many decades on the Coast. I was working in the forests of the northern reaches of the Owena, and the end of one day found me in a Land Rover churning its way south through seas of mud to our first bridge crossing. We reached it and stopped,

thunderstruck. The river, heavily swollen when we had crossed it four hours earlier, had risen a further eight feet and was now rolling over the topmost planks of the bridge surface. Stuck behind the bridge was the most incredible assortment of debris: log ends, tree limbs, great piles of bushes festooned with liane, pit-sawn planks, an upturned canoe, and a massive okwen tree, jammed firmly behind one of the piers. Its huge branches hung high over the bridge and the body of a drowned cow was wedged on top of them.

I would happily have gone straight back up the road and lodged in the timber camp for the night, but my driver was made of sterner stuff. He put the vehicle into gear and moved slowly towards the river.

Most of the decking was under a fast-flowing torrent of brown water, and it was impossible to see whether the bridge still existed beneath it. All the driver could do was to keep his gaze riveted on the point on the opposite bank at which he could just discern the top of the bridge abutment rising above the water, and drive straight towards it. With heart-stopping slowness, he did just that, the bridge shuddering violently under our wheels.

Several lifespans later, a collection of naked urchins standing in the bucketing rain raised a cheer as we pulled up alongside them on the far bank. My driver switched off the engine and lit a cigarette with shaking fingers.

We watched for ten minutes while the waters rose higher and the death groans of the bridge increased in volume. Finally, with one almighty crack, it was gone. Two great concrete piers went tumbling end over end downstream, and ironwood beams weighing several tons each were swept off like matchsticks.

If one had to travel in the rain season, it was better to do so on foot. Even the most powerful vehicles could get bogged down inextricably, and stranded vehicles were sitting ducks for enterprising collectors of vehicle parts. Engines would be removed in short order, and drivers could wake up

to find their cars sitting on blocks, their wheels having vanished during the hours of darkness.

I never had such problems. My legs were my transport and the forest was my home. My life was governed by what was known as 'Africa Time'. If it was impossible for me to get from A to B today, there was always tomorrow. If a river proved impassable and there was no canoe to ferry me across, what of it? The obvious solution was to wait until the waters subsided.

From May to October, it rains and it rains. For six long months Mother Africa hardly ever closes the sluice gates

I was no more fond of the rains than the next man, but I got used to them. My work cataloguing tree species went on throughout the year and I never made the slightest attempt to stay dry when out working: waterproof clothing would have been too hot and cumbersome for the amount of walking I had to do, and the condensation within would have nullified the point of the exercise.

There were some advantages to working in the rain. One got closer to the wildlife. Sometimes, too close. The relentless downpour seemed to have the same brain-deadening effect on wild creatures that it had on human beings. Trudging along a forest path with my eyes on the ground and the rain battering down, I have found myself having close encounters with buffalo, and in the midst of herds of bush pig and giant forest hog.

Some of the less obvious inhabitants of the forest claim the attention most in the rain season. Because of his love of the rain and watery places, the rhinoceros viper is known as the River Jack. He is extraordinarily beautiful, patterned in a striking array of reds and yellows and greens and blues and blacks. He is surprisingly difficult to see on the forest floor. He has a filthy temper, and his strike is lethal.

The African earthworm goes on tour at this time of year, too. The first time I saw this harmless invertebrate writhing down the path towards me, all six slimy feet of it, and one inch thick from beginning to end, I experienced a thrill of horror. I stepped aside and watched as it humped its way blindly past me, moving with surprising speed and agility down the thin runnel of water which flowed along the centre of the path.

Swamp life comes into its own during the rains. Waters that have stagnated during the dry season are revitalised and spawn a new generation of life. Stirring in the murky depths will be the lungfish, an unprepossessing, eel-like creature which hibernates during the dry season in a nest of mud deep down in the swamp. When the water eventually rises and softens the mud enough to enable it to burrow its way back out, it returns to the waters of the swamp.

Swamps are the breeding ground of the malarial mosquito. The onset of the rains sees a rise in the level of the swamps and a consequent increase in the mosquito population. The male is a completely harmless nectar drinker: it is the female of the species that does the damage. West African mosquitoes can shove their needles through denim, and, in addition to transmitting three different types of malaria, they carry such fatal diseases as yellow fever and elephantiasis.

No one has ever travelled through the African rainforest without coming into contact with the driver ant. The first hint of thunder coincides with the start of mass movements over the forest floor by those voracious creatures. They are universally feared, and every able-bodied thing moves quickly out of their path. Driver ants figure prominently in the folklore of the Coast, one popular belief being that before swallowing its victim, the python will always travel in a wide circle around it to ensure that the dreaded driver ants are not in the vicinity and liable to come upon it as it lies comatose after its meal.

The drivers move in columns, flanked by soldiers. The soldiers are formidable warriors: jet-black, about an inch long, with fearsome pincers on their jaws. Millions of them go on the march at any one time, in seemingly endless columns, little more than

a few inches wide. Excessively heavy rain seems to disorientate them, however, scattering them in the surrounding bush, and the unwary traveller may suddenly find himself in a seething mass with no apparent means of escape. The answer is to run like hell with a high-stepping gait, stamping the feet hard on the ground as you go to prevent them from getting a purchase.

Among some tribes the ants are

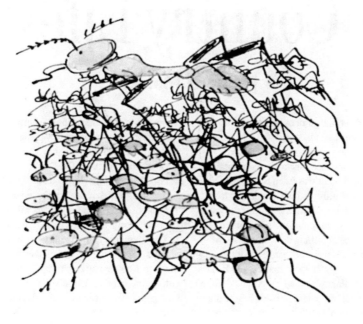

regarded as a blessing. They are the finest pest-control agency in Africa. Huts are abandoned until the ant hordes have passed through, by which time not a single rat, lizard, roach or flea remains. Nothing escapes their attentions. But there are plenty of horror stories about tethered goats, cows in labour, even injured elephants, being reduced to skeletons in short order. Their bite is ferocious, and any unfortunate unable to escape is eaten alive. Even when you pull them off, the body comes away from the head, while their pincers remain buried deep in your flesh.

They are particularly active at night, and are a horrible nuisance to those who have to sleep in the forest during the rains. Moving camp in the middle of the night in bucketing rain, with everything in the vicinity a seething mass of ants, is not for the faint of heart.

There are occasional lulls in the downpour, and these are the times you remember

with the greatest pleasure. You waken one morning to the sound of chimpanzees hooting and screaming their delight as a hazy sun breaks through the clouds and the mist drifts slowly through the branches of the forest giants like puffs of silvery cotton candy.

But these are rare interludes, soon to become a distant memory as the rain comes down again. Once more, you edge your way over rotting tree trunks spanning raging rivers, or flounder through endless swamps. Even when you reach relatively solid ground, there is only the drumming of the rain in your ears as you squelch your way through the sodden forest. You are convinced that you will never be dry again and that this time, the rains are going to last forever…

And suddenly, as abruptly as it started, it is over. Once again the thunder rattles and clatters over the forests and lightning sears through the leaden clouds. But there is a subtle change in the atmosphere. The storms are drifting back to the mangrove swamps of the coastal lagoons. For a few days they will bluster and bellow, but every inhabitant of the Coast knows that this is the end. Soon the skies will once again be blue and cloudless as the dry season returns to the Coast.

The emergent sun will bring new life to the wetness of the woods. For the next few months the treetops will ring to the songs of the birds and the chattering of monkeys, and the forest will become, once more, a paradise of perfume and colour. The cherries are the harbingers of this resurgence of life. *Maesobotrya berteri*, the scientists call them. To me, they will always be November cherries. I can taste them as I write this, and no fruit has tasted half as good.

Country Life

Richard Mabey

The garden stretched out like gardens should at midsummer, as lush and serene as a vicarage lawn. Fledgling blackbirds, deep in heavy-leafed shrubs, chinked monotonously. The comatose cats lay in the grass as placidly as Samson's lion. It was Eden before the Fall. Then out of the corner of my eye I glimpsed what appeared to be an enormous clockwork bird careering down the edge of the lawn. Its broad chocolate-brown wings whirred furiously, making me think for a moment it was a mallard crashing down from one of those rampant courtship fly-pasts. It was less than ten feet from my study window before I realised it was a female sparrowhawk that had just scooped up a young starling. The hawk stood stock-still on the grass, an awesomely beautiful bird with marbled chest feathers and a glittering gold eye. It clenched its talons tighter round the still-living starling, whose beak gaped open in pain and, no doubt, terror (hawks, contrary to belief, aren't always quick or clean killers), then flew off to finish the grisly business elsewhere.

This is the scene, enacted over increasing numbers of the nation's back gardens, which has made a curious common cause between suburban householders, gamekeepers and pigeon-fanciers: piracy on the home patch; the slaughter and – maybe worse – the theft of favourite small birds fondly stoked up with

'My husband eats like a bird - do you have any regurgitated insects?'

peanuts throughout the winter. Many who were appalled at the near extinction of birds of prey by agricultural pesticides are now outraged that their numbers have recovered sufficiently for them to become garden raiders. The Duchess of Devonshire has famously described sparrowhawks as 'using a bird table like the Ritz bar', and campaigns to have them classed as vermin again.

I suppose I see a sparrowhawk kill in the garden once a year. Most of the time they pass rather casually overhead, spying out the land or enjoying the thermals. Only in wildlife documentaries are the lives of birds of prey given over single-mindedly to the chase. So the soft-hearted among us are spared frequent confrontation with the predator's imperative of killing – because that is what it does, neither mercifully nor cruelly, but necessarily. The red kites which have been so successfully introduced to the southern Chilterns are a case in point. They are wonderfully adroit flyers, banking and wheeling like eagles one moment, then heading into the wind with wings shrunk back like falcons, and tilting their forked tails like rudders. But I have never seen one take so much as a worm, let alone a lump of carrion or a mouse. As in their flying, they seem to feed on air. At least hobbies do visibly eat. A pack of six of these dashing falcons, with chestnut thighs and bandit moustachial patches, haunted our local reservoirs throughout May, scything among clouds of swifts, swallows and martins that congregate there in wet and windy weather. But this time the hobbies were hunting only daddy-long-legs and damsel-flies, for which of course not a single sentimental tear is shed. They skimmed over the water, turned cartwheels, stooped and stalled as they caught the flies with their feet. Then they would fly past more leisurely, holding the insect forward in one claw and munching it like an ice-cream cornet. In the autumn it's another matter, and the hobbies feast off the young swallows and martins that gather in thousands just before migration. It's a part of their lives that, as an occasional host to martins, I'm too squeamish to watch. But I console myself with the thought that neither hobbies, hawks, nor any other predators make any difference to the populations of their prey. If they did, they would, of course, wipe themselves out. An abundance of birds of prey, in garden or on grouse-moor, is a kind of benediction, a sign that all's well with the habitat and its food chains.

John Christie

I COULD EASILY have ended my life as a body hidden under the floorboards at Ten Rillington Place.

In 1940 I was doing shuttle service outside the War Office in Whitehall. I was in the ATS. It was a cold day, pouring with rain, when a policeman tapped on my car window. He said, 'Come and have a coffee in the blockhouse, there are other War Office staff there.'

I didn't want a coffee, but the FANYs had a reputation for being snooty, so I agreed. He said he'd go on and for me to follow.

I locked the car and ran back the 100 yards to the blockhouse.

I entered a small low aperture, surrounded by sandbags, and found myself in a narrow passage. I walked to the end and heard a sound. I turned and saw him standing in the entrance, his eyes staring.

I said, 'I came in here for a coffee and nothing else. If you put a finger on me, I'll give such a scream I'll bring the whole War Office out. I have many influential friends.' I hadn't a soul, in fact.

He didn't speak again but dived at me, knocking me back against the wall at the end of the passage, where there was an orange-crate. Then he grabbed my throat with one hand and pinched my nose with the other so that I couldn't breathe. With all my strength I kicked him in the crotch with my army-issue shoe. He staggered back and I dived for the entrance. My heart beating like a sledgehammer, I rushed back to my car and drove off at high speed.

That night I rang my father. 'What shall I do? I was attacked by a policeman.'

My father, full of concern, asked, 'Did he hurt you? Did he touch you? Did you get his number?'

I said I was unhurt; it had been raining, and his cape had covered his number.

'Forget it then, do nothing. Who would believe the word of an ATS girl against that of a policeman?' was my father's advice.

So I forgot it, but I knew that I would never be able to forget those eyes.

The war ended, I got married and had three sons. Then one morning in 1953 I opened the newspaper – and there were those same eyes staring up at me. I screamed for my husband. 'That's the man who attacked me,' I said and pointed to the hateful face.

'Nonsense,' he replied.

'Look in the paper and see if he has ever been a policeman.' I knew I was right.

There were five pages about his awful crimes, with horrific details of all the women who had been strangled.

Eventually he looked up. 'My God, he was a Special Constable in the War Reserve Police in 1940.'

He rang 999 and in seconds was put through to Sir Lionel Heald, who was leading for the Crown. Sir Lionel asked my husband if I had children. He told him that we had three little boys and that we lived in the country. Sir Lionel said, 'Give me your name and address – but I don't want to call your wife. It is the most appalling case and we have enough evidence to hang Christie a hundred times.'

And he duly was hanged – at Pentonville that same year, on 15 July.

I'm 81 now. Last month I saw in the paper that there was to be a repeat of the film *Ten Rillington Place*. My blood ran cold.

Judy Cameron-Wilson

Vive les freebies!

No such thing as a free lunch? Au contraire, says **Wilfred De'Ath**, *who has enjoyed Gallic hospitality for the last five years. Illustrations by* **Derek Rains**

English friends do not believe that I have lived in France for five years without any money. I fell into this way of life by chance in 1992, when, arrested for not paying a hotel bill in Caen, I was dragged, hand-cuffed, in front of the *Procurer de la République* (State Prosecutor) who, after commenting sarcastically, 'I suppose even in England – *même en Angleterre* – people usually settle their hotel bills,' ordered the gendarme to release me to an *asile de nuit* or night shelter.

This was not the most pleasant of places, full of drunks, tramps and neurotics, but it set me on the path which, apart from a few brief intervals in England under legal restraint, I am still treading today. I spent six pretty uncomfortable nights in the *asile*, though the spaghetti they served at supper was the best I have ever tasted. In Angers, three weeks later, in trouble again, I was directed to the Abri de la Providence (literally, providential shelter) where, on my first night, an elderly German resident told me that we had the good fortune to be staying at the equivalent of a two-star family hotel. This turned out to be true. I stayed for three months.

For 15 francs (about £1.50), which you paid only if you could afford it, you were given a comfortable bed and a superb, nourishing meal: soup, salad, boiled beef and carrots, cheese, yoghurt and fruit was a typical menu. The ambience was distinctly familial and the humane director, very pro-British, encouraged me to sing for my supper (since I couldn't pay), by giving English lessons to staff and residents, which I did once a week.

The inmates of the Abri de la Providence were a pretty mixed lot – not so much tramps and drunks (though there were a few of those) as middle-class men who had simply fallen on hard times – deserted by their wives, lost their jobs and had their houses repossessed. They were excellent company, and taught me to speak good French. To a large extent, I identified with them. For several weeks, at supper, I sat next to a former member of Pompidou's government – I didn't believe him at first until he conducted me to the Angers library and proudly showed me a photo of his younger self seated at a table with Pompidou and de Gaulle during the *événements* of 1968.

Even in Angers, however, I knew that *foyer*-wise (*foyer* means 'home' or 'hostel') better things lay ahead. One heard talk of a terrestrial paradise, a *foyer* de luxe named Antipoul, which is situated in the great south-west city of Toulouse. I made it there in February 1993 – I travel free on SNCF – and have lived there, on and off, ever since. For a mere five francs a night – which, again, you don't have to pay if you haven't got it – you share an austere but comfortable and extremely clean room with one other SDF (*Sans Domicile Fixe* or No Fixed Abode) like yourself. This is, admittedly, a bit of a lottery. I have stayed with filthy Arabs, with drunks, tramps, drug addicts, and university professors down on their luck. I am quite ruthless about getting rid of any *voisin* (room-mate) who troubles me too much. I simply complain to the director. As long as the *voisin* doesn't smoke in the room (forbidden anyway) or snore too loudly, then I am content. At present, I am sharing with a Spanish workman who is impeccable, and, as they say, extremely *sage* (well-

behaved).

Breakfast is buffet-style from 6.30am and consists of exactly what you would be served in a three- or four-star French hotel: *café au lait* or *chocolat*, fresh bread, butter and jam. You have to be out during the day for your room to be cleaned (you lunch free at the magnificent, futuristic Restaurant Socials, shaped like a flying saucer), then go back again at five for a shower and a shave and – here we get to the nub – the meal of your gastronomic dreams.

I once read in a food guide that the sign of a really good meal is that you leave the table not merely satisfied but exhilarated, and Antipoul does that for me night after night. Take last night, more or less at random. It happened to be my 60th birthday, which I had spent in Lourdes – two hours away by train – so I was quite tired and hungry when I got back to the *foyer* at 9pm. The staff served soup, a carrot-based salad, two

> **No one will believe that for a mere 20 francs you are given as much quality Norwegian smoked salmon as you can eat**

bowls of spaghetti and two fresh melons – a birthday feast, but nothing special by Antipoul standards.

There are *foyers* in France (every large city has one) where you eat even better than this. In Avignon, a hospital dating from the First World War and once run by Franciscan friars has been taken over by the (extremely rich) town and is now another *foyer* de luxe for the SDF. No one will believe that for a mere 20 francs (again, you pay only if you can afford it) you are given as much quality Norwegian smoked salmon as you can eat. This is normally preceded by a fine soup, deep in pasta, followed by, say, roast chicken on rice salad, Camembert, yoghurt and fruit. The young pro-British director, Roland, has a thing about writers and says it is an honour to have me there. I reply that the honour is all mine.

Limoges is not my favourite French city – rather a grey place – but at 45 Avenue Emile, Labussiere is another *foyer* where I have made friends for life. Michel, the director, an ex-boxer, protects me from the (frequently expressed) anti-British sentiments of the other residents. He is like a brother to me. Françoise, the waitress, cries when I arrive and cries again when I leave – I send her postcards from England, when on remand, which I truly believe she will keep by her bedside until the day she dies. These people offer a warmth and hospitality which I have not encountered under any circumstances in England.

In La Rochelle, at the Foyer des Cordeliers, they ask you, horror of horrors, to do a daily task. So I do not stay there very long – a week at the most – although the food, served by nuns, is excellent.

In La Roche-sur-Yas (almost the perfect French provincial town), at La Halte Foyer, everyone has to pitch in with the cleaning. So I do not stay there for very long either – five days at the most. Again, the *foyer* is superb.

What a selfish, self-indulgent bastard! My daughter, who has priggish tendencies, considers that, since I am living for nothing off the French state, I ought to be paying French *imports* or income tax. But how can I do that without a French income? (It is true that the French are very highly taxed in order to pay for all this.)

I suppose that I feel the world owes me a living. As the possessor of an EC passport and with no means, I am perfectly entitled to stay at these *foyers*. So is anybody else in my situation. So the world is paying its debt to me.

I wish I could say that I felt guilty about all this and that I agree with my daughter. But I don't. I repeat: anyone in possession of an EC passport and with no money is entitled to stay, for as long as they wish, at the French *foyer* – and without payment. Vive la France!

69

Old Boys

You can't always guess how far a classmate will go. **William Trevor** *thinks of one clumsy youth who confounded all expectations. Illustration by* **Peter Bailey**

Mak Choon Moon has gone back to Kuala Lumpur; Ridgeway, P.L.K., is rearing ostriches for meat. D.K. Fisher (1960) harnesses the wind; B.J. Lansdale (1956) is a Justice of the Peace. Southgate, W.M.E, has joined the family business. H.K. McKeever (1984) has assisted in the construction of a dam.

Once a year the Old Boys' Bulletin comes, listing subscribers to the last Appeal, bringing the news from Sligo and County Clare and Cork, from Fakenham and Yeovil, from New South Wales and Chile and Moldavia. T.M. Hopking (1951) has left the tea industry, de Courcy-Hartley is running a hotel. The Revd J.R. Sheill (1931) has retired to Youghal, having always loved the sea. C.C. Roe (1949) writes from Kenya and would welcome visitors.

Is J.M. Kingsmill Moore (1942) the Kingsmill Moore who was in love with Ingrid Bergman for the whole of an Easter term after seeing *For Whom the Bell Tolls*? Is D.C.L. Jameson (1941), now a Canon of the Church of Ireland, the Jameson who was a clever scrum-half, though sometimes slow to pass the ball? Not to be confused with Popeye Jameson of the whiskey family, who was so unjustly expelled? Whatever became of old Popeye? Whatever became of Stuffy Malone, and John Kane Archer in his bookmaker's tweeds? And Poodle Tennyson, and the temporary master who rifled the changing-room lockers? And the Byng brothers – long before my time – reputed to have disturbed a grave in the Moravian cemetery beyond the golf course to see if the Moravians were buried standing up?

I.G. Sainsbury has died. 'You wrote a poem,' Earle reminded me one teatime, a fact he should not have known, since all contributions to the school's alternative magazine were submitted on the understanding that there was confidentiality. Not meaning to hurt, since he was not that kind of boy, Earle said he knew about the poem because Sainsbury – editor of the alternative magazine – had lit his cigarette with it in the Printing Club. Handsome and stagestruck, Earle died too, a long time ago on a tour of Africa, still funny in *Present Laughter*, the first of my friends to go.

Now, they go all the time, age being what it is. The Marriages column, and the Births, once interesting, are less so as the years pile up. Could this Odlum, R.T.G., 1973 – be the son of the Odlum I knew so well? Is the Goodbody of 1967 possibly related to the Goodbody who made inept fags wash the common-room dishes all over again if traces of egg remained on a plate? At one remove too many, such speculations flop limply, before the page is turned.

A few years ago a name sprang out from among the deaths. Easy to forget, this boy, difficult to place. No Widmerpool, no attractive Stringham, no daring Templer. Not even in minor ways defying the school uniform – the knot of his plain grey Stackallan house tie neither too loose nor too tight in its soft grey regulation collar – hair sleeked, apologetic face, he blended so easily with the mass that his unobtrusiveness seems now like art. He would, perhaps, some of us imagined, one day take pride in a Clark Gable moustache, something to cheer those slightly empty features. A watch-chain dangling from a lapel, brown suit and all the buttons of a waistcoat buttoned: for an instant there might have been such an image, filched from a distant middle age.

Something prevents me from naming this boy. There is a privacy to be observed, although in the Bulletin, of course, his identity was clearly stated, and his year of entry. He lived near Monasterevin in County Kildare, a tidy house by the roadside in the country. My father and I used to pick him up at the beginning of term, for although petrol was practically non-existent in Ireland during the War ('the Emergency' as we called it), my father always seemed to be able to lay his hands on some. A battered green trunk was carried from the tidy house, no tuck-box.

'Good holidays?' my father would enquire and be politely told that yes, the holidays had been good. And my father would say something else and be answered, and that, for the remainder of the journey would be that. Years afterwards it was the green trunk, not the boy, that my father remembered.

Disliked by no one, argument or contradiction not his way, the boy we gave a lift to drifted through one term and then another, smiling when a smile was called for by some waggish master, kneeling in Chapel with an upright back, as the requirement was. Neat, ordinary handwriting filled a page with details of Caesar's Gallic War, and listed on another New Zealand's resources. Friendships were mild, no passion there. Never a frequenter of smokers' lairs, not one to find his way to the cupboard where the communion wine was kept, not one to confess outrageously to Brother Charles when once a year he visited, this boy was somehow not a goody-goody: being that would have been to give himself airs. Photography was his hobby – patient photographs of hills and flights of birds.

'He'll come to a sticky end,' we predicted about Piggott-Browne or Anselm. Neither did, in fact, the first rising to great heights in packaging, the second still distinguished in academe. We liked to spot the sticky ends, often seeing ourselves among them. Others we saw as army men and businessmen, solicitors and surgeons and engineers, architects and farmers, painters and journalists. Accountancy we probably guessed for the boys whom no one disliked, if we bothered to guess anything at all.

Perhaps it was because people forgot he was there that he outdid us all in the end. The Bulletin was circumspect, naturally not reporting that he died in gaol, that years before he had released the handbrake and jumped, had stood and watched and heard the screams, as in an old Hollywood film. When a few of us meet now the name bewilders, the face has gone until we drag it back. 'Not the one who'd eat your swedes?' 'Not Colville, who sang in his sleep?' No, not Colville, nor the one who'd finish your turnips for you, although he might have.

'There were initials on that trunk,' my father said when I told him. He had read about the case, he said.

Something went wrong. The corpse was found in a bog, not where it should have been, the grisly story goes. There was no doubt about the guilt, the awful act so clumsily performed that the truth stared the police and judge and jury in the face. Yet he was never one for that – for clumsiness, for murder. You'd swear on oath he wasn't.

I have not been back to look, but in the old school groups that one after another stretch for miles, it seems, on the dark panelling outside Dining Hall, I'm told he's quietly still there. A presence not at all like that of Sealy minor, who manages in his gifted way to appear twice in the same photograph. Kingston has tied his house tie into a bow, Fitzmaurice has turned his back. But taking it all seriously, neat in every detail, the boy we took for granted smiles his polite smile.

> We liked to spot the sticky ends, often seeing ourselves among them. Others we saw as army men and businessmen, solicitors and surgeons and engineers, architects and farmers, painters and journalists

POLICE!

CROOK!

71

Modern Life

What is...
Dumbing down?

I AM WRITING THIS with a smile! In my voice! I have modern hair, as I am writing this, and I am not going to use any long words. Sesquipedalianism – no way! And guess what: I am wearing a woolly jersey! See? I am ordinary! I am as ordinary as you! Maybe even more ordinary... but just because I am more ordinary than you doesn't make me special.

Dumbing down, you see – you do see, don't you? and do stop me if it all gets a bit hard – is where it's at. We can get alongside that one, right? We know where it's coming from? Right. Where it's coming from is a sneering hell, boiled from a vile decoction of snobbery, relativism and raw glossy greed by sharp-suited phoneys; what it is, is the latest in the immemorial line of restrictive and joyless orthodoxies masquerading, as always, as a public benefaction. Its spawning-grounds are politics and the media: the two groups which have most to gain from the peddling of infantilising anodynes to a population which otherwise, God help us, might rise up, smash its televisions, burn down Parliament and wipe its collective arse on the newspapers.

Dumbing down isn't just a con, isn't just an insult; it is, at root, cruel and destructive. At its root is an abject failure of morality. Imagine if our great public reformers had discovered dumbing down. Walking through the stinking streets, strewn with rot and ordure, they would not have been driven to build sewers, to pipe fresh water and clear the slums; instead, they would have cried 'Mmmm! What a lovely smell! That's how we like to live, too! Aren't you lucky!' And next time you hear some bubble-headed 'personality' put on the radio to introduce great music of which he or she knows nothing; next time you watch some fatuous idiot of an unfunny comedian inexplicably presenting a television programme trivialising important matters, or read a newspaper article mocking and snarling at something fine from a position of invincible ignorance, know that behind them lies some cynical, sneering 'executive' crying 'Mmmm! What a lovely smell!'

Because the worst thing about dumbing down is that it is hypocritical. The people responsible for it are educated, calculating men of well-developed sensibilities who have no share in the restricted, snarling, sound-bitten world view they peddle. Most are all too aware, yet count the rewards worth the shame, and are soon so well-rewarded that they lose the capacity for shame in a welter of self-regard.

And so the process continues. As the old gag has it, 'Eat shit; a hundred billion flies can't be wrong.' The peddlers of dumbing down spot a gap in the market, and so sell shit, telling each other that it's what the public want, it's what they like, it's what they understand, it's all they understand. What cannot be reduced to a slogan or have its sting drawn by a mealy-mouthed 'presenter' must be sneered at and dismissed as 'snobbery'. Great music, art and drama are to be condensed and detoxified; tragedy turned into sentiment, history dismissed as irrelevance, religion relieved of the numinous, and politics stripped of statesmanship and transformed into a branch of public relations.

The dumbers-down argue that they are exponents of democracy, but they are either lying or deluded. Democracy turns upon the principle of an informed electorate, not upon its stupefaction. There is nothing democratic about a party political system which battles solely for the control and manipulation of the public's prejudices. The commanders of the Roman Empire knew that after they had won the battle, they had to win hearts and minds; now our politicians seek to win the reptilian hind-brain, as though the exercise of our franchise were co-located with the part that controls our genitals.

Strange and disagreeable as it may be, the slightly improving odour which emanated from H.G. Wells and Bernard Shaw and the Mechanics' Institutes was far less redolent of patronising infantilisation than the sweeter, fruitier, vanilla-and-peachier hogo which shimmers off Disney and Blair, the civety cat-reek of Mandelson, the watermelon insubstantiality of Hague and the honking, faecal, butyric stench of the Murdoch tabloids and their imitators. Those are the real odours of inequality, keeping the proles ticking over in their telly-struck, drum-deadened, dogmeat-pie oubliettes. The do-gooding improvers of a century ago might have been a bit sandals-and-fruit-juice, the tiniest touch oopsie-la, but at least they had more hope than cynicism, did not confuse statistics with judgement, believed perhaps not only that people deserved better, but that there was a better for them to deserve. Now, in the hunt for power and profit and in the name of relativism and market research, instead of being enticed and encouraged, we are indulged, offered spurious and impertinent approval ('Yes! We all like football and fish fingers too!') and treated like children, overwhelmed with slogans, sound-bites, confessional television, proliferating admonitions, vacuous grinning young women, jerks in jerseys, photo-opportunities.

But that's where the money is, so... hey, I'm not one of your snobs. Not me. Rameau, Suetonius, Primo Levi, Shelley, J.S. Mill? Never heard of them! Give me football any day! Look! Still wearing my jersey! Football! Oasis! Still smiling! Modern hair! Hello? Mr Murdoch? I didn't mean it! It was a joke! I'm available...
Michael Bywater

War games

Mike Molloy *recalls a time when school was as thrilling as an old British war film – and dodging prefects meant having to be a master forger*

Recently a friend showed me his newly installed wine cellar. At first I thought it might be a nuclear bunker. Built by a German company, there was a reassuring military quality about the structure, reminiscent of the concrete pillboxes still scattered about Europe as a permanent reminder of the last time the *Wehrmacht* went walkabout. The idea is simple; they just dig a big hole in your garden, lower the whole thing into it and bung a trap-door on top. The user descends a spiral staircase to choose the bottle they want from compartments in the sides.

Not being a wine connoisseur, I have no use for one myself but it got me thinking about some of the things I wish I had laid down over the years. A few black and white vintage British war films would be nice to have, just as a reminder of the way we were before the hideous phrase 'touchy feely' entered the language to so accurately describe the mood of the People's Britain. Nothing set the tone of Old Britain more perfectly than the titles of those masterpieces: *Reach For the Sky*, *In Which We Serve*, *Angels One Five*, *The Way To the Stars*, *The Cruel Sea*, *Ill Met By Moonlight*. One only has to compare them with their US equivalents – *Flying Leathernecks*, *To Hell And Back*, *Hellcats Of The Navy* – to appreciate the differences that once defined our cultures.

British war films gave us heroes to emulate: Richard Todd leading his men forward, stiff

upper lip resolutely thrust towards the enemy, Jack Hawkins on the bridge of a destroyer, John Mills at the periscope of a submarine. And there was always Richard Attenborough as a snivelling cockney showing us how we were definitely not expected to behave.

So strong was their influence that when *The Colditz Story* was released it led to an extraordinary craze sweeping my school. Now all Englishmen of my generation, nurtured by the British film industry, know how to escape from a prisoner-of-war camp. First appoint an escape officer (Eric Portman type), then recruit tunnellers (Michael Medwin types), tailors (Richard Wattis types) to fashion civvy clothing from recycled uniforms ('I've turned your old greatcoat into a very nice three-piece suit, Basil'), and finally – for the most vital bit of kit of all – a forger (Donald Pleasence type) to make the necessary papers. Then you're off, pausing only in Switzerland to send a postcard, supposedly from your Aunt Emily, to the chaps back in the bag. Bostock was the boy who started our school craze. Late one winter afternoon, when we were supposed to be educating ourselves, Bostock was observed cutting up bits of potato. When asked what he was doing, he explained that he was making a Gestapo stamp for a Third Reich railway pass. Immediately a crowd gathered to examine his previous efforts. There was an identity card explaining that he was Jean-Paul Mendes, a toolmaker from Lyon, now employed as an industrial chemist by I.G. Farben, his discharge papers from the French army and a letter from his sweetheart who worked part-time in a *boulangerie*.

The craze was on! Within days our entire year had manufactured papers of their own. My French being weak, I opted to be a Walloon coal miner. Clandestine meetings were held in the lavatories, where we would fantasise about our ultimate bids for freedom.

But fate, always ready to thwart the best-laid plans with a sardonic twist, played a new card. The prefects discovered what we were up to. Noting that we had already cast ourselves in the parts of escaping prisoners of war, they assumed the role nature had always intended them to play: they became agents of the Gestapo. Suddenly we were no longer simply enjoying the fun of examining each other's documents – we had been plunged into a Kafkaesque world where burly thugs would stop us without pretext and demand to see our 'papers'. Those of us who were lucky were merely slapped about a bit, but others, those with unconvincing documents, were less fortunate. They were taken back to the prefects' sanctum, which had been converted into a prison cell, where more leisurely forms of torture

could be employed. So many confessions were extracted that to this day I view 'statements' made under duress with the deepest suspicion.

The horror continued for almost the rest of that term and we plunged ever deeper into despair, but help was to come from the most unexpected source. Before the 'occupation', teachers were regarded as the natural enemy, with prefects as mere co-belligerents, but what we had forgotten was that most of the teaching staff had actually served in the war, and consequently held fairly robust views about 'German' behaviour. Good old British bullying was seen as being character-forming, but Hunnish bullying was not to be tolerated. The teachers in turn formed their own committee under the command of Lieutenant Colonel Arthur Sears, better know to us as 'Trig' Sears, the maths master. It seemed that Trig had actually been on the Control Commission in Germany during the post-war allied occupation. He instigated a programme of de-Nazification for the prefects. It must have been a success; two of those who received the treatment went on to be local councillors in later years. A triumph for democracy – I think.

"That's all we need - the drum solo."

Down Memory Lane

I was sent to work as Richard Crossman's principal private secretary in March 1965. He had become Minister for Housing and Local Government in the new Labour administration in October 1964. It was his first ministerial appointment, but not the job he wanted or expected. His main interest during his first 20 years in Parliament had been foreign affairs, and more recently he had been front-bench spokesman on social security. But he loved his new department: on leaving it two years later, he said it had been the happiest time of his life. His officials were not so enamoured of him. He had no idea of how a minister should behave towards his civil servants. At first he bullied, mistrusted and offended them at every turn. He had already got through two private secretaries before I was sent to him. The permanent secretary, Dame Evelyn Sharp, said to me: 'You'll have to make a go of it: we can't go on like this.' Crossman himself said to me: 'What I want is a sparring partner; everyone here is too deferential.'

Our relationship was a bit stormy at times. Once, at home, my wife heard me shouting angrily at someone on the telephone and was surprised to learn that I had been speaking to Crossman. She said: 'I thought you were talking to the builder.' But Crossman and I settled into a reasonably good working relationship. He realised that he needed an efficient private office, and Dame Evelyn had made it clear to me that the department needed to establish sensible relations with the minister. I never liked him much but I enjoyed his intellectual energy, indiscretion and informality. It was certainly the most entertaining period of my 40 years in Whitehall.

One of my earliest recollections is of being summoned over to his flat in Vincent Square to deliver some urgent papers. Crossman was in his bath, talking loudly to Tam Dalyell (his parliamentary private secretary) who was sitting on the lid of the lavatory. I waited with Mrs Crossman in the living room. Crossman emerged in a cloud of steam, still talking, with a towel round his neck and otherwise naked. He was a large man. Mrs Crossman remonstrated: 'Oh Dick! Don't

My Crossman Diary

As a close aide **John Delafons** *saw the human side of a great political figure*

come in here like that.' Crossman looked down at himself and, somewhat non-plussed, stopped talking and retreated to the bathroom.

I sometimes went down to stay at Crossman's house near Banbury. It was part of a small farm that had belonged to Mrs Crossman's father. On the first occasion I met his two children, who happened to be the same age as mine. After tea we all had to play a game called, I think, 'Dragons'. One person was the dragon and he or she had to find the others, who were hiding around the house, and take them to his cave – which was a gloomy lumber room full of old cupboards and wardrobes. Those captured would be released by others, if they could evade the dragon. I was caught by Patrick Crossman almost immediately and deposited in the cave. After a few minutes one of the wardrobes started wobbling violently and Crossman burst out, shouting 'Free, free!' and thus released me. Afterwards we watched *Dr Who* on television (I had not seen it before and was totally mystified by it). We sat in the dark around the big kitchen table, on which were the remains of tea, including a plate of home-made jam tarts. When the lights went on again all the jam tarts had gone and Crossman's small daughter Virginia had jam all over her face. Crossman cried: 'I name the guilty party!'

I often accompanied him on visits around the country to local authorities or to official speaking engagements. On one occasion he had agreed (reluctantly) to give an after-dinner talk at Ditchley, which is a rather grand country house that seems to exist for no better purpose than to host 'top-level' conferences and seminars, chiefly on defence and foreign affairs. I have no idea who pays for it, but it is supposed to be very posh and, in those days at least, guests

were required to wear dinner jackets in the evening. It was a rule with Crossman that he would never dress for dinner, so he did not on this occasion. We were delayed on our journey and arrived late. The front door was opened by an imposing butler who had been there for many years and was reputed to rule the establishment with a rod of iron. Crossman asked to visit the Gents. The butler led the way down a wide corridor and threw open a huge door inside which was a rather small WC with a mahogany seat. I hesitated

He was in his bath, talking loudly to Tam Dalyell, who was sitting on the lavatory lid

outside and Crossman said over his shoulder, 'Come on John, don't be shy'. So we both peed into the bowl with the door open, under the astonished gaze of the butler.

There was a famous occasion when Crossman left some official papers under his chair after dining on his own late one evening at Prunier's. Someone picked the papers up after

Crossman had left and, instead of returning them, took them to the *Daily Express*, which resulted in a front-page scandal. George Wigg, who was the prime minister's self-appointed security expert, at once learnt of this from his Fleet Street sources and spent most of that night trying to trace me so that he could blame me for letting my minister take papers out of the office, not in an official box. In fact this happened while I was out of the office and Crossman had failed to tell the staff what he was taking. What seemed to infuriate Wigg was that I had not been at my post at 10pm and could not be contacted at my home address. 'Where were you?' he roared. 'I was at the theatre,' I replied. I suspect it suited Wigg (and the *Express*) to let it be thought that the papers Crossman had left in Prunier's were 'Top Secret'. In fact they were a set of out-of-date housing statistics which Crossman had wanted to use for a speech he was due to make later that week.

I can't remember any more about Crossman at present. Perhaps I will later.

PENSIONS-
THE WAY
FORWARD

The new earnings related scheme

Marrying Sean

When you're stuck in a grotty bedsit and the bailiffs are at the door, it makes sense to marry a film star. A short story by **Zenga Longmore.** *Illustrations by* **Larry**

9 April, 11am

Uggh! I knew the day was going to be awful, because it began with a call from the landlord: 'Still 'aven't paid the rent, luv?'

'Erm, no, that is to say, yes. Hasn't the cheque arrived yet?'

I may even have added a 'tut-tut-tut' for authenticity.

'Right, that's it. Three months overdue, an' still no sign of payin' up. I'm takin' you to court and you're out by the end of the month. Don't take this personal, but…'

'Oh no! No offence taken, personal or otherwise. Must dash, there's a knock at the door.'

It was the postman, asking me to sign for no fewer than three summonses. I was about to go straight back to bed when I noticed a fourth letter. A luscious blue padded envelope. Inside I found a wedding invitation. Lucky and Ingrid, that ghastly couple who moved to a swanky semi in Kingsbury last year, are showing off a step further by holding their reception in the Palm Court Hotel. They moved out of Harlesden, claiming it had become too run-down. Run-down! The nerve. And what a pretentious card, gilt-edged with turquoise cherubs at the top. But the most ridiculous thing of all was a note pinned to the card

saying, 'Please do not send gifts, but a cash donation would be welcome.' How can these people, whose sole purpose in life is flashing their wealth in the faces of us Harlesdenites, have the temerity to ask us for money. Ask for money… Ha-a-ang on…

To race down to the corner shop and spend my entire week's dole money on wedding invitations was the work of a moment. Pen between lips, I pondered on whom I could possibly be marrying. Someone capable of dazzling the world with a splendid wedding reception. Someone whom all my friends and family would financially cripple themselves to impress. Then I'll simply call the whole thing off at the last moment, and ring-a-ding-ding!

Now, before I forget, who's hubby going to be? An Arab sheik? Hmmm, the Pentecostal members of the family wouldn't approve, and the godless ones would shun the wedding, fearing there wouldn't be alcohol at the reception. Richard Branson? Too litigious. A film star? Aha! They're glamorous, rich, and get married so often that even if my chosen fiancé decides to have a well-publicised wedding the week before we get hitched, I can quite plausibly say, 'He's marrying her this week, and me the next.' So, who's it to be? Sylvester Stallone? Too beefy. Jack Nicholson? Too dangerous, might scare rich Uncle Aubrey away. Arnold Schwarzenegger? Woo! Too many letters to write on all those cards, I'd be shaken by the end of all that writing. Shaken. Shaken, not stirred.

9 April, 11pm Have sent off 120 wedding invitations to friends, relatives, neighbours and third acquaintances twice removed:

Bluebell Campbell and Sean Connery (the film star) invite you to their wedding at St Paul's Cathedral, 3pm, 30th April. Reception at Café Royal Hotel at 8pm. Don't send gifts, but a generous cash donation would come in handy

Impressive, eh? I thought the film star bit was an especially good touch. After all, it's important that no one goes away with the idea that I'm marrying just any old Sean Connery; the Sean Connery who works in the King's Head, for instance, or the potty Sean Connery who stands outside Budgen's with a mongrel tied to a piece of string. The cards look a bit tacky but, after all, Sean's filming in America, and I can't be expected to afford swish invitations like Lucky and Ingrid. With all the money I get, maybe I too could afford to move out of Harlesden. On the way to the post-box just now, I did notice the streets are looking a bit – how can I put it? – run-down.

10 April Washing machine broke down. Kitchen flooded. Ate nothing but dry toast all day 'cause spent dole on cards yesterday. Bit fed up, no cash, no job, life has no point. Lay in bed all day, watching boring programme about Euro currency and G7 summit.

11 April Wow! What a day! Just as well I managed to soft-soap the BT bloke out of cutting off my phone, 'cause it's been ringing non-stop. First caller was Uncle Aubrey in a state of high hysteria.

'Eh eh, darlin'! Is true, ah true? You a-go marry James Bond?'

'Yep.'

'Is how you meet him?'

'In the library in Harlesden. He was researching for a new film – set in Harlesden – about Brent Town Hall politics. He plays a housing officer who gets involved in a Housing Benefit scandal.'

'Rockstone! Who would have thought it! Well, listen, sweetheart, you book a photographer yet? 'cause Jason [his goofy son] say he'll do the photos for free. So, who'll be there at the Café Royal Hotel?'

'My friends, the family – oh, and of course Sean and all his showbiz chums. I expect you'll be able to wangle a dance with Julie Andrews.'

A sort of fizzing exploded from the other end of the phone, like a burst Coca-Cola can. The upshot was, he's sending me 300 smackeroonies. This must be the most ingenious idea I've had in my life! I didn't even have time to eat, so busy was I all day on the phone embellishing, embroidering, and listening to screamed congratulations. Cousin Noreen, Bev and Winsome are doing the catering. I swore to them that Sean adores rice'n'peas, and all the forms of Jamaican food they cook. Aunt May's doing the cake, and Daffodil and Dandy are going to ice it.

The only unnerving call was from Ingrid.

'Sean Connery, eh? How very strange, Bluebell. Where you pick 'im up?' she asked in her ice-cold Jamaican/ Kingsbury accent.

'In Harlesden library,' I replied, rather lamely.

'I see. Funny ting, I read this morning that he married a'ready.'

'Divorcing, you mean.'

'Whatever. An' another funny ting, me never knew the Café Royal was a hotel. When last I go there for the Christmas office party, it was a restaurant. Well, congratulations, Bluebell, see you at St Paul's. Oh, an' by the way, if Sean's there with you now in your Harlesden bedsit, tell him a big "Good evening, Mr Bond" from me, won't you?'

'I will.'

Trust Ingrid to be the only non-believer in my midst. Probably jealous that I'll upstage her vulgar wedding. I shall just dismiss her from my mind. There – gone!

What would Sean say if he knew he was setting Harlesden on fire with as much brilliance as Raj Patel, who burnt down three of his shops last week for the insurance?

12 April Mum called from Jamaica. She's a stern member of the Brotherhood of the Twelve Martyrs, and I imagined the news of my wedding would give her a heart attack; her only child about to become a backsliding Hollywood wife. I was just about to confess that the whole thing wasn't quite true when she sobbed, 'Oh, me sweet, sweet pickney! Jesum Piece! Me always thought you-a-gonna stay sunk into an 'orrible mire of failure alla you life, an' now you-a-go wed Roger Moore! This is the proudest day of me whole life! Praise be!' and she continued to weep for a few more minutes. Thank goodness I wasn't paying for the call!

'Now look 'ere,' she finally said, collecting herself, 'Aunty Cray's flyin' over from Brooklyn two days before the wedding with you grandma's lace. She gon' fit you up with a nice-nice wedding dress. An' I've been been able to borrow the money for a flight from me neighbours, so I'm comin' on the mornin' of the wedding. I tell everyone Sean'll pay 'em back threefold.'

Then she began to scream, 'Lawd

Pen between lips, I pondered on whom I could possibly be marrying. Someone capable of dazzling the world with a splendid wedding reception

Lawd! A daughter of mine! Mercy! Lamb of Calvary!'

I glowed with pride. Yet somewhere, niggling at the back of my mind, there lurked a certain… I can't put my finger on it.

14 April This morning, the floor was littered with cards stuffed with cheques. I put them all in the bank, and marched straight off to African Wave Crescendo. Decided to buy a new washing machine.

21 April Someone from the *Daily Star* phoned to ask if there was any truth in the allegations that I was about to marry Timothy Dalton. Noreen says that her mum in Kingston has spent a fortune getting her house done up in case we decide to drop in. Her eyes shone really brightly when I told her we were going to live in three houses: the Hampstead mansion, the Hollywood ranch and the villa in the south of France. She told me I've always been her favourite cousin.

25 April Money continues to flow through the letterbox like vodka martinis into James Bond's cocktail glass. I never noticed before that I had so many friends. By the way, the court case was heard in my absence yesterday, and apparently I've been evicted. I'm supposed to move out today. Just as I was leaving the house to escape the constant ringing of the phone, Pearl called round. She looked fantastic in a gold wig and silver acrylic fingernails decorated with the Stars and Stripes. I must get my nails done like that.

'Where's Seany?' she yelled.

'In my Beverly Hills home,' I replied smugly.

'Flippin' 'eck, man. Well, no matter. Let's go West End an' buy some clothes. I need a nice outfit to wear for the wedding.'

So off we trotted to every department store in Oxford Street. Pearl tried on scarlet strapless shift dresses and see-through crotchet numbers. Afterwards, we had drinks at the Waldorf. We couldn't stop giggling about the new life I was about to lead. I promised Pearl I'd get Sean to make her a Bond Girl. After a while, we got a bit tipsy and began to cry, saying how much we'd miss each other. I told her I'm sure Sean wouldn't mind if she lived in the Hampstead mansion with her three kids

while we're away. Then she cheered up.

'Just think,' she laughed, 'you got no more worries about bills and debts ever again, girl!'

I didn't need Pearl to tell me that!

28 April, noon Two days to go. Aunt Cray's here from New York. She's sleeping on the floor with Uncle Sinai and Cousin Horace. We've had an exhausting day measuring, tucking, tacking and trimming, and we've come up with the most beautiful wedding dress I've ever set eyes upon. The flowers have arrived a bit early, but Horace says they'll keep. Pompous Pastor Leap turned up uninvited to deliver a dull lecture on the sanctity of marriage. I was too busy arranging the veil to listen properly.

'You must not henter the 'oly state of weddingship with avarice inna ya heart!' he droned.

Then he had the cheek to ask for ten quid for his church, and asked if Sean could pay for his son Vernon to go to college. They've cut the phone off, and I got a letter from the bailiffs to say they're coming on Saturday. I'm very tired. I'll just try on the wedding dress one more time, then I'm turning in.

30 April, 1pm Well, here it is! The big day! Pearl came round early in the morning to do my hair. Uncle Aubrey's arranged for a limo to call at two. All the catering's fixed up. Noreen and the gang left ten minutes ago bound for the Café Royal Hotel. It took three minicabs to transport all those steaming pots and pans. This wedding has cost much more than we expected, but everyone's happy with IOUs until Sean arrives.

A rather horrible thing happened this morning. The bailiffs burst in and took all the furniture, the telly, the video, half my clothes and the new washing machine. I asked them how they could treat a girl like this on her wedding day, but they said, 'A job's a job, darlin'.'

Not that it really matters. Mum arrived safely this morning. She's gone straight to St Paul's because her plane was late. I haven't heard from Sean yet, but I expect he's having problems with his flight too, and anyway, isn't it unlucky to speak to the bride on the morning of the wedding?

Ah! Here's the limo! I must compose myself. Mustn't get too nervous in front of all those cameras at St Paul's. Pearl's yelling that I should stop writing now. It's time to go.

Illustrated by John O'Connor

Santus Circus

SANTUS CIRCUS could be in any suburban backwater on the edge of some East Anglian town or inland from the straggling bungalows of a Kentish seaside resort. On this particular burning July evening, it is lost in London's outback. We travelled through the East End on the District Line, and out into the full sun at Bromley-by-Bow, where there were butterflies on the buddleia all along the side of the track. The carriage emptied gradually onto eastward platforms, and we journeyed past wastelands of rosebay willow-herb, council tower blocks and allotments; past poplars and parks and back gardens stuffed with rows of runner beans and washing lines and sheds, towards Upney where nobody at all gets on or off.

The local taxi driver at Dagenham East station, who doesn't know there's a circus out on the A13, speeds us out beyond solid-looking pubs on roundabouts to marshy, willowy fields, pylons, rows of second-hand lorries for sale, an ancient church in the distance and then, suddenly, beside the road, the big top rising triumphant.

When you walk in from reassuringly ordinary England to a huge, bright blue, gold-starred other world, the old magic feeling takes you by surprise. It made me want to cry, I found it so beautiful. In the red velour ringside seats there is a middle-aged couple, a father and his child, and on the tiered seats behind, two more children. The lights dim, the drums roll and through the spot-lighted curtains on the other side of the ring a palamino stallion bursts through and canters round the small, scarlet-sided ring alarmingly fast, ridden by a glorious blonde, spangle-skirted ring mistress… 'Mesdames et messieurs,' she proclaims in perfect French, 'Welcome to Santus Circus.'

What ensues is the happiest, jolliest show to keep us smiling and the children's faces in a constant state of wonderment – from the Bulgarian clown, who trained in the Moscow circus, the Moroccan acrobats and a knife-throwing act, to Ann Marie Santus (who sold us our tickets and served us refreshments in the interval) climbing to dizzy heights up a rope in a skimpy leotard and spinning like a top from her neck, or being swung through the air on a metal frame by a circling motorbike, or asking four goats and two geese to do simple tricks. Roget, her husband, also asks little of the elephant Rani (who clearly adores him), or of the African bull. The feather-plumed Shetland ponies trot round and pirouette in perfect unison. Ernest Santus, the circus manager, smiles radiantly as the ringmistress, in her third change of sequinned leotard, top hat and tails orchestrates the final bow.

The circus coming to town is Unwrecked England. You can still find it if you look hard enough, but it has been driven into hiding by Political Correctness. If the Santuses put a poster up in a shop, the shop windows are smashed by animal rights people; no council will afford them an open space, no schoolteachers a mention.

It is Ernest Santus's determination which keeps the spirit of this circus going. The take tonight is barely enough to feed the animals – which incidentally are loved to distraction – let alone pay the exhausted artists who have just shifted the show from King's Lynn and put up the tent. When the animals are fed and watered, we sit and drink outside the caravans in the crimson glow of the Essex sky while the dogs bark and the elephant pushes her trunk under the side of her tent to graze. Ernest describes the trouble he has keeping the show on the road, how the trapeze artist has just left, how he can't hang on much longer: 'They are trying to kill it, they are breaking our hearts,' he says. Then he describes his parents' flying trapeze act, how his grandfather trained horses, how his other four brothers are all in the circus and his smile and his grit return. At its best, circus is art. If it is considered politically incorrect then teaching dogs to sit should be illegal.

Sir James Goldsmith

IN 1959 I WAS a student in need of a lucrative summer job. For reasons that are now unclear, I believed that the *Times* personal column was the best source of well-paid employment. My intuition proved correct when I spotted an advertisement for 'Attractive young ladies, outdoor types, needed for exciting project, duration three months. Excellent remuneration.' I applied, emphasising my love of the outdoors and enthusiasm for riding, and shortly afterwards was invited to an interview by the sales manager of Ellanby Laboratories.

He commented that I was rather pale for one so much in the open air, but supposed it had been a damp spring. He then told me that my employer would be Jimmy Goldsmith, 'of whom you may have heard'. Indeed I had. A year or so earlier, Goldsmith, well-known as an extremely rich playboy and gambler, had eloped with the 17-year-old daughter of a Bolivian tycoon. Following a hasty marriage, she had tragically died in childbirth, leaving a baby daughter. Now it seemed that the bereaved husband had put his flamboyant past behind him. He was to devote himself to his daughter and start a business career. As a first step he had bought a respected but unprofitable chain of chemists called Lewis & Burroughs. They were also manufacturing chemists, and it was this aspect of the business that Mr Goldsmith was anxious to expand. Hence Ellanby Laboratories, and the exciting new product that I, and five other attractive, healthy outdoor types, had been hired to promote.

Jimmy Goldsmith himself presided over the first meeting of his new sales force. He asked about our recent holidays – it appeared that I was the only one of the group who had not recently returned from the Mediterranean. I remember the eligible widower as thin and rather pale – not an

outdoor type himself. Our product, he said, looking carefully at our complexions, was something quite new, a lotion to make you tan without the sun. It was called Night Tan, and you applied it before you went to bed at night, waking up to find yourself with a deep copper tan. He then went over the economics of Night Tan. It was to retail at 25s, a very large sum in 1959. However, the more expensive a beauty product, the better it sold. Purchase tax accounted for five shillings of the cost, as did the retailer's margin, production and marketing (us)

'Right hand down a bit.'

were 2/3 and the actual ingredients cost 3d. A whacking 12/6, said Jimmy proudly, was profit. There were no competitors. The sales strategy was simple. Ellanby Laboratories had mailed six bottles of Night Tan to every retail chemist in the country, along with an invoice for £6. If they sold them all, they would make 30s, and hopefully order more. If they did not sell, they could be returned.

Returns were to be strongly discouraged, and this was where we came in. Attractively tanned, we were to call on all the chemists, exulting in the effectiveness of Night Tan. In 1959 most people spent their holidays in damp Britain, and sun-lamps were unheard of. Only a few sales were needed for the secret to be out, and Night Tan would fly from the shops. Or so the theory went. Unfortunately, there was just one flaw, which explained Goldsmith's insistence on horsey outdoor types. Night Tan did not turn you a deep copper bronze. It made you bright yellow, as if you had jaundice. I discovered this before the rest of the sales force. Being paler than the others, I went straight home and covered myself in the stuff. My first calls on the chemists were very unsuccessful. When Jimmy Goldsmith saw me, he was quite cross. I obviously needed to relax and ride more in my spare time – without a cap on. The summer progressed. I visited every chemist in Kent and Sussex. As my natural tan deepened I made a few sales and some commission, but it was hardly 'excellent remuneration'.

By the end of the summer there were at least six other tan-without-the-sun products in the shops, all of them much cheaper than Night Tan. Nevertheless, Jimmy Goldsmith was pleased with the success of his business venture. He quietly killed off Night Tan and went on to buy Cavendish Foods and Marmite. **Kim Clark**

Bert & Dotty

BERT LIKES A LAUGH. 'Life and soul, that's me,' he says, with a chuckle. Down at the social club he regales his mates with a torrent of old jokes and anecdotes. Bert has seen it, Bert has done it, but most of all Bert has talked about it, over and over again. Barmen rarely survive in the job more than a couple of weeks. Casual visitors to the club leave fast and do not return. The committee sits glumly in the corner and wonders what to do. Membership figures are declining as more and more of the club's stalwarts take the only way out, and die of old age. Only Bert seems to last the course. His body is strong, his mind is alert. 'I should write a book about it,' he tells everyone, and everyone wishes he would. At least it would keep him out of the club for a few hours each day.

Everyone assumes Bert is lonely. His wife passed on several years ago, more in relief than in suffering, and Bert seems to be perpetually at a loose end. His friends are desperate. Even when they manage to evade his company, they can talk of nothing else. He has become a menace.

'I know,' says Ken, in a moment of inspiration. '*Blind Date*.'

'What?' say the others.

'We'll send him on *Blind Date*,' says Ken. 'They have the occasional line-up of old blokes looking for a bride. Well, one of those old blokes can be Bert.'

Everyone agrees: it is a brilliant idea. Bert is the ideal candidate. He has what only TV researchers would call 'a lively personality'. The studio audience will lap him up. The woman on the other side of the screen won't be able to resist him. They will fly off somewhere for a week. They might get on. They might fall madly in love with each other, get married on prime-time TV and retire to a quiet little house far away. The committee basks in the warmth of this absurd dream.

Bert responds positively to Ken's suggestion, assuring him, not for the first time, that he likes a laugh. Ken is deputed to acquire the appropriate forms, and a few weeks later Bert is called to London for an audition. In the silence he leaves behind, some of the more spiritually inclined members pray for a successful outcome.

Bert passes the audition, and several committee members accompany him to the recording. They know how crucial it is that the studio audience fall in love with him. They cheer as Cilla trots on stage.

They yell as the three competing old wrecks are introduced. They scream and bawl and stamp their feet each time Bert opens his mouth. Before long everybody else does too.

The chooser is Dotty, a tiny furious Scotswoman with over-permed hair. She looks a match for any of the contenders, or indeed all three of them put together. She smiles and laughs, but her eyes do neither.

Bert tap-dances and flatters Dotty with a gentlemanly flourish, for he knows that the usual *Blind Date* innuendoes cut no ice with the more mature female. He is right. Dotty, it becomes clear, disapproves of the other two men even more than she does of Bert. She chooses him by default. The screen rolls back. The two of them grin expertly and walk off holding hands, just as the floor manager told them to.

A week in the Dordogne: at the club it's the shortest week of their lives. Back for the recording the following Tuesday, the committee can't wait to find out what happened. Had the Dordogne been the river of their dreams? Or had it turned out to be more of a white water ride?

81

'Have you been going through my pockets again?'

Bert thinks Dotty is 'beautifully turned out'. Dotty thinks Bert is 'a real gentleman'. Dotty says Bert told her everything. Bert says Dotty listened to everything he said. 'Will you see each other again?' asks Cilla. 'Oh I think so,' says Bert, with a grin. But Ken and the committee are looking at Dotty. She looks older than she did a week ago – frailer, and far less formidable. Her eyes do not smile. And she says nothing.

In the car on the way home Bert is unstoppable. The Dordogne – marvellous. Cilla – couldn't be nicer. Everyone treated him like a king. And as for the pretty make-up artist…

'Sounds great,' says Ken. 'But what about Dotty?'

'Oh, her,' says Bert. 'Stupid old trout.'

The committee members look at one another. This does not sound promising.

'But you looked so happy together.'

'Well we were. We were on telly with Cilla. And we knew we'd never see each other again.'

'But I thought…'

'Yes I bet you did. Do you think I have lived this long without knowing how to play *Blind Date*? If you hate each other they crucify you. But if you play along…'

'But you looked so well matched,' says Ken, who can't admit defeat.

'What? Me and that old bag?' Bert shudders. 'What on earth did you think we had in common? Besides, if I want company, I've got my mates, haven't I?' Bert smiles maliciously, and puts his arms around the two committee members sharing the back seat. 'My old mates.'

Back at the social club Bert has a whole new repertoire to exhaust: my friend Cilla, the funny Frenchies in the Dordogne, the horrible old trout, the pretty little make-up girl.

The committee sits glumly in the corner and waits for death.

Marcus Berkmann

Max Glatt is a social drinker with a 40-year-old alcohol problem. When the consultant psychiatrist first came across alcoholism as a young man in the Fifties it was not recognised as a social disease. The government refused to countenance its existence and doctors had no idea what to do with the addicts who came to them for help.

Two decades later, partly thanks to Glatt's work in the field, alcoholism was universally acknowledged as a disease. There were over 30 regional National Health Service alcoholism units complementing hundreds of Alcoholics Anonymous groups. But that wasn't the end of the problem. Once recognition of the illness was achieved, the political will to treat it withered, the number of units shrank and during the Eighties more and more costly private clinics opened.

Glatt, a German Jew, has become renowned for fighting for help and funding for sufferers, as well as advancing understanding of the illness. He first came across 'drinkers', as he calls them, while working at Warlingham Park Hospital, Surrey. A dental surgeon was a patient on one of Glatt's wards. 'When he was not drinking he was noticeably different from the other patients. More intelligent, a very interesting case. In particular, he displayed none of the attributes that society associated with drinkers. He wasn't workshy or stupid and he wanted to stop drinking.'

Glatt formed a group of four drinkers. Group therapy was in its infancy and Glatt admits that he had little idea of what he was doing. 'I asked the group at the end of an hour, "Has anything come out of this?" They said that they had no idea, but talking was certainly better than making paper elephants in occupational therapy classes. So we went on.' After a few sessions it was clear that something was happening. The group's search for its members' salvation continued. They wrote a monthly journal and, once rehabilitated, they arranged yearly reunions.

Warlingham Park became the prototype for the treatment of alcoholics within the National Health Service. Until then the

Max Glatt

government line had been 'What drink problem?' If politicians acknowledged the existence of alcoholics it was only to insist that they could be treated by mental hospitals. The medical establishment was looking at the treatment of alcoholism via the combined Committee for Alcoholics and Vagrants – 'That title was very indicative of their perspective at the time,' Glatt remarks.

Glatt is a master of understatement about his achievements. He claims he drifted into medicine as a young Berliner who wanted to become a journalist but didn't know how. Later he drifted again into psychiatry, partly because he was fearful that as a German in wartime England he'd be deported when English doctors returned from service. Psychiatry was an unpopular discipline at the time. 'I thought they wouldn't throw me out so quickly if I was a psychiatrist.' Now he lives in a quiet suburban street in Hendon, north London, with his wife. He is small and neatly turned out with white hair carefully combed above a high forehead. His most noticeable characteristic is his voice. 'It's embarrassing,' he explains, 'the vay my accent is not improved in 50 years.' He went to a conference in Germany recently where the host finished his speech of thanks by saying, 'I would like to congratulate Max Glatt on his excellent German.' Glatt says: 'I have had the misfortune of forgetting my own language and not learning yours.'

The psychiatrist is coy about his age. 'I'm still working, so I think it's better that I'm discreet.' But considering that he had already gained his medical degree by 1938 it is easy to work out that he could have enjoyed many years of retirement by now. Instead he still has patients, including famous names (about whom he is even more coy, although he admits he once counted Peter Cook amongst his celebrity patients) and visits a prisoners' alcohol therapy group in Wormwood Scrubs once a week. 'I tell the prisoners I have a lot in common with them. After all, I spent four years in prison too.' In 1938 Glatt had tried to leave Germany but was caught and imprisoned in the Dachau camp. Soon after that he was deported to Britain and lived in Sandwich, Kent. 'When Hitler invaded the lowlands, people got panicky and I was moved to the Isle of Man.' From there Glatt was transported to Australia aboard a prison ship. He was horribly seasick for the two-month journey but survived to live in internment. Later he returned to England, intending to go back to Germany after the war. Once he discovered that his parents had died in Belsen, he decided to make England his home.

By the Sixties Glatt had a new field of interest – drug addiction. Up until then the only drug addicts had been patients addicted to their painkillers, and doctors and pharmacologists who had experimented with their own medicine chests. Suddenly young people were introduced to cannabis. Then amphetamines caught on, quickly followed by heroin and cocaine.

Glatt was working at St Bernard's Hospital in London during the swinging Sixties. The era's casualties poured into his wards. He lobbied the World Health Organisation to consider drug and alcohol addiction under the same umbrella but he came up against a powerful opposition – Alcoholics Anonymous. AA hadn't fought to have alcoholics recognised as sufferers of an illness only to have them lumped together with 'dope fiends' and 'criminals'. Eventually the WHO ignored AA's argument. This was the first of many differences of opinion between the alcoholism specialist and AA.

Although Glatt insists that 'AA has done more for alcoholics than all the professionals together,' he also points out, 'I come from Nazi Germany, so I have seen what having only one party line can do to you. Anyone can become an alcoholic. It follows that there are very different personalities among them, so to think there's only one method for treating all alcoholics doesn't make sense.'

Max Glatt went on to become a member of the WHO's expert advisory panel on drug dependence. He has chaired international congresses on addiction, edited journals on the topic and taught on the subject at University College Hospital, Middlesex Hospital and the Royal Free. He has even had treatment centres named after him.

Yet he has never succumbed to the demon drink himself. 'I have many problems, but drinking is not one of them,' he concludes, with a wry smile.

Sarah Shannon

The wink

To suck the excess cheer out of Christmas, a chilling short story
by **Ruth Rendell**. *Illustrated by* **Robert Geary**

The woman in reception gave her directions. Go through the day room, then the double doors at the back, turn left and Elsie's room is the third on the right. Unless she's in the day room.

Elsie wasn't, but the beast was. Jean always called him that, she had never known his name. He was sitting with the others, watching television. A semi-circle of chairs was arranged in front of the television, mostly armchairs but some wheelchairs, and some of the old people had fallen asleep. He was in a wheelchair and he was awake, staring at the screen, where celebrities were taking part in a game show.

It was at least ten years since she had last seen him but she knew him, changed and aged though he was. He must be well over eighty. Seeing him was always a shock but seeing him in here was a surprise. A not unpleasant surprise. He must be in that chair because he couldn't walk. He had been brought low, his life was coming to an end.

She knew what he would do when he saw her. He always did. But possibly he wouldn't see her, he wouldn't turn round. The game show would continue to hold his attention. She walked as softly as she could, short of tiptoeing, round the edge of the semi-circle. Her mistake was to look back just before she reached the double doors. His eyes were on her and he did what he always did. He winked.

Jean turned sharply away. She went down the corridor and found Elsie's room, the third on the right. Elsie was asleep, sitting in an armchair by the window. Jean put the flowers she had brought on the bed and sat down on the only other chair, an upright one without arms. Then she got up again and drew the curtain a little way across to keep the sunshine off Elsie's face.

Elsie had been at Sweetling Manor for two weeks and Jean knew she would never come out again. She would die here – and why not? It was clean and comfortable and everything was done for you and probably it was ridiculous to feel as Jean did, that she would prefer anything to being here, including being helpless and cold and starving and finally dying alone.

They were the same age, she and Elsie, but she felt younger and thought she looked it. They had always known each other, had been at school together, had been each other's bridesmaids. Well, Elsie had been her matron-of-honour, having been married a year by then. It was Elsie she had gone to the pictures with that evening, Elsie and another girl whose name she couldn't remember. She remembered the film, though. It had been Deanna Durbin in *Three Smart Girls*. Sixty years ago – well, fifty-nine.

When Elsie woke up she would ask her what the other girl was called. Christine? Kathleen? Never mind. Did Elsie know the beast was in here? Jean remembered then that Elsie didn't know him, had never heard what happened that night, no one had. She had told no one. It was different in those days, you couldn't tell because you would get the blame. Somehow, ignorant though she had been, she had known that even then.

Ignorant. They all were, she and Elsie and the girl called Christine or Kathleen. Or perhaps they were just afraid. Afraid of what people would say, would think of them. Those were the days of blame, of good behaviour expected from everyone, of taking responsibility, and often punishment, for one's own actions. You put up with things and you got on with things. Complaining got you nowhere.

Over the years there had been extraordinary changes. You were no longer blamed or punished, you got something called empathy. What the beast did would have been her fault then. Now it was a crime. She read about it in the papers, saw about things called helplines on television, and counselling and specially trained women police officers. This was to avoid your being marked for life, your whole life ruined, though you could never forget.

That was true, that last part, though she had forgotten for weeks on end, months. And then, always, she had seen him again. It came of living in the country, in a small town, it came of her living there and his going on living there. Once she saw him in a shop, once out in the street, another time he got on a bus as she was getting off it. He always winked. He didn't say anything, just looked at her and winked.

Elsie had looked like Deanna Durbin.

The resemblance was quite marked. They were about the same age, both born in 1921. Jean remembered how they had talked about it, she and Elsie and Christine-Kathleen, as they left the cinema and the others walked with her to the bus stop. Elsie wanted to know what you had to do to get a screen test and the other girl said it would help to be in Hollywood, not Yorkshire. Both of them lived in the town, five minutes walk away, and Elsie said she could stay the night if she wanted. But there was no way of letting her parents know. Elsie's had a phone but hers didn't.

Deanna Durbin was still alive, Jean had read somewhere. She wondered if she still looked like Elsie or if she had had her face lifted and her hair dyed and gone on diets. Elsie's face was plump and soft, very wrinkled about the eyes, and her hair was white and thin. She smiled faintly in her sleep and gave a little snore. Jean moved her chair closer and took hold of Elsie's hand. That made the smile come back but Elsie didn't wake.

The beast had come along in his car about ten minutes after the girls had gone and Jean was certain the bus wasn't coming. It was the last bus and she hadn't known what to do. This had happened before, the driver just hadn't turned up and had got the sack for it, but that hadn't made the bus come. On that occasion she had gone to Elsie's and Elsie's mother had phoned her parents' next-door neighbours. She thought that if she did that for a second time and put Mr and Mrs Rawlings to that sort of trouble, her dad would probably stop her ever going to the pictures again.

It wasn't dark. At midsummer it wouldn't get dark till after ten. If it had been, she mightn't have gone with the beast. Of course he didn't seem a beast then, but young, a boy really, and handsome and quite nice. And it was only five miles. Mr Rawlings was always saying five miles was nothing, he used to walk five miles to school every day and five miles back. But she couldn't face the walk and besides, she wanted a ride in a car. It would only be the third time she had ever been in one. Still, she would have refused his offer if he hadn't said what he had when she told him where she lived.

'You'll know the Rawlings then. Mrs Rawlings is my sister.'

It wasn't true but it sounded true. She got in beside him. The car wasn't really his, it belonged to the man he worked for, he was a chauffeur, but she found that out a lot later.

'Lovely evening,' he said. 'You been gallivanting?'

'I've been to the pictures,' she said.

After a couple of miles he turned a little way down a lane and stopped the car outside a derelict cottage. It looked as if no one could possibly live there but he said he had to see someone, it would only take a minute and she could come too. By now it was dusk but there were no lights on in the cottage. She remembered he was Mrs Rawlings's brother. There must have been a good ten years between them but that hadn't bothered her. Her own sister was ten years older than she.

She followed him up the path, which was overgrown with weeds and brambles. Instead of going to the front door he led her round the back where old apple trees grew among waist-high grass. The back of the house was a ruin, half its rear wall tumbled down.

'There's no one here,' she said.

He didn't say anything. He took hold of her and pulled her down into the long grass, one hand pressed hard down over her mouth. She hadn't known anyone could be so strong. He took his hand away to pull her clothes off and she screamed then, but the screaming was just a reflex, a release of fear, and otherwise useless for there was no one to hear.

What he did was rape. She knew that now – well, had known it soon after it happened, only no one called it that then. No one spoke of it. Nowadays the word was on everyone's lips. It seemed to her that nine out of ten police serials on television were about it. Rape, the crime against women. Rape, that these days you went into court and talked about. You went to self-defence classes to stop it happening to you. You attended groups and shared your experience with other victims.

At first she had been most concerned to find out if he had injured her. Torn her, broken bones. But there was nothing like that. Because she was all right, whole, and he was gone, she stopped crying. She heard the car start up and then move away. Walking home wasn't exactly painful,

more a stiff, achy business, rather the way she had felt the day after she and Elsie had been learning to do the splits. She had to do it, anyway, she had no choice. As it was, her father was in a rage, wanting to know what time she thought this was.

'Anything could have happened to you,' her mother said.

Something had. She had been raped. She went up to bed so that they wouldn't see she couldn't stop shivering. She didn't sleep at all that night. In the morning she told herself it could have been worse, at least she wasn't dead. It never crossed her mind to say anything to anyone about what had happened, she was too ashamed, too afraid of what they would think. It was past, she kept telling herself, it was all over.

One thing worried her most. A baby. Suppose she had a baby. Never in all her life was she so relieved about anything, so happy, as when she saw that first drop of blood run down the inside of her leg a day early. She shouted for joy. She was all right, the blood cleansed her of it, and now no one need ever know.

Trauma? That was the word they used nowadays. It meant a scar. There was no scar that you could see and no scar she could feel in her body, but it was years before she would let a man come near her. Afterwards she was glad about that, glad that she had waited, that she hadn't met someone else before Kenneth. But at the time she thought about what had happened every day, she relived what had happened, the shock and the pain and the fear, and she called the man who had done that to her the beast.

Eight years went by before she saw him again. She was out with Kenneth; he had just been demobbed from the Air Force and they were walking down the High Street arm-in-arm. Kenneth had asked her to marry him and they were going to buy the engagement ring. It was a big jewellers with several aisles and the beast was quite a long way away, on some errand for his employer, she supposed, but she saw him and he saw her. He winked.

He winked just as he had just now in the day room. Jean shut her eyes.

When she opened them again Elsie was awake.

'How long have you been there, dear?'

'About half an hour,' Jean said.

'Are those flowers for me? You know how I love freesias. We'll get someone to put them in water. I don't have to do a thing in here, don't lift a finger, I'm a lady of leisure.'

'Elsie,' said Jean, 'what was the name of that girl we went to the pictures with when we saw *Three Smart Girls*?'

'What?'

'It was 1938. In the summer.'

'I don't know, I shall have to think. My memory's not what it was. Bob used to say I looked like Deanna Durbin.'

'We all said you did.'

'Constance, her name was. We called her Connie.'

'So we did,' said Jean.

Elsie began talking of the girls they had been to school with. She could remember all their Christian names and most of their surnames. Jean found a vase, filled it with water and put the freesias into it because they showed signs of wilting. Her engagement ring still fitted on her finger, though it was a shade tighter. How worried she had been that Kenneth would be able to tell she wasn't a virgin! They said men could always tell. But of course, when the time came, he

couldn't. It was just another old wives' tale.

Elsie, who had already had her first baby, had worn rose-coloured taffeta at their wedding. And her husband had been Kenneth's best man. John was born nine months later and the twins eighteen months after that. She had had her hands full. That was the time, when the children were little, that she thought less about the beast and what had happened than at any other time in her life. She forgot him for months on end. Anne, her youngest, was just five when she saw him again.

She was meeting the other children from school. They hadn't got a car then, it was years before they had a car. On the way to the school they were going to the shoe shop to buy Anne a new pair of shoes. The Red Lion was just closing for the afternoon. He came out of the public bar, not too steady on his feet, and he almost bumped into her. She said, 'Do you mind?' before she saw who it was. He stepped back, looked into her face and winked. She was outraged. For two pins she'd have told Kenneth the whole tale that evening.

But of course she couldn't. Not now.

'I don't know what you mean about your memory,' she said to Elsie. 'You've got a wonderful memory.'

Elsie smiled. It was the same pretty teenager's smile, only they didn't use that word then. You were just a person between twelve and twenty. 'What do you think of this place, then?'

'It's lovely,' said Jean. 'I'm sure you've done the right thing.'

She kissed Elsie goodbye and said she'd come back next week.

'Use the short cut next time,' said Elsie. 'Through the garden and in by the French windows next door.'

'I'll remember.'

She wasn't going to leave that way, though. She went back down the corridor and hesitated outside the day-room door. The last time she'd seen the beast, up till an hour ago, they were both growing old. Kenneth was dead. John was a grandfather himself, though a young one, the twins were joint directors of a prosperous business in Australia, and Anne was a surgeon in London. Jean had never learned to drive and the car was given up when Kenneth

died. She was waiting at that very bus stop, the one where he had picked her up all those years before. The bus came and he got off it, an old man with white hair, his face yellowish and wrinkled. But she knew him, she would have known him anywhere. He gave her one of his rude stares and he winked. This time it was an exaggerated, calculated wink, the whole side of his face screwed up and he squeezed his eye shut.

She pushed open the day-room door. The television was still on but he wasn't there. His wheelchair was empty. Then she saw him. He was being brought back from the bathroom, she supposed. A nurse held

him tightly by one arm and he leaned on her. His other arm rested, it seemed just as heavily, on the padded top of a crutch. His legs, in pyjama trousers, were half-buckled, and on his face was an expression of torment as, with the nurse's help and to the nurse's whispered encouragement, he took small tottering steps.

Jean looked at him. She stared at him and his eyes met hers. Then she winked. She saw what she had never thought to see happen to an old person. A rich dark blush spread across his face. He turned away his eyes. Jean tripped across the room towards the outer door, like a sixteen-year-old.

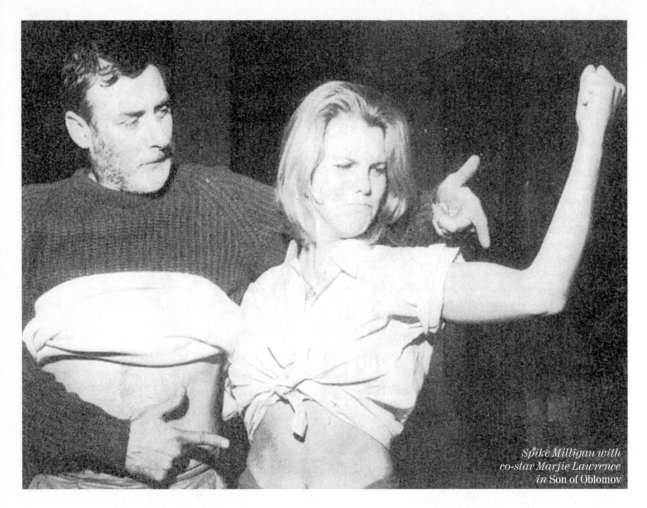

Spike Milligan with co-star Marjie Lawrence in Son of Oblomov

Ad lib – ad infinitum

On the opening night of Oblomov, *Spike Milligan walked on stage, forgot all his lines, and turned a serious drama into an unprecedented comic triumph.* **Ian Flintoff** *was in the cast*

The curtain came down for the interval, and Spike Milligan walked off stage while the standing-room-only house clapped, laughed and roared. He got into his Mini – parked near the stage door – drove home to Finchley and did not return. Spike Milligan's 80th birthday brought back to mind a couple of years I spent as a very young actor in a West End play of which he was the star.

Oblomov had been adapted by the Italian writer Riccardo Aragno from the 19th-century Russian novel by Goncharov. Spike's firm had bought the script to launch him as a straight and

sensitive actor, playing the part of a Russian aristocrat who couldn't be bothered to get out of bed. Joan Greenwood took the female lead, and other major parts were played by Bill Owen and Valentine Dyall. It was a major production for a young impresario, Michael White. The director was Frank Dunlop, who went on to do magnificent work at the Edinburgh Festival.

On the morning of the read-through, Frank spoke of the delicate and sensitive Chekhovian nature of the piece and, for the six or seven weeks of rehearsal, that was the kind of production we were all aiming for. We opened at the Lyric Hammersmith. On the first night Spike, overwhelmed by stage fright, forgot every line. The rest of us were thrown, but he kept going, making up the missing lines as he went along. Spotting the *Evening Standard*'s critic, Milton Shulman, in the audience, and in gratitude for previous rave notices, he declared: 'Thank God, Milton Shulman's in!'

The notices were generally unkind, but since the show was booked for several weeks, Michael White and Frank Dunlop proposed to save it by allowing Spike complete *carte blanche* on stage. Spike ad-libbed his way through every performance. *Oblomov*, changed beyond recognition, ran for five weeks and broke all the Lyric's box-office records, before being transferred to the West End as *Son of Oblomov*. It could still be running to this day had the exhausting job that Spike took upon himself not made this humanly impossible. No two performances were the same. Audiences – including the Prince of Wales – could return time and again and see a different show. As a result, there was never a feeling of audiences falling off. *Son of Oblomov* epitomised Spike at his best: inventive, unpredictable and indefatigable.

My first scene was alone with him on stage, and any stage fright I might have had was banished after a couple of weeks in the West End. I'd dutifully learned my lines in response to fixed cues, but, since Spike couldn't be bothered with anything like cues, you got what you were given – which was invariably followed by drowning laughter from the audience. If you were tempted to come in a millisecond too soon and kill the laugh, he'd gently mumble from the side of his mouth: 'Wait for it, wait for it.'

Once I entered stage right to find that Spike was sitting in the stalls, in his nightgown costume, calling up to me, 'Come on then, Ian, give us a show!'

Another time I did the routine business – came on, sat down, extended my hand without looking to shake his as I'd done 100 times – and his hand came off in mine.

The Queen and family came on her birthday, with Peter Sellers and Britt Ekland. Spike set up a double-act routine with Sellers across the heads in the front stalls – 'Why does the Duke of Edinburgh wear red, white and blue braces?' 'I don't know. Why does the Duke of Edinburgh wear red, white and blue braces?' 'To keep his trousers up!' The show overran by 45 minutes.

Spike was kind and generous to younger members of the cast, myself included. My first impression of him was of a painfully shy, quiet, gentle, almost diffident man – though an old mate of his, the Australian Bill Kerr, who was later co-opted into the cast, once said to me, 'We have to put up with all the shit, mate, because it pays the rent.'

I suspect that Spike was then searching for a full expression of another side of himself: the man who personally repainted the children's Elfin Oak in Kensington Gardens, at his own expense and with an anonymous plaque claiming that the work was 'done by the fairies'; who sat down on pavements in protest against the threats of extinction to wildlife; who never forgot his friends when they needed work and he could help.

All this happened a quarter of a century ago. I've forgotten none of it, and I never will. Next time I'm on stage Spike's 'Wait for it, wait for it' will whisper to me still.

Two poems

Ancient Yoof

On my desk, gathering dust
Is an alabaster bust
Bought at a country fair
And marked Horace – a beardless Roman youth
Of about seventeen
With a supercilious air
Quite unlike the imagined man I once translated.
Last night in the firelight he seemed to wink
And I thought I heard him say, 'So you think
I'm the poet? Well, I'm not. I'm his son
(I bet you never knew he'd fathered one),
And, if you want the truth,
I loathed his crappy Odes. The Golden Mean?
I never mess with Mister In-between.
"It's great to die for your country"? Hopelessly dated.
"Keep your balance when the going gets tough"?
That sort of stuff
Went out with Cato. But one thing he wrote was okay:
Carpe Diem. Have a nice day!'

Very Small Point Scored

'Look,' I cried, 'at that copper beech
Against the blue of the sky!
Doesn't it, almost, answer the question *Why*?'
But my old duchess said, 'Why do you always preach
About nature? It's a topic
Which, being myopic,
You can't really know much about.
Aren't you being a tiny bit pretentious?'
Stalled in self-doubt
(I don't know the difference between
A broad and a French bean),
I rallied pedantically: 'My dear, you meant "sententious".'

James Michie

Vicars from Hell

Priests weren't always woolly atheists. **Paul Pickering** *remembers a darker and more satanic breed. Illustration by* **Martin Honeysett**

I was enjoying the lesson at my local church by the M4 about Shadrach, Meshach and Abednego being thrown into the fiery furnace and then rescued by a mysterious fourth figure, who is obviously an angel, when up jumped the vicar with a Judy Garland smile on his face. After a quick pout at his nails, followed by some of those theatrical little dance steps they seem to teach at ecclesiastical college these days, he demolished, nay, deconstructed the whole wonderful story in a Cambridge sort of way. The 'myth' should not be seen as a piece of magic, oh no. It was, ho hum, political. Just a nice piece of spin-doctoring to make the Jews in Babylon feel good about themselves.

It almost made me yearn for the vicars of my Yorkshire childhood where God was in his heaven, which was 'up there', and anyone falling asleep was prodded with the churchwarden's brass-headed pole; the sort of vicar that is every bit the measure of, and often far worse than, the sin he is combating.

My present priest offers counselling to single-parent families in a manner far different to when my mother lost her first baby and became concerned that it had not had a proper funeral or been 'churched'. She went to see the vicar in a terrible state and said she had been told the baby would be in purgatory until she herself died. 'Nay,' said the vicar. 'You've got it wrong. Your baby will suffer purgatory until the last judgment.'

Yet that vicar was nothing compared to a man, now dead, called Halford, who took over the parish further up the hill. He had

been in the RAF and, having nothing else planned, gave religion a go when the war ended. Like all the really top-notch bad vicars, his intention was to do good, in his case in the little village of Kimberworth outside Rotherham. At first he did nothing much out of the ordinary. Unlike a minister in Attercliffe, he did not pick fights with his congregation to prove whose side God was on. Halford merely wore strange clothes: a black cloak affair of his own design and a three-cornered hat, which was sullenly disapproved of, as was asking parishioners for ten per cent of their income.

But his sermons were so unremittingly horrific that the congregation forgave him. Hard men who had come through two world wars were apt to stagger out of St Thomas's a little pale. There was no fannying around and shaking hands and the vicar asking what colour you'd painted the kitchen. Everyone went down the semi-perpendicular hill thinking very seriously about Hell and how to avoid it.

The fiery furnace text was always popular in a steel-working area, but during the Cuban missile crisis Halford surpassed himself. He used the tale of Shadrach, Meshach and Abednego to talk about the effects of a heat flash from a nuclear weapon hitting Sheffield and what this might do to Kimberworth, Wentworth and Thorpe Hesley. Several people had to leave.

His message was that nuclear war, although unpleasant, was nothing compared to the wrath of God. In fact, Mr Kennedy should not shy away from pressing the button. The 'responsible folk' under their kitchen tables reading the Bible and cheery MoD pamphlets about why not to look at the blast would have the angel sitting by them. 'Unreliable types', which included those in the pub, those who liked Communists, Malcolm Muggeridge, Elvis Presley, and the makers of ungodly radio programmes such as *Hancock's Half Hour*, not to mention 'louts' in milk bars, could expect to run down Kimberworth Hill faster than a fried egg on hot dripping.

Later, drunk on his own popularity, the preacher fell from grace. In the mid-Sixties, as an ill-judged concession to the times, probably brought on by one too many conferences on the New Testament, he decided to turn the churchyard into a nature reserve. He banned the old men and their terriers who sat on the churchyard benches. The men were the backbone of his congregation. The terriers kept down the rats in an area with the highest congregation of rodents in England. Soon the thickets were overrun by a rat population of biblical proportions. There were large, evil-smelling holes in graves, from which we used to try to ignite the gases.

> **His message was that nuclear war, although unpleasant, was nothing compared to the wrath of God**

Shunned, Halford took up with a local spinster who owned a spoil heap. Many nights he was to be found in her farmhouse, bandaging her phlebitis. He then got himself national publicity by turning away a funeral which had not paid the arbitrary fee he imposed to employ a rat-catcher.

The worst priest I have ever known was also a bad man trying to be godly. An ex-South African Air Force officer, he was loosely part of the *Verbo Divino* Catholic sect in the little town of Hohenau in Paraguay.

One day when I arrived in the town, a hymn was in progress in the small church in this mainly German area. Then there was a sharp crack like wood splitting. Next a man was being carried from the church, swearing. Father Wolfgang filled the doorway with his hands clasped in front of him and an expression of tender regret on his face in the manner of priests all over the world. Except Wolfgang's hands contained a smoking Colt 45.

I learned later that he had shot the man – 'only in the leg' – for talking in church. Naturally Wolfgang, who did not have a symbolic bone in his body, believed Christ paid for all our sins on the cross, which, like the fiery furnace, was as real as his warm gun. Very soon Wolfgang himself expected to be searching for the exit and the angel. Is this more reassuring than my present C of E atheist? Well, as my granddad used to say, 'If that's the sort of help God employs then there's hope for the rest of us.'

Strangers, who obviously take me for an imbecile, ask again and again: 'You mean to say you come to London for the winter months?' Yes I do. Born and bred in Montreal, I have, all the same, long looked on London as my second home. I first sailed for England on the *Franconia* in 1950, my intended short stay broken up by lengthy sojourns on the continent, extending to more than 20 years. I met my wife in London and four of our five children were born here. We returned to Canada in 1972. In 1993, our children grown up, Florence and I acquired a flat in SW3, which we have made our winter quarters.

Natives of this island who regard our choice as bizarre are happily unaware of the alternative. Six months of punishing winter. Icy streets. Frozen pipes. Cars that won't start. Three-day blizzards. Never mind this winter's Great Ice Storm, which paralysed Montreal for ten days, leaving it without light or heat, but also rendering it fairyland postcard gorgeous, everything shrouded in ice. It is also good to escape Quebec's loopy language laws.

Among other petty-minded strictures, the French Language Charter, which was introduced by our separatist provincial government in 1977, prohibits English on outdoor commercial signs, unless the English lettering is half the size of the French. In the absence of Keystone Cops, this is enforced by our language police – or tongue-troopers as they have been dubbed – armed with tape measures. Pondering corruptions of the language of Racine, Voltaire and Brigitte Bardot, alert Québecois lexicographers have legislated the humble 'hamburger' edible by renaming it the 'hambourgeois'.

In the spring of 1996 an alert inspector from the Office de la Langue Française was responsible for what became celebrated as the 'Matzoh Bust'. Weeks before Passover he espied boxes of imported matzohs, labelled in English only, on the shelves of a kosher grocery in Montreal, and ordered them removed. The story, a real knee-slapper, was carried round the world, embarrassing Quebecers. So the government had second thoughts. It exempted matzohs from French labelling regulations for 40 days before Passover and 20 days after. Those Jewish felons who, like me, might fancy a delicious matzoh omelette on the illegal 68th day have the satisfaction of knowing that we are bonding with the *conversos* of 15th-century Spain, who also had to practise their religious rites in secret.

No sooner was the matzoh crisis settled than another francophone zealot struck. An indignant customer of a Montreal pet shop threatened to complain to the Commission de Protection de la Langue Française, because a parrot called

More than a man can bear

It's cold as hell, tough guys eat squirrels, and parrots are forbidden to speak in English. No wonder **Mordecai Richler** *prefers London to Quebec in the winter. Illustration by* **Geoff Waterhouse**

Peekaboo spoke English only.

Our separatist Parti Québecois government has succeeded in dividing Quebecers into the *pure laine* and *les autres*, that is to say, the pure and impure woollies. The former is composed of old-stock francophones, the overwhelming majority, and the latter of anglophones and so-called allophones (Italians, Greeks, Portuguese and so on). I'm proud to report that Quebec's Jews, most of us descended from East European *shtetls*, pass muster as anglophones, even as we are incongruously dubbed 'Anglo-Saxon Jews' in Israel.

The French Language Charter's ultimate goal is to make French the common language of all Quebecers. So, understandably, alarm bells went off when a government report revealed that sneaky impure woollies still read English-language newspapers and magazines, sometimes even books, and watched English-language TV and videos at home. Worse news. There was damning evidence that the ungrateful children of anglophone immigrants, who were obliged to attend French-language schools, *preferred to flirt in English* in their schoolyards.

I would be remiss if I suggested that all francophone Quebecers were intolerant of anglophones. Or were intimidated by anglophone royalty for that matter. Take, for instance, the case of pop singer Charlesbois, a Québecois *vedette*. It has been reported that, seated next to the Duchess of York at a dinner party last year, he said: 'It has to be easy for the Queen to go to the hairdresser.'

'I don't understand,' said Fergie.

'She just has to point to a stamp, or her picture on a £20 note, and say "I want it done like that".'

Neither would it be fair to suggest that life is a misery for an English-speaking novelist in *la belle province*. I enjoy a certain frisson, scribbling in a language that affronts Quebec's *visage linguistique*.

Until 1993, Florence and I saw out the long winters rooted in our dacha on the shores of Lake Memphremagog, in Quebec's Eastern Townships, hard by the Vermont border. Giving up the Townships for London has deprived us of a number of social-cum-cultural events, among them the annual Wild Game Dinner at The Owl's Nest, an unassuming watering hole perched on cinder blocks out on Highway 242.

The Owl's Nest banquet is not for vegans. Tables are laden with wild turkey. Deer livers sizzle in pans, while porcupine, grey squirrel and black bear bubble in cauldrons (coyote is eschewed for being too chewy). The delicacies are washed down with quarts of Molson's Ex and a brand of Ontario *vino* that could, at a pinch, clear car windshields of frost. Smoking, bawdy language, and sexual harassment are encouraged, but 'wacky baccy' is not tolerated.

In the absence of a string quartet, the management provides a fiddler, screechy beyond compare, or somebody who can master the battered piano with the six missing keys. This long, enchanted evening usually culminates in one of the celebrants breaking a chair over the head of a neighbour, his hollered explanation charged with baffling sexual contradictions, as in, 'You've been screwing my woman, you fucken little faggot.'

Among my good companions in the Townships I count Big Foot. Big Foot winters in a remote cabin high in the hills, but once a week he descends through the snowdrifts to The Hooter, another bar on the 242. Attired in a shiny black suit and soiled white shirt with a ruffled collar, sporting an enormous bejewelled crucifix in place of a necktie, he will sit down at a table and order three quarts of Molson's. Then he will bet anybody a dollar that he can lift him off the floor by his trouser belt 'wiff my teef'. One week Big Foot did not appear at The Hooter, so a bunch of regulars piled into a four-wheel drive, laden with cases of beer, and headed for the hills. A distraught Big Foot was discovered staring into space at his kitchen table. 'My wife must be very angry wiff me,' he said. 'She hasn't spoken to me for two nights. I can't get her out of bed.'

One of the regulars went into the bedroom and returned to tell Big Foot: 'She ain't angry with you. She's dead.'

'Oh, so that's it,' said Big Foot, enormously relieved.

I once met...

Laurens van der Post

IN 1958 I WAS teaching at a mixed boarding school on the Ammersee in Bavaria and was sent into Munich one morning to collect the lecturer for the school's weekly sixth-form talk. He was staying at the Bayerischer Hof, even in those days a hotel of extraordinary luxury. The lecturer was Laurens van der Post.

He came down the thickly carpeted stairs, past a gigantic display of flowers, and seemed to me to be more expensively dressed than anyone I had ever seen. He was wearing a beautifully made pale grey flannel suit, a silk tie, what I imagined were hand-made brown shoes, and he was carrying a small brown felt hat. Altogether he was small, neat and spruce, his sparse hair combed across the top of his sun-tanned bald head, but there was a suppressed extravagance about him, like an actor playing a small duke.

He spent about 20 minutes talking to local reporters, then I introduced myself and took him to the car, driven by the school driver. On the 30-minute trip back to Schondorf he talked a great deal. I was sufficiently impressed to put down what he had said in my next weekly letter home, though until then I had never heard of him. He was, I told my parents, 'a fantastically interesting man, and quite charming'.

He said his first language had been Zulu, his second Afrikaans, that he had captained his school hockey team and led their first hunger-strike. Some of his fellow pupils had beards, and one was married. At the age of 19, he had captained the South African hockey team, and soon afterwards set sail for England and learned to speak English for the first time.

On his first visit he became friends with Stephen Spender, Graham Greene, Benjamin Britten and Rose Macaulay. Questioned later by our headmaster, he

admitted that he did not know the Queen herself, but he was a close friend of the Queen Mother, and from his conversations with her had formed a 'very good impression of the Queen's character'.

Back in South Africa, he founded the magazine *Whiplash* with Roy Campbell, in which he openly attacked apartheid: it was closed when Campbell had a row with their backer. Van der Post told many stories about Campbell, including one in which he

tried to murder Epstein in a fight over a woman; the sculptor's wife later dropped one of her husband's works on Campbell's head as he passed beneath her window.

Van der Post had then, he told me, travelled to Japan, and become fluent in the language. This had stood him in good stead at the outbreak of the Second World War, as he recounts in his book *A Bar of Shadow*, when he was parachuted behind the Japanese lines in Java.

There, he told us that 'without any supplies or radio communication', he had carried on a guerrilla war against the Japanese 'in the company of a Swiss geologist and a beautiful Javanese princess'. Deserted by his doctor, he was visiting the sick one morning when he found himself surrounded by a Japanese patrol, who charged at him with fixed bayonets. Only his request to them in faultless formal Japanese to 'wait an honourable minute' had stopped them. At the end of the war he acted as negotiator between the Javanese rebels and the Dutch, and remembered being present as 'the only white man in a crowd of 20,000 yellow men' as an old Javanese rebel returning from Russia had begged them with tears in his eyes never to have anything to do with the Russians, 'who stole one's heart and one's mind'.

His talk to the school concentrated mainly on the Kalahari, about which he told what even I in my innocence described to my parents as 'fantastic stories'. Witch doctors consulted invisible crowds, machinery jammed on sacred mountains, and he himself had paddled through swamps in a bark canoe when two giant crocodiles rose from the water only feet away, locked in a death-struggle.

I think what I remember most clearly, but did not include in my letter home, is the way his eyes flashed when he told the children about his prowess as a hunter. When he was in London, he said, he was always finding shillings and half-crowns lying on the pavement, being trained and alert to the threat of snakes on the jungle paths. Before he left, we walked down through the village, and he raised his brown hat in greeting to the lake. In Africa, he said, it was the custom to raise your hat to the Great Spirit of the Water.

John Wells

Miles Kington

Gaudy by name, tiresome by nature

I had always said that I would never go to a school or college reunion, and until June this year I think I had kept that promise. My three years at Oxford left me with surprisingly little nostalgia for the place. Although I played a lot of jazz there, met my first wife there, learnt a bit of French there and even learnt to jive after a fashion there, I never really felt an integral part of the place. Nor did Oxford treat me as someone to cherish. Now, 40 years on, I find there are only two college people from my Oxford days that I am still glad to keep regularly in touch with, and it was, in fact, to see those two again that I went back to Oxford for a Gaudy, as they call the old boy reunions at some colleges.

It wasn't meant to be like that. The whole point of going to Oxford was to get plugged into the old boy network and make hundreds of friends who would be useful to me in later life, and failing that, to whom I could be useful. This theory has been proved wildly wanting through all my educational years. The only person from the dreadful prep school I was sent to who achieved anything was a younger boy called Douglas Hogg, whom I dimly remember as a bit of a wet in a junior form. No change there, then. The school I went to in Scotland produced nobody of note outside the maverick journalist Alex Cockburn and Robbie Coltrane, who unfortunately didn't arrive until after I had left. As for my college at Oxford, I have to say that I wasn't particularly drawn to anyone there, apart from a few immediate friends. My college seemed to attract minor sprigs of the aristocracy who were too dim to get into Christ Church and others who seemed to have arrived solely because of their double-barrelled names. (Indeed, one man in my modern languages year had a treble-barrelled name, something I had never encountered before. Montagu Curzon-Howe-Herrick he was called, or Monny for short, and a rather nice, amiable bloke he was too, though I don't recall him lasting the full three years.)

If I had wanted to join an old-boy network at Oxford I should have arrived a year or two earlier with Ingrams and all the *Private Eye* mob. I did, it's true, establish a foothold with the Monty Python crowd, but only because I made friends with Terry Jones, a contemporary of mine at Oxford whom I met for the first time a week after he and I had left the university.

By the time I left Oxford I had made quite a lot of friends, but they were all from colleges other than mine, so this 1997 college reunion wasn't likely to be a milestone in my life. Indeed, as the braying noise of 100 middle-aged ex-undergraduates rose in the hall, and later, more drunkenly, in the cellar bar, and the self-congratulatory speeches limped loudly along, I found myself thinking that I was now surrounded by all the people I had tried to avoid at Oxford and asking: 'What on earth am I doing here?'

Come to think of it, this is something I remember asking myself frequently at Oxford back in the days when I was an undergraduate. What was I there for? To learn French and German, certainly, but a lot of what I learnt was too recondite to be of any subsequent use. Put it this way: I learnt quite a lot about medieval French while at Oxford, but NEVER at any point in three years were we required to speak a word of the modern language as used today in France. What we were taught was for the syllabus, and the syllabus was there for the degree course, and the degree course was there to make the dons feel they were doing something to justify their existence…

I remember bumping into my tutor a week before Finals and saying that I was seriously thinking of not doing the exams. He was aghast. Why ever not? Because, I said, I had learnt all I was going to learn and the exams would teach me nothing more. They might give me a degree, but I had no need of a degree. What use was a degree? He finally talked me into doing Finals, but in retrospect I think he was wrong and I was right. I got a third-class degree. I never collected it. It is still lying waiting for me somewhere, I expect. Nobody in this world, employer or otherwise, has ever shown the slightest interest in my degree, and quite right too.

The only regret I have, looking back, was that I didn't take the year off abroad which modern languages people sometimes took. But then, I suppose, you might say that I took three years off, and spent them all at Oxford.

'Start again, Ned, you were in tune.'

Around the world in a batey daze

Dung heaps, discomfort and injury greeted **Joan Wyndham** *on a Jules Verne trip to India. Illustrations by* **Geoff Waterhouse**

of the three palaces dropped, and others substituted. The final blow was the closing down of Agra airport, which meant that our whole trip was changed. We were to fly to Delhi, and no fewer than eight of the royal residences mentioned by Jules Verne had been cancelled!

However, my mood improved at Gatwick, especially when I discovered that two of our fellow travellers were in their eighties, and at least three (like me!) were on sticks. There was also a helpful lady from Jules Verne, to check us in – our guide perhaps? No such luck, she soon disappeared and was never seen again. Instead, we were met at Delhi by Ajit, our real guide, an Indian who seemed friendly and capable, but whose English was almost incomprehensible.

He first showed us the filthy back-streets of Delhi, a dilapidated dung heap where the poor lived in broken-down shacks, or tents made from rags. Sometimes there were just four posts supporting a sheet of corrugated iron, held down by rusty old bicycles.

By now Ajit felt we had had enough squalor, so he took us to the town centre. 'The Garment Centre!' he proudly cried, 'grand houses of the garment officials!' For the first half-hour we were convinced Delhi was the capital of the rag trade, until we realised that 'garment' meant 'government' in Ajit-speak.

Early next morning we set out on the seven-hour coach-ride to Mandawa, our first castle in Rajasthan. This, said the guide-book, is the place to stay, with every room a work of art, and beautiful views of the desert beyond. According to Jules Verne, 'you have the feeling of having come home'.

Greeted by musicians and a guard of honour of lance-toting veterans, we sat down exhausted on the terrace, and waited to be offered a drink. Instead we saw Ajit approaching with a nervous smile on his face.

'Sorry, castle full-up! No reservation for Jules Verne party!' For a moment we sat in stunned silence, then all hell broke loose. We argued with Ajit, we screamed at the manager, but to no avail. Ignominiously thrown out, our bags packed onto a donkey-cart, we stayed the night at a nearby Holiday Centre with clay huts and beds like

concrete. So much for the feeling of having come home!

Two days later we boarded our coach for a six-hour drive to Jaisalmer. More of an instrument of torture than a means of conveyance, this coach was built to give you maximum pain. The seats sloped forward, so you were constantly slipping down and banging your knees on the seat in front. The window frames cut into your arms like knives, and the air-conditioning froze you to ice.

The only compensations were the fascinating glimpses of local life – both animal and human – seen through the coach windows. Wild peacocks, chipmunks clicking their tails, sinister vultures hopping up and down and fluttering their umbrella-spoke wings at the sight of a dead sacred cow. These beautiful creatures, with their sad, brown eyes and long silky ears, wandered at will, even among the traffic. Although they are holy, nobody seemed to feed them – they even munched plastic bags lying in the gutter. Camels were everywhere, with their sneering expressions and elegant gait unchanged, even when pulling a dung cart.

Hordes of beggar-boys and pedlars descended like blow-flies on any foreigner they spotted. Schoolboys wanted Biros (a status symbol) and lighters were popular, but some merely pointed to their open mouths, indicating hunger. For a gipsy woman, a sickly-looking baby was mandatory, even if she had to borrow one.

'Hello, hello!' the boys yelled, banging on our windows. Luckily I had been taught the local word for 'F—k off' – 'Chello'. 'Hello, hello!' 'Chello, chello!' soon saw them off. On one occasion only I gave my precious lighter to a nice-looking boy, who snorted with disgust. 'Nasty, cheap lighter, made in India,' he said, and threw it back at me. That put an end to my charitable phase.

Approaching towns, there was much to amuse us; a factory called Inertia Industries and, our personal favourite, a hoarding on which two Indian boys cavorted happily together, labelled 'BUM CHUMS'. We never found out exactly what they were advertising!

Finally we reached Jaisalmer, the 'Golden City', its medieval beauty marred only by the hordes of Germans, Americans and Japanese lensing their way through the narrow alleys. Our hotel was comfortable,

W e were looking for an unusual kind of holiday – something new and exciting – and Jules Verne's 'The Royal Cities of Rajasthan' sounded just the ticket. The brochure promised us accommodation in no fewer than seven forts and royal palaces, some restored as hotels, others with royalty still in residence. There was talk of regal bedrooms, stud farms, camel safaris, swimming pools, billiard rooms and vintage cars. Fired with enthusiasm, we booked right away.

Then came a second itinerary, with two

but with the usual awful food which we were to find in every place we visited. Imagine a central buffet with six pots, each containing a mahogany-brown, red-hot gunge, topped with an inch of grease. One mouthful guaranteed you the dreaded 'Delhi belly'. There were, of course, beautiful, tempting mounds of fresh fruit and salad, but we had been forbidden to eat anything that had not been boiled, on pain of death! For 12 days I lived on omelettes, the only non-Indian food available, until I began to look like an egg. On the rare occasions when curried chicken sandwiches were on the menu the chicken consisted of nothing but bare bones!

By now Ajit had realised our plight, so one day he stopped the coach at a wayside café, promising us good English snacks and a nice, hygienic loo. We were not impressed by the menu, which was headed 'Coffy, Tea and Cold Snakes'. The loo was guarded by an evil-looking, one-legged Cerberus, brandishing his crutch in one hand, and holding a few sheets of pink loo paper in the other: we were forced to pay three rupees per sheet before he would let us in but, being desperate, we paid up. By now at least half of us had Delhi belly, and were living on Immodium.

In Jodhpur, hoping for a hint of grandeur, we stayed at the Ajit Bhawan Palace, a former royal residence. The first thing we saw was a long, dusty corridor, lined with ancestral portraits, which led to a totally blocked loo. When we came back from sightseeing it had overflowed, covering the floor (and part of the corridor) with evil-smelling effluents.

After breakfast we were due to visit Chittorgarh Fort, the most historically significant in Rajasthan – 'epitomising the whole romantic, doomed ideal of Rajput chivalry'. From it, the saffron-clad warriors rode out to their deaths, while their wives committed suttee on a vast funeral pyre. Hardly able to contain my excitement, I asked Ajit how soon we would get there. 'Where? Chittorgarh? We no go Chittorgarh!' A murmur ran round the coach – 'But it's on our Jules Verne itinerary!' Ajit shrugged his shoulders. 'I have never seen a Jules Verne itinerary,' he said, to our utter amazement. The same thing happened with Pushkar – 'an enchanting town' said the guide-book, 'many fall so deeply in love with it that they never leave.' We were to stay in the most luxurious hotel, the Pushkar Palace, with views over the lake. 'Pushkar? We no go Pushkar. We go Ajmer instead,' announced Ajit. At this point a fellow traveller from the BBC started to stride up and down the coach, shouting, 'This trip is a f–king nightmare!' We couldn't have agreed more.

The hotel in Ajmer was so awful that even the guide-book warned us against it. Its only note of grandeur was our bath, shaped like a marble coffin. Being used to rubber mats, I slipped and fell heavily, damaging my ribs. Although in great pain, I managed the trip to Jaipur, where my husband called in the hotel doctor. He turned out to be one of the most caring and efficient doctors that I have ever come across. Although it was the great feast of Holi, he visited me at least four times. Next morning he drove me to his clinic, where I lay on a hospital bed having every test under the sun, while my happy fellow travellers were climbing the Amber Fort on the backs of elephants. Although the clinic was spotless, the loo, needless to say, was a hole in the ground. Realising I could get neither down nor up, the ingenious doctor brought in a huge metal chair with no seat. Two orderlies perched me on top of it, but I was far too embarrassed to pee.

There was talk of flying me to Delhi for further tests, but I refused firmly: 'Certainly not, I'm seeing the Taj Mahal tomorrow.' 'And which is more important to you, your life or the Taj Mahal?' 'Oh, the Taj, definitely!' Funnily enough, Dr Garg seemed rather pleased by this answer.

And so Agra, our last stop. I suppose many people fear that the Taj may prove an anti-climax after so much hype, but in fact it was more beautiful than we had expected. If you sit and look at it for long enough, the perfection of its symmetry can hypnotise you into a kind of happy, relaxed trance.

The flight home was long, and the fatal word 'turbulence' was heard too often. As a result, quite a few succumbed to Delhi belly, but luckily there was a doctor on the plane.

We were not sorry that we went to Rajasthan, for the interesting bits more than made up for all the blunders. Nevertheless, we were both overjoyed to be home again, thanking our household gods for clean loos and baked beans on toast.

Modern Life

What is...
Empathy?

DO YOU THINK that children learning to read should be taught the sound of individual letters? That children learning to add should not be allowed to use a calculator? That children learning history should be taught facts? That children should be taught in rows, and not be left to wander around, learning from 'experience'? If you believe any of these things, watch out. You might be labelled a 'traditionalist', the very worst form of abuse that the Education Establishment can hurl at you.

These 'traditional' beliefs have been exiled from Britain's schools for a generation, expelled by the fanatical egalitarianism of 'progressive' theorists who have managed to ruin the education of thousands of children. Their greatest coup was the slow subversion of the National Curriculum and the examination system; and nowhere have they left a clearer mark than on the history syllabus.

The Party slogan in Orwell's *1984* encapsulates why history matters: 'Who controls the past controls the future. Who controls the present controls the past.' Those who control the history syllabus currently taught in many schools do not like Britain, and they want to change it. New Britain requires New History.

Evidence of New History is easy to find. British history – particularly political and military history – no longer forms the cornerstone of what children learn. It has been elbowed out of schools by ersatz themes, such as 'Race Relations in Multicultural Society since 1945'. Gone is the notion that history should impart the narrative of our past in a methodical manner. Empathy and interpretation of sources, not dates and events, now underpin the teaching of history in our schools.

The analysis of sources is a sophisticated skill. Students need a mental framework of dates and events so they can put the source in context. To be examined properly, students should be expected to construct an argument, supported by factual knowledge, which explains the source's relevance. The GCSE does not demand this of students. Many questions ask simply for students' views, not their knowledge.

Consider one question on 'Aspects of British Social and Economic History', for those who have studied 'Cinema, Radio and TV since 1945'. Of the five questions that follow, three could be answered without any knowledge whatsoever. Pupils are asked, for example, whether they agree that, before 1980, television was 'more of a curse than a blessing to British society'.

These absurd questions are the consequence of children being taught not periods of history, but historical themes, such as 'Poverty 1815-1990'. For a proper understanding, teenagers would need to know much more than could ever be expected of them: some basic economic theory, the philosophical theories which underpinned the Victorian approach to poverty, the political landscape, the changing social fabric – the list is long. As they cannot know all this at the age of 16, they are asked instead to empathise with those who lived in poverty. The questions are fatuous and leading: 'Why did unemployed people in the 1930s resent the means test?', or 'Why did the poor hate the New Poor Law?'

To answer these questions, children need to empathise with what it was like to

"Remember, your job is to hit the one who isn't wearing a bow tie..."

be means-tested and poor. This risks a subtle form of indoctrination: the means test was 'bad', the New Poor Law 'bad'. There are no questions like 'Why did the middle classes like the capitalist system?' Not that there should be: values and 'feelings' should not be allowed to push facts and knowledge out of the window.

'Themes' have conquered the history syllabus and gradually evicted British political history, which has been reduced to claiming squatters' rights in various syllabuses. Our nation's past has succumbed to the cultural relativism of the politically correct, by whose diktat it is wrong to teach teenagers British history to the exclusion of other cultures. Yet if history does anything, it should give children an understanding of how the present relates to the past. It should impart knowledge which acts as a grid reference, thereby helping children to understand other cultures.

Why has the teaching of knowledge become so unpopular? Knowledge stands for tradition, experience, heritage, authority. These values fly in the face of child-centred theories, which have indoctrinated countless teachers into believing that children should be free to express themselves; that a child's opinion, however idiotic, is just as valid as anyone else's; and that tradition is something that a child should learn from his or her own 'experience'. Knowledge can also be tested, exposing the harsh reality that some children are better-informed than others – a fact which egalitarians cannot stomach. And learning facts requires effort and discipline: children need to be taught them in a structured manner, requiring a return to whole-class teaching. The teacher cannot be a 'facilitator'.

Worst of all, real history exposes harsh realities that some on the left would prefer to ignore and cannot afford to admit. The world is unfair; humans are unequal.

'History is the handmaiden of authority,' wrote J.H. Plumb. The authority of the history that used to be taught in schools was grounded in the purity of factual knowledge. It is now being abused by educationists who think 'their' history is superior, and who are forcing children to learn about Britain's past from the progressive perspective. L.P. Hartley's description of the past is being realised: it is indeed 'a foreign country'.

George Bridges

Simon Raven

The novelist, dramatist, memoirist, critic, gambler and epicurean in conversation with **Naim Attallah**. *Portrait by* **Jane Bown**

I have the impression that your passion for the classics and your respect for the teaching of the Ancients has shielded you to some extent against the realities of the modern world. Would you agree?

They have certainly shielded me against a lot of nonsense that is spoken in the modern world. Both the Greeks and the Romans were full of direct and pithily expressed commonsense, much of which would be considered unacceptable today. Also the study of the classics is a very absorbing matter, involving quite a lot of concentration and hard work, which in itself shields one from all the follies going on outside. I hardly ever read a newspaper these days except for the racing sections. Newspapers contain so much sentimental rubbish and self-pitying whining about this and that, rape and murder, or photos of politicians in silly positions sucking up to rows of proletarian children. I just don't have time for that. The trouble with this is that when the modern world does break through, which it is bound to do from time to time, it is uniquely unpleasant.

You are very grateful for your classical education and the civilised values which it taught you. I think you would be the first to admit that you have not yourself always adhered to these values. Is it enough to know them and to recognise them?

If you can know them and recognise them, you've obviously gone a considerable way. Apart from Socrates, the only person I've ever heard of who's actually practised what he's preached is Jack Jones, a great nuisance figure in the trade unions, but a man I've always admired, and absolutely deserving of the Companion of Honour. When everybody else was getting into the best hotels in Brighton or Blackpool, there was Jack Jones staying in the bed-and-breakfast joint. But Socrates and Jack Jones aside, there are very few people who practise what they preach.

In your book An English Gentleman, *you say that by becoming a writer one bade farewell at once to ethical restraint and to any kind of conventional status in society.*

Have those two factors been the cornerstones of your writing?

They were advantages that came with the trade. The point I was trying to make was that if one was a regular army man, or a don, or a schoolmaster, or a Foreign Office man, one had to observe the code, largely a Christian code – and this still applies. Writers did not have to observe a code, and I was very grateful for this.

You say that you don't expect your novels to be remembered – indeed your sequence Alms for Oblivion *takes its title from* Troilus and Cressida, *referring to the scraps which are 'devoured as fast as they are made'. Is this something you regret?*

I would very much like some of my work to be remembered, but when I consider what has happened to better novelists in my own lifetime, it's extremely unlikely that my own work will last. If you take a novelist such as Francis Brett Young, who was very important in my parents' day – whoever hears of him now? It seems to me that

in order to be remembered as a novelist you have to be of supreme merit and also to enjoy a lot of luck. I could still hope in a corner of my mind not to be forgotten, but the omens are not good.

Have you always been able to be quite clear about the boundaries between fact and fiction or do they sometimes merge one into the other in your life?

They do merge. Even when I think I am absolutely clear about something, I am often very surprised by how wrong I am. I once won £200 on a bet at Warwick racecourse, and I distinctly remember the horses coming round towards me in a clockwise direction. My own horse was in the lead and going on to win. When I went to Warwick again 30 years later, I discovered that the horses go round in an anti-clockwise direction and always have done. Well, if one can be wrong about which way a horse that won you £200 was going – in other words, a serious matter – one is unlikely to be strictly accurate about anything.

In an article in the Listener *in 1962 you gave an account of your addiction to gambling in which you spoke of 'the treasury of terror, guilt and perversity' which it entailed. You suggested that the principal motive for gambling in your case was the desire to be punished when things went badly, and the 'almost sexual satisfaction' to be derived from an evening of disastrous losses. If it is indeed sexual, it is surely masochistic…*

Yes, I think it is. It is quite true that all those things accompanied my gambling, and there was definite sexual excitement, an erection in my case, though never orgasm. But I do know of several people who, when doing very badly, actually come in their trousers. That is partly to do with fear, I

think. I can remember when I was a very young boy doing a long-division sum for an exam and I couldn't get it to work out. Time went on and I had no time left for other questions, and I found myself becoming distinctly sexually aroused. I also remember getting a huge erection underneath one of Aspinall's gambling tables when I was still allowed to go there. I now see that the only form of gambling which is really amusing is horse racing. You can't hope to win at horse racing because you don't know how the horse feels. That's why hot favourites lose to 33-1 numbers, and a wail of self-pity goes up from the crowd. It's my favourite thing, particularly if I've backed the 33-1 number. The point about horse racing is that it is just fun, it's an exciting sporting spectacle, you don't know what is going to happen, the colours are beautiful, the band plays, there are blue hills in the background, and so it becomes almost a cultural obligation to go to the horse races. Toulouse Lautrec and Degas knew this, as did lots of fine artists. The gambling side is just fun; you know you're almost certain to lose, but you also know that every now and again you have a streak of luck. Roulette, which I used to play a lot, is stylish in its way, but it's mechanical. The odds at roulette are very fair, but with horse racing it's different. Sometimes the horse is constipated and has had a nasty journey. That's why I always back a horse when I see it crap in the paddock.

When you were at prep school you were a victim of what it is fashionable to call 'sexual abuse' at the hands of the games master. You obviously didn't see yourself as a victim; indeed you felt what you called 'great erotic fascination' with what went on. Is that how you choose to remember it, or do you think that is how it actually felt at the time?

> Like everybody else I've had a lot of experience of the foolishness of women, and the foolishness of men too. On the one hand, men tend to be sexually vain and greedy. Women, on the other hand, tend to be possessive and domestic

It's certainly how I choose to remember it, and I think it actually felt that way at the time. One knew, of course, that there was something not quite right about it, but what made it feel more right than it possibly was, was the fact that Colonel K, as I call him, was a very good schoolmaster, a very charming man, kind, pleasant, and representing the best of the prep school system. He taught mathematics, English literature and geography with imagination and esprit. And as regards sex, what he did was very pleasant, no two ways about it. Small children can be sexually excited, and certainly by the time I was nine or ten I was having a sort of orgasm, whereby the thing juddered about, and the whole business was very enjoyable. He played with the other boys too, and we all did it to each other, and also to him. And great fun it was too.

I think I'm right in saying that you regarded yourself as bisexual, which, in the 1950s, was not exactly fashionable. Did you ever wish that you were one thing or the other, so to speak?

No, I've been very happy being bisexual. It seemed to me the intelligent and civilised solution. It was the position taken up by all my favourite classical authors, and a lot of my favourite more modern authors, who, even if they themselves weren't bisexual, certainly condoned the condition and sometimes actively approved it. It's so matchlessly convenient to be able to help yourself either way if the opportunity presents.

You have a reputation for misogyny. Does it have a rational basis? You obviously have strong feelings about the worthlessness of women, their 'inability to act sensibly', as you put it. Are these principally feelings, or are they part of a thesis, as it were?

These answers are not to be oversimplified. Like everybody else I've had a lot of experience of the foolishness of women, and the foolishness of men too. On the one hand, men tend to be sexually vain and greedy. Women, on the other hand, tend to be possessive and domestic. This is quite simply biological, since nature tells us that women are there to have babies; they are naturally possessive of men so that a family can be formed. This can make them in any number of ways very tiresome. They don't want their husbands to go out on a drunken evening or do jolly things like racing, because that uses up money which is meant for babies. I find this aspect of women particularly tedious. Also this business of wanting to be in on male things. Women have gone to endless trouble to penetrate male clubs. Well, if they want clubs, why can't they have their own? After all, it's very good for people to be able to get away from the opposite sex, for women as well as men. Why do they go to such lengths to go on ships? They're not needed on ships, they're a perfect nuisance on ships, stirring up all kinds of trouble. It's bad enough having men trying to seduce the cabin boys, so to speak, but when you've got a whole load of women there as well, you just don't need it.

While you were at King's it came as a shock when your girlfriend Susan Kilner announced she was pregnant. The prospect of marriage appalled you, yet you caved in under pressure 'to do the decent thing'. Was this not uncharacteristic behaviour – I mean, to do what was expected of you?

No. I was afraid that her parents might make a row and that I might as a consequence lose the studentship I'd just got, and that I would be expelled. Obviously something had to be done, but it was very much on my own conditions. I never lived a day under the same roof with Susan after we married. It was on my own terms that I married her, and the whole thing quietened down very nicely, largely because of her great good sense and co-operation.

Do you think your son was psychologically damaged by this arrangement?

I don't see why he should have been. He always knew where I was, even if he didn't see me very often, and I've always been on friendly terms with him. He's now well over 40, and we go racing together quite often, and we travel abroad together sometimes. He's a very good driver and a good chap to have on a trip, as long as he doesn't drink too much and ask for all the most expensive things on the menu.

About 25 years ago you said: 'The English, by and large, are the last decently behaved people in the world.' Do you still believe that to be true?

I do, despite all the nonsense that goes on. The great danger is so-called political correctness, which could make Nazis of us all in the end. All the informing which goes on, and all the silly judgments which interfere and undermine. I don't think it's too bad in England yet, and on the whole we're still a very decent, tolerant lot.

In your own obituary, which you were invited to write some years ago, you complimented yourself on your loathing for what Orwell called 'smelly little orthodoxies' and what are sometimes called

My son is a very good driver and a good chap to have on a trip, as long as he doesn't drink too much and ask for all the most expensive things on the menu

'modern sensitivities'. What would you include on your list?

The whole bother about race – that's one smelly orthodoxy. I'm perfectly prepared to accept the fact that I need to call anybody of any creed or race equal, but I see no reason why they should be subjects of special consideration. Why on earth should they be? They've got to put up with things like anybody else. The whole business of equality can be solved by decency and commonsense, instead of all this going round making doctrinaire fusses and having special institutions. The Race Relations Board does nothing except make trouble.

Another orthodoxy I have nothing to do with is this matter of equal opportunities for women. If women are as good as men, then let them have the job by all means, but don't make a great sort of fuss about it and say there's got to be a quota. That's a big smelly orthodoxy. And as far as I am concerned, Christianity is another. Belief in Christ is not necessarily smelly, nor is belief in God, but Christianity as it stands is most definitely smelly, from the clap-happies to the most severe Catholics. There are inquisitors in our midst; they may not use heated tongs, but they are inquisitors just the same.

"Look's like Christmas again"

On the Sixth Day of Creation God caused a great mist to fall on the earth, moistening the dust to form a clay. God moulded the first man, breathing life into his nostrils. Adam was indescribably beautiful, though compared with God he was as ugly as an ape. He was so large that when the living creatures of the earth saw him they mistook him for their Creator. Lying down he stretched from one end of the flat earth to the other. When he stood up he could see into Heaven. At the first sight of his head peering into Paradise the angels trembled and called him 'Holy One'. But they were puzzled how there could be two Creators. God, understanding their concern, cut Adam down to a height of a thousand cubits and after the Fall he was trimmed still further. Many thousands of flakes were sliced from his flesh, reducing him to a mere hundred cubits. Adam complained: 'Why do You diminish me?' God replied: 'I take only to give again. Gather these trimmings, scatter them far and wide. Wherever you cast them, there they shall return to dust, so that your seed may fill the whole earth.'

God gave Adam the task of naming every living thing. All the animals of creation paraded before him in pairs, male and female. Adam, interested that all the other animals had partners, coupled with each female in turn, but found no satisfaction. He raised the matter with God: 'Every creature but I has a proper mate!' So God created the first woman, Lileth. As He had made Adam from the pure dust of the earth, so He fashioned the first Woman from the filth and sediment. But Adam and Lileth could find no peace together. When Adam wished to couple with her she objected to him being on top. 'Why must I lie beneath you?' When Adam tried to compel her she flew into a terrible rage, uttered the magic name of God, rose into the air and disappeared in a clap of thunder. Adam again complained to God: 'I have been deserted!' A band of angels were sent to bring her back from where she was sulking beside the Dead Sea, but she refused to return.

God then attempted to fashion another partner from Adam's tail. He took most of it off, leaving the stump we still carry at the base of our spines. Adam sat with God, greatly interested, as He made many attempts to shape a woman – from bones, tissue, muscles, blood and glandular secretions, adding skin and tufts of hair. These attempts did not please Adam. God realised each time that He had failed and sent them away. Finally God grew impatient. He put Adam into a deep sleep, took a rib from his side, shaped a comely woman, plaited her hair and adorned her as a bride in a gown, with 24 pieces of jewellery. When Adam awoke he was entranced by what he saw. This was Eve. It is a pity those other females got lost from Genesis. If they had remained it would have been possible to explain where Cain got a wife.

Lileth had developed from the Sumerian demon Lilitu, a winged creature with clawed feet. Screaming through the night, she seduced men while they slept, drinking their blood. Magic, sacramental rites, charms, incantations and exorcism were needed for protection against her. She was the archetype of the Western witch.

In 1484 Pope Innocent VIII's bull declared open war on witches and in 1486 two German Dominicans published their *Malleus Maleficarum*. In it they reported finding a nest of penises in a tree, stolen by witches. They decreed that most witches were female because women were more foolish, inconstant, feeble and lustful than men.

And so the executions began. One hundred and twenty witches were burned at the instructions of an archbishop, having confessed under duress to prolonging the winter by their spells. Estimates of the killings range from 100,000 to 300,000. James I published a book, *Daemonologie*, introducing into England Continental beliefs about their evil powers. He was responsible for the hanging of more witches than any other English king, before ordering a new translation of the Bible in 1611. In the introduction the translators refer to him as 'most dread sovereign', and deliberately mistranslated the Hebrew word *kashaph* – a sorcerer, diviner or magician – as 'witch' to provide Biblical warrant for their king's obsession. Witches were detected by finding parts of their bodies immune to pain. If they sank when tied up and thrown into a pond they were innocent. If they floated they were not.

Females had a bad press in early Scripture. In Leviticus, Jehovah informed Moses that a woman was unclean for 33 days after bearing a son. But after the birth of a girl she was defiled for 66 days.

The stain associated with child-bearing has lasted to this day. Some churches still perform the ceremony of 'churching' women – the process of ecclesiastical cleansing after childbirth. Women are also unclean during their menstrual cycles, a matter not overlooked by those who oppose the ordination of women.

Women needed to evade angels lusting after them, descending to earth and seducing them, procreating demons. To ward off angelic attention, they covered their hair. St Paul ruled that women should remain quiet in church – another reference used to oppose female ordination.

After the trouble He had had in Eden, God was on the side of those who defended themselves against the monstrous regiment of women. Lileth had been a bad start and the others a series of disasters. When Eve led Adam astray that must have been the last straw.

It was a man's world, and not without good reason – especially if that report about the nest of stolen penises was true. God was not on the side of Women's Liberation. Lileth and Eve in those First Days had caused enough trouble to last until the End of Time.

Would you Adam and Eve it?

'Would you please turn her back into a rib?'

Early Hebrew stories show that Eden was no paradise when Adam's first wife was around. Words and pictures by **Hugh Burnett**

On 18 May, in Dorchester, I was imprisoned for six months by the local magistrates for making off without payment from two hotels and for failing to attend an earlier hearing at their court. I was transported in handcuffs to the nearby Dorchester jail, a crumbling Victorian edifice built to house 200 prisoners. It now holds nearly twice that number in conditions of noise, stench and squalor. I spent three miserable weeks there, sharing a tiny cell with an extremely disturbed heroin addict (and dealer) who was going through 'cold turkey'.

Early in June, a senior 'screw' entered our cell and offered us both a choice of transfer to either HMP Dartmoor, or HMP Weare, the new 'floating prison' in Portland harbour (motto: Who Swims Wins!). We both, with alacrity, chose the boat. Originally built for oil-rig workers, then used to transport troops during the Falklands War (quite a few of the 'screws' had made that trip as servicemen), it was eventually sold as scrap to the Americans for £10,000. The Yanks sold it back for £5 million and another £9 million was spent on refurbishing it as a prison. £14 million! (In fairness, though, to build a brand-new prison would cost £60 million.)

On a bleak, rainy Monday morning, heavily chained and double-handcuffed, we were driven the short distance from Dorchester to Portland. Our spirits sank down to our prison-issue trainers as the grey steel hulk loomed over us in the mist. It looked like Auschwitz-on-Sea. Furthermore, the reception screws seemed to have, in prison parlance, 'a bad attitude' towards us. We were kept for several hours in a claustrophobic holding cell before being conducted to the B2 'Induction' deck. Suddenly, life was transformed. I was shown to a large single cabin with a sea view. There was an en suite lavatory and shower, carpet, all kinds of furniture and a selection of toiletries. A polite screw brought me that evening's menu: a choice of roast turkey and stuffing, spaghetti bolognaise, or a vegetarian dish. He returned a few minutes later with a complimentary copy of that day's *Telegraph*. Had I booked onto a luxury cruise?

Marine heaven continued for three more days, during which I read books from the well-stocked prison library and drew and painted the splendid view across Portland harbour. I had to pinch myself to make sure I wasn't dreaming. This had to be the most cushy establishment in the whole of the prison service. No wonder, as the governor mendaciously claimed in a notorious *Sun* article, no inmates had ever requested a transfer.

It was too good to last, of course. Reality replaced false paradise four days after we boarded. We were abruptly and brutally told to pack up all our things and proceed to the A4 landing, the noisiest and most violent – 'boisterous' was the screws' euphemism – on HMP Weare. I was given an inner (no sea view) cabin with yet another drug addict – the entire boat was awash with drugs – who played his music at full volume and danced around in the nude. On my first evening, I was 'kidnapped' by five enormous black men at the far end of the landing and made to play chess with

them. They told me they would 'beat the living shit out of you, Whitey' if I won – or even if I lost. I kept my nerve and shrewdly went for a stalemate, so they let me go. Another evening, they challenged me to Scrabble, but bottled out when they realised how good I was.

Life aboard the floating prison slowly evolved a weird rhythm of its own. We could feel the heave and swell during the summer storms, but nobody was ever seasick. HMP Weare would be hell for anyone who suffers from claustrophobia, since apart from one's 'cabin' and a minute association area with a single pool table, there was absolutely nowhere to go. All the air was recycled, which was fine until the air-conditioning broke down, which it frequently did. Ditto the toilets. Exercise was difficult to get because it invariably clashed with other activities. One Saturday morning, I took it all alone in the rain on top deck, the only one of 400 prisoners to do so. (The screws solemnly stood guard over me.) Due to the cramped conditions, everything had to be carefully organised, which was fine until the computer broke down – again, not uncommon – and then the boat became confusion at sea.

Education, presided over by a scatterbrained naval wife, was particularly chaotic. I won't pretend I didn't enjoy the art classes (we had two excellent teachers, Nina and Judith, and three hours in their studio was like being given 'shore leave' for the afternoon) but, due to computer failure, one never knew which class one was supposed to be at, and prisoners wandered around the boat like lost souls in limbo and then found themselves being put on report for being out of bounds.

Worst of all was the sheer boredom and an odd feeling of being manipulated; at times, it felt like actual sensory deprivation. I am not so paranoid as to think that this was a deliberate ploy on the part of the prison authorities, but it was hard not to believe that one was a guinea pig in some kind of penal experiment. (HMP Weare has been adjudged a 'success', whatever that means, and two more floating prisons are to open soon.)

I was unlucky with my shipmates. After the crack addict and the nude dancer, there was a Scots burglar named Phil who claimed to have an original Turner hidden away in his loft insulation. Worst of all was a particularly vicious young car thief named Montgomery, known as Full Monty for his habit of playing 'rave' music at full volume all day and all night. I couldn't handle this (or him) for very long, so arranged to move to another cell with a very sulky inmate named Ian. When I asked him what he was in for, he replied 'Murder' – the only word he addressed to me in four weeks. From other sources I learned that Ian had tried to blow his wife's lover's head off with a shotgun, a crime of passion which, in 'Lucky' Court 13 at the Old Bailey, had earned him only three years. I tried not to think about this more than once a day.

Most of the inmates on HMP Weare were hardened criminals reaching the end of long sentences, and so not wanting too much trouble. The officers had all volunteered to work on the ship and, with the usual exceptions, had a pleasant and helpful attitude. My

> A polite screw brought me that evening's menu ... He returned a few minutes later with a complimentary copy of that day's *Telegraph*. Had I booked onto a luxury cruise?

Ship of De'Ath

*No stranger to incarceration, oldie crook **Wilfred De'Ath** finds that life on the 'floating prison' is not plain sailing*

personal officer, Mr Phillpott, was well-meaning, if ineffectual, and there was another, Steve Hollett, whom I would happily employ as a valet if ever I make it rich. I was genuinely sorry to say goodbye to him when I left. I had an ambivalent relationship with one officer, known all over the ship as Little Hitler. Small of stature, and not unlike Adolf in appearance, he was one of those curious individuals who manages to be both absurd and sinister at the same time. He remained deeply suspicious of me for many weeks until one day, checking the mail, he discovered that we shared the same, rather upmarket, local solicitor. From then on, he couldn't do enough for me. (He was to be further impressed by personal notes from the newly ennobled Melvyn Bragg, an old friend, and from *The Oldie* editor – thank you, by the way, to those readers who wrote to me on board.)

The jewel in the crown on the ship was the thrice-weekly chaplaincy service. With a Roman Catholic Mass on Friday, Anglican church on Sunday, a chaplain's class on Tuesday, one was never more than three days away from spiritual consolation. I liked all the chaplains, but the Anglican, Bill Cave (all Anglican prison chaplains are called Bill), was in a class of his own. He had once been a university chaplain but didn't consider ministering to 400 tattooed gorillas with drug problems to be a step down.

Towards the end of my sentence, I was sent on a P-R (Pre-Release) course, two-thirds of which was spent watching videos about conditions in other prisons. When I complained to the officer in charge about the relevance of this, he said: 'Well, 75 per cent of the guys will be coming back soon, so they might as well know what to expect.' How cynical can you get?

One Tuesday evening in July, Bill Cave asked me to give a talk on God, which I did, reaching the rather unexpected conclusion that I had felt closer to Him during these two months in the steel womb of HMP Weare than at any other period of my interesting life. After all, in the womb one either sinks or swims, dies or grows, and I think I most definitely swam and grew during this summer. As Peter Ustinov said of his time in the army, I loathed every moment of it, and I wouldn't have missed it for the world.

'I hope you don't mind. We started without you'

Douglas Byng

I didn't start it. The phone rang in the early 1980s. It was a nice lady in Bournemouth. 'We want a 1930s star to be in our forthcoming summer festival – can you supply one?' 'Douglas Byng,' I replied sharply. 'Who's he?' she asked. 'Look him up in *Who's Who in the Theatre*,' I said, more sharply. 'He's got three pages.'

Douglas Byng – or Dougie, as he was affectionately known – was a great panto dame and revue artiste who scored notable hits with his risqué songs in the 1930s, for instance 'I'm Millie a Messy Old Mermaid' and 'Doris, the Goddess of Wind' ('My life's been one long blow from morning till night'), and was championed in later life by George Melly and John Betjeman. He'd long since retired but even in his late eighties could easily be coaxed out for an appearance. The lure of an audience proved irresistible.

The nice lady from Bournemouth phoned again the next day. 'I had no idea that Douglas Byng was so famous. We'd like him for two weeks, twice daily.'

The telephone nearly dropped from my mouth. 'You do realise he's nearly 90?' I spluttered. 'Will that be a problem?' came the reply. 'Not really, but he'll need somebody to work with him. May I suggest the performer and pianist Billy Milton?' 'Who's he?' 'Look him up in *Who's Who in the Theatre*. He's got three pages.'

Dougie was excited. So was Billy, and he was only 83. We all met up at the National Film Theatre before taking our first-class seats on the train from Waterloo to Bournemouth. Dougie arrived in a hired limousine and Billy came on the bus. Each was dressed

Great dames

Patrick Newley *arranged for Dougie Byng and Billy Milton to perform together in Bournemouth, and found no love lost between the old luvvies*

immaculately. Dougie had brought five suitcases and Billy a small holdall with his toiletries and a pile of sheet music. We had a splendid compartment to ourselves and excellent service. It was then that I discovered that they hated each other. And always had.

I sat next to Dougie, who was somewhat deaf, and Billy sat facing us.

Dougie: 'You know, dearie [shouting at me], I'm very surprised they booked Billy – he was never a star. You don't mean he's going to do an act?'

Billy (turning to me): 'I can't really bear the thought of two weeks with Dougie. You will keep him out of my way, won't you?'

Dougie: 'Is he saying something about me, dearie? Tell him to speak up, will you.'

Billy: 'If she goes on like this any longer, I'm getting off at the next stop.'

We arrived at Bournemouth and were greeted like visiting royalty by the theatre's management. Happiness prevailed until we were shown backstage to the dressing-rooms. Dougie insisted on the number one and Billy ended up in the number two. Later that afternoon he placed a note on the door which read 'Number one dressing-room – Billy Milton'.

The show opened to a large audience including the Mayor of Bournemouth and a gaggle of seaside landladies, all on free tickets. Billy played the piano to perfection, interspersing his own compositions with anecdotes about Noël Coward, Mistinguett and Maurice Chevalier. The audience loved him. But Dougie did not. 'Why does he go on and on?' he asked me in the dressing-room, where he could hear the show on the Tannoy. 'I mean, are they really interested in all those old stories?'

When Dougie went on, some members of the audience gave him a standing ovation. He told some extremely risqué gags and sang some of his best-known songs. He overran by 15 minutes, and the audience couldn't get enough of him. Except Billy. 'Why, oh why, does she go on and on?' he asked me in the dressing-room. 'I mean, who's interested in all those old stories?'

This went on for the whole two weeks, but worse still were the evenings when fans came backstage, clutching books and records to be signed. If there were more fans in Dougie's dressing-room, there would be a loud shout from Billy: 'Why are people going in there? They've come to see me!' When an admirer went into Billy's dressing-room, Dougie went white and screamed, 'He's gone to the wrong room! Quick, tell him I'm in here!'

They rarely spoke off-stage, despite staying in the same hotel and in next-door rooms. The walls were paper-thin, so they could hear each other's telephone conversations. 'You wouldn't think that Billy had any friends,' Dougie once remarked.

There was an exception when, one Sunday, we were invited to afternoon tea at the Royal Bath Hotel. The three of us sat in the sunshine in the gardens, drinking champagne at Dougie's insistence. There was no arguing, and they began to remember past glories. They fell asleep, and when the afternoon became chilly Billy woke up, patted Dougie on the hand and said, 'Dougie dear, we've a show to do tonight.' Dougie stirred and muttered, 'Oh, I suppose we should be getting along, dearie.' They helped each other up and as they walked through the hotel Dougie said to Billy, 'You know, it's been a long time. We must be the oldest performers in the business and still working. No one can criticise us any more.'

Dougie Byng died at the age of 94. Shortly before he died I visited him at the actors' rest home, Denville Hall in Middlesex. He was frail and confined to his bed. He turned to me brightly on this occasion and said loudly, 'You know, I wouldn't mind doing another show with Billy. I mean, he's not that bad really.' Billy Milton died a few years later, after writing me a letter in which he said, 'Do you think we could do another of those shows with Dougie? He's bloody difficult, but not that bad.'

Billy Milton

A German lesson in racial tolerance

In the space of a few weeks **Zenga Longmore** *was racially abused on trains in both Berlin and London. In Berlin outraged fellow passengers rushed to her aid; in London they pretended nothing was happening*

THE WORD 'EFFERVESCENT' just about summed up the mood of our little party as we travelled on the metro train in East Berlin. Andrew Gimson, the writer, and his hospitable wife Sally had taken us out on a visit to Potsdam Palace. My German friend Helga and I were busily munching away at the remains of the day's picnic. Omalara, my six-year-old daughter, and Helga's half-Nigerian son, Freddy, were scattering crisps over the floor of the train, to the accompaniment of fond chuckles from the German passengers.

There was a time, I thought, when one never read accounts of the former East Berlin without gasping at the horrific tales of neo-fascism and racist attacks. A few years ago, I would not have set foot in the area, because it seemed as if the lives of black people were no longer safe. But now it appeared we had found ourselves in one of the most welcoming cities in Europe. East Berlin had a serene, ethereal quality; tall grey houses swathed in the scent of *Linden*. Far from fending off crazed skinheads, Omalara and Freddy had been plied with free sweets and cake. The *kinder* had been spoiled rotten. After two days, I had decided that East Berlin was right up my *strasse*. Until…

A derelict, inebriated German man staggered onto the train, slumped opposite us, and directed a fishy gaze in my direction with a somewhat inflamed eye.

'Here we go,' I thought, 'he's about to ask for my telephone number.' So thinking, I pursed my lips and assumed that expression one wears when about to be chatted up by a former East Berliner.

I neither speak nor understand German, so I hope no German will be offended when I say that the man uttered something in a drunken slur, which sounded very much like, '*Einen sveinen biffen boffen!*' Being of dignified persuasion, I merely raised my eyebrows and stared coldly, but the other passengers on the train drew a collective intake of breath. A moment later, the drunkard rose to his full height of five foot three and began to proclaim, '*Einen sveinen biffen boffen!*' in a mighty Hitlerian roar, lurching back and forth, waving a fist inches from Omalara's nose. It was at that point I realised that my telephone number was the least of his concerns.

'What's he saying?' asked a quivering Omalara.

'He's saying he's never seen such beautiful children in his life,' I hazarded. Omalara was instantly pacified. Freddy, on the other hand, who spoke fluent German, grasped that I was not being strictly truthful. Clinging to my arm, he began to shake uncontrollably. 'Don't worry,' I whispered, 'he's just a very silly man who should be ignored.' But the other passengers on the train did not share my sentiments. Old ladies with cats, middle-aged couples with

> **Yet more people sprang to our rescue, wagging angry fingers in the drunkard's face**

dogs, strapping young men and even teenage girls surrounded the drunkard to voice their displeasure. Far from appeasing him, their words of disgust inspired him to scream abuse with Wagnerian frenzy, his fish-like eyes bulging as if possessed by some Nordic god of yore.

'What's he ranting about?' I asked Helga, whose face had become a twitching green mask.

Helga explained that the man was wondering aloud why he should have to pay taxes so that children like Omalara and Freddy could live in his country. What, he wanted to know, were the likes of two black children doing in his country in the first place?

Freddy explained further that the man's language was littered with expressions not fit to be uttered outside the *toiletten*, and that he was threatening to shoot the children with a mysterious pistol which he apparently kept hidden in a secret pocket.

I recalled how a German Jewish friend of my mother once told me that, during the early Thirties, the first signs of anti-Semitism had been felt by the Jewish children. She had been barred from the local schools, and had been sworn at and spat at in the streets. Striking at children is an effective and cowardly way of tyrannising the adults.

'And he says we're all very shitty,' wailed Freddy.

'He's saying *what*?' asked an outraged Omalara.

'We're all very pretty,' I responded, nervously.

But I had no need to be nervous that day. A fellow passenger thrust his hand over the drunkard's mouth, and yet more people sprang to our rescue, wagging angry fingers in his face. When the train finally stopped at the next station, an efficient guard restrained the man, and the driver marched onto the platform to announce that the train was going no further until the sot was removed.

'Do you wish to press charges?' inquired the earnest stationmaster. After a long period of deliberation, Helga decided to let the matter rest, because she would not be staying long enough in Berlin to see the whole thing through. Freddy continued to shake and scream. I sat in a state of wonder. The violence of a drunken man had not shocked me. I have travelled to apartheid-ridden South Africa, the Deep South of America, and Worthing, West Sussex, so racial abuse has lost much of its shock value. What surprised me was the number of people who came to our aid, not to mention the train driver and guard, who had urged us to press charges against this broken-down wreck of a toper. After all, he had only shouted at us.

Andrew Gimson began a very sweet but uncalled-for apology.

'But he didn't actually hurt us,' I replied, 'and it was quite wonderful that so many people voiced their disapproval.'

'Well, you see,' said Andrew in a wise tone of voice, 'racial hatred once flared up here in Germany, and people are anxious to prevent it from happening again.'

The English have never gone a bundle on this Third Reich business, so maybe that is why passengers on the London Tube view racist attacks in a somewhat different light.

About two months ago, I was travelling on the Piccadilly Line, happily craning my neck to gain a clearer view of someone else's *Independent*. Just as I was about to get to the meaty part of the article, ping! A cigarette butt hit my cheek.

Looking up, I noticed a group of four teenage Irish travellers had entered the train and were diverting themselves with the sport of throwing little pieces of rubbish at the black passengers. One by one, the human targets drifted from the carriage. One would have thought from their expressions that they wanted to leave the carriage anyway, for there was no flicker of annoyance, and no concern from the white passengers who sat walled behind various newspapers.

When a broken Biro became tangled in my hair, I decided enough was enough. Trying to keep the vocal wobble at bay, I said: 'Now listen, kids, stop that at once!'

'Did you hear that, now?' a pop-eyed 18-year-old girl asked of her chums. 'She's only told us to feckin' stop!'

'She did that, now did she? Who the feck is she to tell us what to do? Why, the feckin' black whore!'

I'm not sure what became of the Scarlet Whore of Babylon, but if she was stoned to death, it seemed that I was about to receive a similar fate. Bottles, Coca-Cola cans and screwed-up copies of the *Evening Standard* were hurled with a good deal of ferocity in my direction. Racial abuse rent the air, every word prefixed and suffixed by the term 'feckin' '.

In a flurry of bluff I cried: 'That's it, children. I'm going to fetch the guard.'

'Hurry up! I've only got time for a sound-bite!'

The teenagers were diverting themselves by throwing pieces of rubbish at the black passengers

'What feckin' guard might that be?' enquired a freckle-faced 17-year-old boy. 'And why are you thinking he's going to want to do anything for a feckin' black whore like yourself?'

The youth had a point. No guards were available, and a barricade of paper continued to shield the faces of the other passengers, who, unlike the Berliners, appeared to be thinking only – 'thank goodness it's you and not me!'

I stumbled out at the next station and hid behind a stairwell, praying to what I hoped was a benevolent God that the children had not followed to continue stoning me to death.

But luckily, as the train rattled away, they could be seen rollicking uproariously, throwing apple cores at a hapless Indian woman. If I am not mistaken, the word 'feckin' ' echoed through the empty station. Or maybe it was ringing in my ears. I do not know, but one thing is clear, let it never be said that Irish travellers are feckless.

No one can really explain racial hatred, an emotion as random as Cupid's arrow. If it is to do with power over oppressed classes, why the Holocaust? And if it is about fear of the unfamiliar, why do people of different religions who have been living side by side for centuries suddenly attack one another?

What harm could Freddy and Omalara have done to that East Berliner to have merited such fury? Maybe the drunkard had lost his job and self-respect since the unification of Germany, but only a highly perverted sense of logic could have convinced him that black people were to blame, and black children at that.

The London and Berlin incidents were very different. In London, a group of teenagers were attacking a grown-up, and in Berlin, a grown-up was abusing children. Germany, as Andrew Gimson pointed out, has a recent history of unimaginable racial violence, whereas in England we are all supposed to be liberal. Perhaps that is why the so-called racist East Berliners rush to the defence of innocent victims of prejudice, and the tolerant English happily tolerate it.

W henever I come back to this utterly enslaving, beautiful, sinking, sometimes stinking, dying city, I do so with the hope that this time it will yield up its secrets to me. But when the time comes for me to leave I realise that, even if I stayed in it for the rest of my life, this could never be. If Venice is a labyrinth, it is one in which you can wander forever without any hope of reaching the centre, for the simple reason that, as a labyrinth, it has no centre and, as in a labyrinth, you will be lucky to escape from it without a pair of fallen arches. But really Venice is not sufficiently substantial to be compared with a labyrinth. It is much more like the mirage which so often confronts the passenger as the ship sweeps in towards the city up the dredged channel from the Adriatic, who first sees its domes and campaniles looming up larger than life in the air, then liquefying, dissolving and sometimes dispersing completely before taking on some semblance of substance.

In *Albertine Disparue*, Proust writes of entering a network of *calli*, the little alleyways of the city, and coming by chance upon a great open *campo* in the moonlight and failing to

In the valleys of San Toma the cats of Venice reign supreme and there is scarcely a dog to be seen

find it again the next day, wondering whether it was part of a dream, or a place like one of those oriental palaces 'to which mysterious agents convey by night a person who, taken home again before daybreak, can never again find his way back to the magic dwelling which he ends by supposing that he visited only in a dream.'

This feeling of a lack of substance, which even the largest Venetian buildings possess, perhaps because they literally rise from the water, is heightened by the apparent emptiness of so many of them…. An emptiness you can experience only at night.

Great *palazzi*, some of which are big enough to house a hundred persons, have water gates which look as if they have not been opened for a hundred years. The steps leading up to them are covered with long, green weed. Inside, the vast hall is lit, if at all, by a 40-watt bulb. Sometimes there is another, equally feeble, light in another room high up under the highest cornice, belonging to the caretaker, or perhaps a hermit. The feeling of emptiness extends far beyond the Grand Canal. It is especially strong in those parts of the city which tourists rarely visit, up in the Quartiere Grimani, in the territory around the Arsenale, in the alleys of San Toma where the cats of Venice reign supreme and there is scarcely a dog to be seen.

Lost in Venice

*Visit the sinking, stinking beautiful city before it dies,
says* **Eric Newby**. *Illustrations by* **John Ward, RA**

At night, especially in winter, when they have made their ritual, obligatory *passeggiata* in the principal *calli*, *piazze*, *campi* and *salizade* of whatever neighbourhood they inhabit, the ordinary Venetians disappear completely, leaving the city to visitors and those who live off them. They do this because most of them have to get up hideously early in order to get to work on the terra firma at Mestre or Marghera. So the best way of seeing some is by chugging down the lesser waterways, when you will have fleeting glimpses of them through windows that are almost always barred: a custodian asleep at a desk in some important archive, a man and a girl kissing, a family sitting round a table to which a risotto is coming in a cloud of steam – like a series of not very modern pictures hung in the open air on walls of leprous stone.

What can you do in Venice? By day, armed with Antonio Salvadori's book *101 Buildings to See in Venice*, you can discover a lot that you would probably otherwise pass by, including that remarkable enclave of Venetian skyscrapers in the Ghetto.

In Venice, according to the French authors of *Guide Julliard de l'Europe*, there are four intelligent ways to spend the evening.

The first, and most costly, is to hire a gondola (a closed model if one has improper thoughts and the means to gratify them); the

> **Really wintry weather can be a bit much and the fogs are something Jack the Ripper would have got lost in**

second to instal oneself at a table in the Piazza San Marco; the third to look for adventure in the streets and alleys; the fourth to go to bed with a good book and a bottle of Scotch. When one has tried all these, the authors say, there are the nightclubs.

Venice is a city, nightclubs or not, in which it is useful to have enough money. Being penniless in Venice conjures up visions of Baron Corvo, past even pederasty, sleeping on mud banks in the Lagoon and being gnawed by crabs and rodents. Having too much brings Hemingway to mind, with his awful *Across the River and into the Trees*, and his dreadful Colonel Cantwell.

When should one go to Venice? May is lovely; June is good; July and August insufferable – the greatest crowds, the smelliest smells; the first half of September is culture time, with music and cinema at the Lido; October is also good. Winter is strange and exciting, but really wintry weather can be a bit much and the fogs are something Jack the Ripper would have got lost in. Many of the city's hotels and restaurants close from the end of October until April. The *vaporetti*, the passenger boats that take you around Venice, have become very expensive. How long should one stay in Venice? Never long, but return often to make sure that it has not sunk beneath the waves.

Olden Life

What were...
The Clangers?

THEY WERE THE Teletubbies of their day (1969-74) except for being about a million times more inventive and stimulating – a family of mouse-like creatures who lived on a lonely moon and conversed in fluting squeaks and descants which sounded so like human speech that I assumed (wrongly) that actors' voices were being fed through some electronic comb-and-paper device. They dwelt in caves protected by iron doors which clanged shut like dustbin lids, hence their name. There was Major Clanger, Mother Clanger, Small Clanger and Tiny Clanger, plus various uncles and aunts making guest appearances. They subsisted mainly on soup which bubbled up from the interior of their kindly world and was dispensed by the Soup Dragon. Early in the run an iron chicken which had dropped in laid them an egg, but it hatched out teeming notes of music rather than food. Music was, in general, a key element in the show. In one story the Clangers were menaced by sinister trumpet-beings who descended from the sky. My eight-year-old grandson was highly alarmed when he watched it (on a video) last Christmas.

'Don't worry – it terrified me, too,' says Oliver Postgate, who dreamed up *The Clangers* and, with Peter Firmin, wrote, produced and animated every episode. A son of Raymond Postgate, the Labour Party historian, he'd tried his hand both as artist and actor, and was a studio manager at BBC Television when, in 1959, he stumbled on his true niche in life. Children's programmes, especially those for young children, he decided after working on some of them, were simply not good enough. Money was so tight that animation, then costing about £100 a minute, was beyond the department's means.

He and Firmin set up shop to see if they could produce an affordable ten-minute series. Firmin was the artist and model-maker. Vernon Elliott wrote the music. Postgate wrote the scripts and taught himself the laborious skills of frame-by-frame animation. They turned out *The Saga of Noggin the Nog* for an astonishing £10 a minute, followed by *Ivor the Engine*, *Pogles' Wood* and *Bagpuss*. *The Clangers* came in response to a sudden demand by the BBC to go into colour. Their isolated little world was chosen because space and space travel were much in the news and in young imaginations. They were mouse-like persons because one *Noggin* story had already featured an astronaut mouse, and their diet was soup because Oliver Postgate's little sons had told him

Still with us: Small Clanger, Soup Dragon, Tiny Clanger and Baby Soup Dragon

authoritatively that our moon was full of hot soup which a giant called Edward, who lived on the far side, sucked up through a straw he poked down any convenient volcano.

'Our studio,' says Postgate, 'was first a cowshed, then a row of pigsties, on Peter's farm in Kent. He made the sets and the skeletons of all the creatures, beautiful bits of engineering. His wife Joan knitted the bodies. I wrote dialogue for every time a Clanger opened his or her mouth, but no, it was never actually spoken. Vernon Elliott, who sadly died last year, turned the rhythms of each line into music, and Stephen Sylvester and I played it on Swanee whistles, which are tin whistles with a slide. You could get them from Boosey and Hawkes.'

Gratifyingly, the result sounded so much like speech that I wasn't alone in believing it to be processed human voices. Germans were convinced that the Clangers were speaking perfect German, Swedes that it was Swedish. The BBC got cold feet when in one episode Major Clanger had to struggle to open the lid to his cave. 'Oh sod it! The bloody thing's stuck again!' he grumbled in the script. We *can't* say things like that on children's television, Postgate was told. It wasn't going to be said, he pointed out, only whistled. But people would know! 'Not if they have nice minds,' said Oliver. 'They will only hear him say, "Oh dear me, the naughty thing has jammed again!".'

Looking back, the charm and also the strength of the entertainment lay in this mixture of mischievousness and innocence. There were sinister overtones, as in the descent of the trumpets. There were frailties of character – but also a goodness, a civic quality, to the Clangers as they strove to live peacefully on their moon, perhaps deriving from Oliver Postgate's own pacifism. (In the Second World War he went to prison for his beliefs.) He is now a cheerful and lively 72-year-old who would like to substitute 'What are the Clangers?' for 'What were…'. They live on in video cassettes and on cable TV, and a new set of Clanger figurines has just come onto the market. But, having seen how some old TV favourites have been revived he is not keen, on a Clangers' resurrection. **Philip Purser**

116

Still With Us

Sir Stanley Matthews

I was lucky enough to have a *tête-à-tête* lunch with Sir Stanley Matthews in a small bistro in Notting Hill Gate, over 20 years after his retirement from professional soccer at the age of 50. He was wearing a brown suede jacket, and his hair was startlingly white. He chose carefully from the menu: he has always been very wary about what he eats and drinks, so much so that, during his playing days, his reluctance to enjoy sumptuous fare at after-match banquets became something of a joke among his team-mates. Nat Lofthouse, the England and Bolton centre-forward, remembered the maestro pulling all the dough out of a roll and eating only the crust. He refused the offer of a roll, and went for a simple salad – a gastronomic favourite of his during his long playing career, when fasting over a weekend was often a major preoccupation – washed down with a glass of water.

We talked, of course, about football and the state of the modern game. Like all fans in the company of their heroes, I talked too much. I wanted to tell him that I was born in 1932, the year that Matthews, the son of a Potteries featherweight pugilist, made his League debut for Stoke City for the princely sum of five pounds a week. I wanted to tell him about the first time I saw him play for Blackpool at Stamford Bridge, when he mercilessly teased Chelsea's Welsh full-back, Billy Hughes,

in front of a crowd of some 70,000. I wanted to tell him about the wet, chilly afternoon in 1954 when I sat among the photographers at White Hart Lane, Tottenham, and could have shaken his hand as he wiggled by, and the straining and pushing in the Spurs penalty area as the defenders struggled to keep Matthews away from his Blackpool partner, Stan Mortensen.

I wanted to tell him how I had thrown a cushion through my host's cocktail cabinet when he mesmerised Bolton in the late stages of the 1953 FA Cup Final. I wanted to tell him about his magical performance for England against Brazil at Wembley in 1956, when he turned left-back Nilton Santos into a wobbly jelly. And I wanted to remind him that I had covered his last league game in 1965 at the Victoria Ground, Stoke, against Fulham, amid tears and high emotion.

Instead, Sir Stanley disrupted my fantasies by nearly losing his temper. As far as I know, the maestro has never shown a trace of public temper in his life, but now he almost sliced his lettuce into a mass of pulp. Mention had been made of another footballing genius, Diego Maradona, the Neapolitan coke-snorter. What made Sir Stanley react so violently was the incident in the 1986 World Cup in Mexico, when the darling of Buenos Aires knocked the ball into the England goal with his palm – an incident which became known as 'the hand of God'.

'I was sickened by some of Maradona's actions in Mexico, especially the "hand of God" business.' Sir Stanley raised his fist, an action he never did on the pitch, even when heavy-metal left-backs like Tiger Shaw of Scotland tried to kick him off the park. 'Why did Maradona have to do it? What I saw him do against England was unbelievable. And he followed this up against Belgium with other nasty tricks.'

'Didn't you play in a match before the war when an Italian centre-forward punched the ball into the England net?'

'Remember it well. The chap was called Piola. Not only did he cheat, but he managed to give our right-back, George Male, a black eye at the same time.'

As president of Stoke City, Sir Stanley has to suffer in his seat in the stand while the highly paid robots of modern soccer show scant regard for the ethics of our national game. He admits that cheating did go on during his younger days as an international, though it was generally motivated by politics rather than pampered avariciousness.

'I remember that international well. The Italians were determined to win at all costs

to please Mussolini. They were helped by a German referee who allowed Piola's goal to stand.' Matthews modestly failed to reveal that it was his dazzling run which allowed England to force a late equaliser.

The maestro's show of petulance about football's cheats came and went in a flash. Questioned about his choice of the game's great players, he responded like a star-struck ten-year-old. Some of them had played in his farewell match at Stoke following his retirement – Alfredo Di Stefano, Puskas, Greaves, 'all wonderful players'. Picking a dream team – which naturally did not include himself – he named some British players who followed in his twinkle-toe footsteps.

He singled out for mention Pat Jennings, the Northern Ireland goalkeeper, Bobby Moore, George Best, Sir Bobby Charlton and Jimmy Greaves, as well as some of those he had played with and against during his 33-year career – Eddie Hapgood, Alex James, John Charles, Danny Blanchflower, Sir Tom Finney, Billy Wright, Neil Franklin and his old chum Tommy Lawton, recipient of so many goals from Matthews's centres.

It had been a pleasure meeting Sir Stanley in such cosy circumstances – and hang Maradona. Since then I have had the occasional telephone conversation with the only player to be knighted while he was still playing. His voice is shy but firm. He still has a zest for the game which made him famous, though he has his reservations about its business side, especially vast takeovers like the recently proposed Murdoch-Manchester United deal. 'It won't be the last, you see – Chelsea, Newcastle, it could happen to them.' He is also critical of modern players who can't take press criticism. 'We were treated just as harshly in my day – but we didn't complain and got on playing. And look at the salaries we got then compared with today.'

He sounded chuffed because his club, Stoke City, had been leading the Nationwide Second Division. Sir Stanley, however, spent most of his playing career in the old First Division. Where else?

John Moynihan

The Richter scale

Pianist **John Bingham** *pays tribute to his Ukrainian mentor*

Sviatoslav Richter

The great Ukrainian pianist Sviatoslav Richter died recently in Moscow. His name first became known in England during the mid-Fifties. Those who had heard him play in Eastern Europe spoke of him as 'the greatest pianist in the world', 'a super-Horowitz'; Emil Gilels sang Richter's praises whenever he played in the West; the legend was being created. We all awaited the first records. One day, when I was 16, my father came home with recordings of Schumann's *Fantasiestücke*, *Waldszenen* and astonishing live performances of Liszt's *Études* and Mussorgsky's *Pictures at an Exhibition*.

In 1961 Richter was to give his first London recitals. With some of my fellow Royal Academy of Music students I slept the night outside the Royal Festival Hall to get tickets. His first recital of Haydn and Prokofiev came as something of a shock: there was amazing vision and virtuosity, but he played more quietly than anyone I had ever heard. His platform presence was one of extraordinary lightness for such a tall man. The whole hall was mesmerised, despite some idiot in a box shouting: 'For God's sake, play some Beethoven!'. The critics were not all kind. This angered me to such an extent that around midnight I phoned Neville Cardus to protest.

The sheer physical attack and the temperament of the young Richter were amazing. I remember him upon impulse charging into the opening of Schumann's C-major Fantasy before he had even sat down. Years later, in Moscow's Tchaikovsky Hall, after the orchestral exposition of the Brahms Second Concerto, Richter came in with such panache that the Steinway – its brakes unsecured – rolled away into the cello section of the orchestra.

From an early age I had dreams of studying in Russia. I had grown up surrounded by great recordings of Rachmaninov, Heifetz and Horowitz; now Richter added fuel to the fire. In 1966, on the advice of the pianist Tatiana Nikolaeva, I accepted a Soviet government scholarship and entered the Moscow Conservatoire for two years. The question was with whom to study. My original idea was to go to Gilels. Richter was 'permitted not to teach'. The students told me that the strongest class was that of Stanislav Neuhaus. I auditioned for him and was accepted. I was not fully aware of the great tradition into which I was entering.

Stanislav's father, Heinrich Neuhaus, had been the teacher of both Richter and Gilels. As a child he had grown up with his cousin Karol Szymanowski, who later became a great Polish composer. He then studied piano with Leopold Godowski in Vienna. Listening to old recordings of Godowski playing Schubert *Transcriptions*, one hears the tonal beauty which was inherited by all the succeeding generations of Neuhaus students. Neuhaus was surrounded in Russia by such people as the composer Scriabin; the painter Leonid Pasternak and his son the writer Boris Pasternak; as well as his uncle Blumenfeld, the teacher of Horowitz; and Vladimir Sofronitzky, whom I regard as the greatest Russian pianist since Rachmaninov.

Richter adored Heinrich Neuhaus, and would interrupt a concert rehearsal to greet and embrace him. After Neuhaus' death, his class at the Moscow Conservatoire was divided and his students were transferred to Malinin, Naumov and his son Stanislav. Stanislav (Stasik) Neuhaus's importance as a pianist has yet to be discovered by the Western world. He was a poetic artist with an enormous range of tone and pianistic colour. Memories of his Chopin and Scriabin recitals will remain with me always. As a teacher I can say simply that he was the greatest musician I ever had the privilege to work with and a person of incredible culture and warmth. He died

tragically in Moscow in 1980, aged 53.

This 'elite' society was made up of very humble, informal and dedicated people who were – to quote Neuhaus – 'working together for art'. Richter was extremely courteous and encouraging, with a high-pitched, melodious voice. He gave concerts rarely in Moscow. On one occasion word flew round that he had decided to play all the Book Two *Preludes* of Debussy in the large hall of the Conservatoire that afternoon. There was no official notification or publicity, yet Richter played to a full hall.

Richter's dedication was obsessive. His housekeeper once told me that he had been practising the same phrase of a Haydn Sonata for hour after hour. The rest of the day he spent painting landscapes. I remember him playing the Mozart Concerto K.449 in Moscow. At the end he was obviously unhappy, so the last movement was repeated as an encore. It was worse. During the interval he stormed through the swing doors into the foyer in a rage, his huge forehead red and shining.

Years later Richter was recording in

> **In Moscow's Tchaikovsky Hall, after the orchestral exposition of the Brahms Second Concerto, Richter came in with such panache that the Steinway, its brakes unsecured, rolled away into the cello section**

London. By that time I knew him quite well and took some of my students to the sessions. He treated them with respect and sensitivity, and showed interest in their comments about the alternative recording takes.

Stanislav Neuhaus mentioned to me that Richter had once played all the Liszt *Transcendental Études* in Moscow. I enquired about the existence of a recording, expecting a lot of bureaucracy. The Conservatoire archive director looked through his tape libraries and found it. I was thrilled. He gave me a copy and I gave him a Ronson cigarette lighter. He was equally thrilled.

Richter was one of the century's great individual pianists. However much one might sometimes question his interpretations, he was always unique and honest. This is something that many brilliant young pianists could emulate. To be sensational is easy; without dedication and honesty it is futile. I used to visit Neuhaus at his country house near Moscow, formerly Boris Pasternak's dacha. His mother had married both Heinrich Neuhaus and Pasternak, and Stanislav regarded the writer as a second father. There we would chat and sometimes drink vodka, as if inhabiting a Chekhov play. On one occasion a student played the 4th Prokofiev Sonata. It was clear that one passage was causing her problems. I remember Neuhaus saying, with sudden impatience: 'You know, Slava would practice that part until it is perfect. That is why he is Richter!'

'Almost finished'

119

Miles Kington

Cut off in my prime

Recently I terminated my agreement with Orange telephones. I had been giving them money and they had been lending me an Orange mobile phone. Well, it didn't say 'Orange' on the phone, it said 'Motorola', but I am sure they knew what they were doing. No, I take that back. I am not sure they knew what they were doing. I say that, because it rapidly transpired that in the house where I live, which is down in a valley, I cannot use my Orange phone in any meaningful way, because it will not link up with the outside world.This strikes me as a good enough reason not to want an Orange phone, as I mentioned in my letter of resignation.

It took me some time to get an answer back from the mighty Orange empire. When I did get one, it said that they had been trying to contact me by telephone, but failed. This suggests to me that they do not read letters very closely at Orange, as the very thing I had been complaining of was that they couldn't reach me by phone. Another hint that they do not read letters very closely came in the next letter from Orange to me – yes, they still keep on sending me letters – which said among other things that they regarded me as a valued client.

Now, if a month or two after I have resigned from our arrangement they still regard me as a valued client, it strikes me that news travels slowly round the Orange grapevine. Perhaps they phone each other at the bottom of valleys to tell each other the latest news…

Actually, it wasn't me who got the phone in the first place. My wife bought it because she was working in Bristol, where there was no telephone. I don't mean to say that there are no telephones in Bristol, only that there was none in the part of Bristol University where she and a small troupe of actors were rehearsing the play she was directing. Very often she wanted to get in touch to ask important questions such as whether I had collected the child from school, whether there was anything for supper, and whether I knew what day Tchaikovsky's birthday was. (The play she was working on was about Tchaikovsky.)

She came back from the rehearsals quite impressed with the capability of the phone. She was less impressed when she found that although it operated tolerably well out of Bristol University, she could not make a call to anywhere from our house. We had committed ourselves to 60 minutes of free calls each month, the Orange people no doubt assuming that once we had used up our free quota we would go on using the phone for calls we would have to pay extra for. However, as we could so seldom use the phone, I don't think we ever exceeded our free allocation of monthly chat, even when my wife wanted to find out exactly

where the Reichenbach Falls were in real life (the play was about Sherlock Holmes as well as about Tchaikovsky).

This left us with two choices. Either we could ignore the presence of the phone, except on occasional trips out, or we could move to somewhere on top of a hill, like Bristol University. We opted for the former. So I would sometimes take the phone to London on the train, or on car journeys to Wales, where I have been working for the BBC, and I would bring it back unused. This was because, on trains, I always seemed to attempt to use the phone in Box Tunnel and because there are large stretches of Wales where the Orange empire doesn't reach. The last place I tried to use my Orange phone was near Bala in Merioneth, but a kindly onlooker called Price said: 'I wouldn't bother if I were you – you'll never get in touch with the outside world on one of those things. You can't from here, you know.'

I suddenly woke up to the fact that in trying to call my home in Wiltshire from Bala, I was dialling from a place where you couldn't use an Orange phone to a place where you couldn't use an Orange phone, and a still, small voice said somewhere inside me: 'Why not jack it in?' Later, another voice, which was bigger and stronger and which I identified as my wife's, said: 'Why don't we jack it in?' So now we have jacked it in and retreated one step from the modern world. Yes, for the last month or more I have been operating entirely without a mobile phone. The difference has been huge.

No, hold on, the difference has been absolutely minimal. The only difference is that I can once again look down on mobile phone users, which I couldn't before. For a while, if I was in a train, and one of those braying voices started telling George he was on a train and was probably going to be late for the meeting, or telling his wife that was on a train and probably going to be on time for supper, I couldn't exchange glances with other people as if to say 'What a wally!'. Well, I could, but only at the expense of being uneasily aware that I, too, had an Orange phone stuck in my luggage.

I once got a round of applause in a crowded coach by saying to a woman who was talking at the top of her voice on her mobile: 'If you're going to talk so loud, could you please have more interesting conversations?'. This was gratifying, but it meant I couldn't get out my mobile and ring my wife to say that I was on a train. At least, not without going into the next coach and doing it surreptitiously. I wonder if I would have the nerve to do it again…

He should have stopped

Nell Dunn *met a brave woman on the number 14 bus*

I am on the number 14 bus riding up the Fulham Road, sitting downstairs in the front left seat (the one I try to get if I am carrying too much to go upstairs at the front left, my favourite). We approach a request stop and a black woman holds up her hand. She realises the bus is not slowing and steps out into the road, her hand held high to hail the driver. He drives straight past her but is forced to stop at the lights 50 yards on. She belts up the road. She is thin and wiry and about 50 years old. She just makes it to leap on to the platform as he pulls away.

'Why didn't he stop for me?' she asks the long-haired, laidback white conductor. He shrugs and points to his temple. She marches up the aisle and knocks, rapperty-tap, on the glass partition behind the driver. He turns around.

'Why didn't you stop for me?' she asks.

'You didn't put your hand up,' he says, turning back. She raps again, harder this time. He turns around.

'Why didn't you stop for me?' she asks again. He stops the bus, jumps down from his cab, goes round, gets on the platform and hurtles up the aisle to where she is sitting. He is ugly, fat and white.

'Get off this bus,' he says.

'Why didn't you stop for me?' she says.

He leans over her, almost drooling in fury. The conductor stays on his platform.

'Get off, now!' he shouts.

'No,' she says, 'this is a public bus. I'm not getting off.'

He pushes his face still closer. 'Get off!' he shouts.

'I'm not frightened of you,' she coolly says.

Almost crazy with rage now, 'If you don't get off this bus now I'll make everyone get off!' he yells.

'I don't care,' she lightly returns.

'You don't care?' he screams.

'No,' she says, 'I don't care. Why didn't you stop for me?'

To my amazement he is defeated. He turns and stomps back down the aisle, gets back into his cab and drives on.

'You were very brave,' I say.

'He should have stopped for me,' she says.

Masai Mara mayhem

The intrepid **Joan Wyndham** *tackles Africa and Mauritius.*
Illustration by **Larry**

'Going on safari? You must be mad!' The dread words 'At your age?' hung in the air, unspoken but all too plain. 'And what's more,' continued my helpful friend, 'there's a cholera epidemic, and rioting in the streets over the election.'

Nothing daunted, we set off for Kenya, seeing nothing more sinister than a sign saying 'Joy Hotel, Lucky Bar and Butchery'. Our only harassment came from hordes of beggar boys – 'You buy banana? No? Then give me free money!'

Our lodge in northern Kenya was a mini-safari in itself, with crocodiles dozing on the river bank, and monkeys leaping along the parapets. Brilliantly coloured birds shared our breakfast, and black and white genet cats swished their long spotted tails from the rafters above our dinner tables.

The meal was announced by a dancing procession of kitchen staff, headed by the chef beating time on a saucepan. The food,

after this, was a bit of an anti-climax, so there were plenty of left-overs for the ritual feeding of the crocodiles, who waited below with gaping jaws, their yellow eyes gleaming in the dusk. Nearby were some rickety steps marked 'To the Crocodile Bar'. Unfortunately, the staff had forgotten to mention that the bar had been swept away in the last floods – they must have lost quite a few guests that way.

Our first safari was a great success, with zebras running beside the car, cheetahs loping through the bush, giraffes, bison and gazelles. Unfortunately, all the leopards seemed to be up trees, eating something, with a hideous pack of hyenas waiting below for the left-overs. Your first elephant always causes shrieks of excitement, even if it's only a glimpse of a large grey bum with twitching tail vanishing into the bushes. Little do you realise that in a few minutes you'll come across a huge herd of them, and soon will be saying scornfully, 'Oh no, not another elephant.'

Our next stop was Tree Tops, famous as the lodge where Princess Elizabeth first heard she was Queen. Before we were even

offered a drink, we had to Ooh and Aah over her bedroom. Our own tiny room overlooked the lake, where hundreds of animals gathered at night, lured by the salt-licks. The finest sight of all was a whole herd of elephants who dived into the lake for a swim.

I had always thought of the elephant as a rather boring, static creature but once in the water he was like a pachydermous Esther Williams, gambolling joyously, spraying friends and dunking foes.

My husband was glued to the window, so I sneaked off to the bar for a whisky. The barman looked amazingly small, but then I am very short-sighted. 'A large whisky,' I demanded. 'No ice.' No reply. I tried again and got an odd sort of chattering noise and a flash of yellow teeth. It was only then that I realised that it was, in fact, a baboon.

'Don't worry, he's a regular,' explained the returning barman, giving me my drink while the baboon watched with interest from a nearby table. I almost expected him to cross his legs and light up a cigar.

Our next stop was the Masai Mara and we had been warned that the road might be

'Ask for just one hand to be lopped off – they expect you to haggle.'

'a little bumpy'. In fact it was over 100 miles of rutted mud, interspersed with deep pools of water. We were tossed around, and thrown violently in every direction, cracking our heads on the roof or being hurled to the floor. All along the route were overturned cars and buses stuck in the mud, with the hysterical passengers being told that they had to spend the night there.

At our lodge, the phones were jammed with enraged tourists telling their agents that it was a bloody disgrace, and that they were flying home immediately.

We, however, were made of sterner stuff, fascinated by the prospect of seeing the Masai Mara and its legendary tribesmen. They are great hunters, warriors and dancers, and also a beautiful people, lean and muscular. There is apparently no such thing as a fat Masai, due no doubt to their politically incorrect diet of beef-on-the-bone, fresh milk and warm blood.

Our safari ended on a note of triumph – our first sighting of the elusive lions. The whole pride was lounging happily by the roadside, so near you could have stroked their noses – provided you didn't mind losing an arm.

It was a great way to say goodbye to Africa.

We had planned to spend the final week of our trip relaxing in Mauritius. It was only five days to Christmas, and the airport was ringing with carols. We sat in the waiting-room with our fellow travellers, singing along with the festive music belting out of loudspeakers. Suddenly the door burst open and in came about 50 Muslim pilgrims returning from Mecca, all in spotless white, their wives adorned like brides. They seemed a little taken aback to be greeted by a rousing chorus of 'O Come, All Ye Faithful'.

Mauritius was beautiful, but unexpectedly hot and humid, so I spent most of the day lurking in my air-conditioned chalet.

'Why on earth aren't you out sunbathing?' demanded my husband, hurtling out to the beach in his smart new swimming trunks. 'You might just as well be in Cheam!' I ignored him, surrounded by all my favourite things – a bottle of malt whisky, an American crime novel, a packet of Silk Cut, and a bar of Toblerone. Who needs the beach? In any case the sea was full of sharp shards of coral, and the swimming pool monopolised by screaming kids and people learning to scuba-dive.

Dinner was a very impressive-looking buffet, but after sampling my third cotton-wool crayfish tail, I had a suspicion that I might have lost my sense of taste. Perhaps the oil of cloves that I'd used for toothache had burnt out my palate. 'Don't worry,' said my husband, 'we're all in the same boat. I think there must be a machine in the kitchen labelled "Taste Extractor".'

The evenings were the only really enjoyable time, with an open-air dance floor and a fabulous local band with phoney dreadlocks. All ages raved together. I watched a six-foot Mauritian teaching an ecstatic English child of five the samba, while in another corner her parents were rehearsing for the next day's rock and roll competition.

Unable to sit still any longer, I abandoned my stick and joined in, jumping around like a teenager on Ecstasy. A French lady in the audience was clapping, and I glowed with pride until she brought me down to earth with a loud cry of 'Bravo les Anciennes!'

Christmas Day came and, after a gruesome turkey dinner (no plum pudding, no mince pies) we sat outside, hoping to glimpse the Star of Bethlehem shining through the palm trees, listening to a black band playing 'White Christmas'.

On our last night there was a midnight beach party, but my husband wasn't keen so I went on my own. I wasn't the least bit embarrassed to be sitting alone at two in the morning sipping genteelly on my White Lady and smoking a small cigar. On the sands they were dancing round a bonfire, while in the bar I was surrounded by a noisy gang of young Mauritian boys, stripped to the waist and throwing back Planter's Punches by the gallon. Anywhere else I might have felt nervous, expecting any moment to be either mugged or chatted up (I should be so lucky).

But here I felt totally at ease, with warm friendly people who didn't give a damn about age or sex, provided that, like them, you were happy.

For that alone I might one day go back to Mauritius.

'I really look forward to our baby-racing days.'

125

Enoch Powell

IT WAS THE SUMMER of 1983, and I was a year out of Oxford, working for a public relations agency in central London where my main task was to edit *Airfix Magazine* for its proprietors, the Palitoy Company. The tube journey to work took me from Victoria to Oxford Circus, and it was midway between these stations, early one July morning, that I stared across a crowded carriage and registered that the man standing next to me was the Rt Hon J. Enoch Powell MP.

Regardless of the stifling heat, Powell was togged up in full morning dress, complete with briefcase and furled umbrella. On his head was a curious item, a bit bigger than a bowler with an odd, curving brim, that may have been a Homburg hat. He looked grim, weather-beaten, somehow brooding and ground down. For some reason, prompted perhaps by my father's quaint notion that famous people 'like to be recognised', or the memory of having stood, if not in the same circle of talking heads, then at any rate in the same room as him at a *Spectator* party a week or two before, I decided to say hello.

What followed is engraved on my mind with painful clarity. From the moment I caught the glint in Powell's eye as I introduced myself, I divined that this was not merely a bad idea, but the worst idea, as Martin Amis might have put it, the very worst idea of all. As I prattled on about our non-encounter of the previous week, Powell fixed me with a look that was not at all benevolent, a look of absolute awful gravity. Whatever composure I may have possessed at the start of our interview vanished into the ether. In fact I simply babbled, while Powell – still stony-faced – deflected each advance with a single precisely articulated sentence. Unusual to see Mr Powell travelling in the opposite direc-

tion to the House of Commons, I wittered nervously, but then, er, Parliament was in recess, wasn't it? No, Powell tersely corrected, Parliament was not in recess and he was off to the BBC to deliver a talk on Schopenhauer.

The rest of the carriage had woken up to the conversation by now, and was silently enjoying the spectacle of this young twit undergoing ritual humiliation. Somehow the question of my *alma mater* came up. 'Of course, you're an Oxford man yourself,

aren't you, Mr Powell?' I proposed, gamely misremembering a vital nugget of biographical data. 'I regret that I did not have the pleasure of attending that university.' The novels of A N Wilson found him no more forthcoming. In the end I gave up and just looked at him hopelessly as the train pulled into Oxford Circus.

On the platform he turned stiffly towards me. 'I regret that when we began this conversation I omitted to enquire your name.' I supplied it. 'Mr Taylor,' Powell enunciated – and I have an idea that he may even have raised the Homburg in valediction – 'I wish you success.'

Oddly enough, we never kept up after that, though I used to be amused by the stories of a literary editor chum whose least-liked job was phoning up Powell to ask him to review a book: Powell would always answer on the first ring, then return remorselessly logical replies to routine pleasantries. This reduced my friend to a state of nervous terror. 'I believe I have your telephone number, Mr Powell?' he rambled desperately on one of these occasions. 'Yes,' Powell assured him, 'otherwise you could not have telephoned me.'

D J Taylor

Modern Life

What is...
A Focus Group?

'ENGLAND HAS DONE one thing: it has invented and established public opinion which is an attempt to organise the ignorance of the community and to elevate it to the dignity of physical force,' Oscar Wilde wrote of late Victorian Britain. His words seem even more appropriate to our own age, where the views of the public on every possible subject are now treated with grotesque reverence. So, attempting to match the ever-shifting moods of public opinion, the Established Church feels compelled to abandon its traditions. The monarchy watches the vast, lachrymose crowds outside Buckingham Palace and promises to change, while the leader of the Conservative Party dons a baseball cap.

In this constant drive to be 'in tune' with the public, institutions, political parties and businesses increasingly rely on market research to tell them what 'ordinary people' are thinking. It is not surprising, therefore, that market research has become one of the great growth industries of the last decade. 'Real growth has continued at levels of around 10 per cent for some years now,' says the Association of Market Survey Organisations. It is estimated that the total size of the industry – led by companies such as National Opinion Polls and Taylor Nelson AGB – could be more than £750 million.

Market research can be divided into two types of methodology. First, there is the 'quantitative research' which relies on asking a large, representative sample of the public their opinions on a certain product or issue. It is from such research that we get all those statistics which so intrigue the media, such as '41 per cent of couples have had sex in the kitchen' or '88 per cent of the public think Louise Woodward (the Cheshire-born killer nanny) is innocent.' The problem with such numbers, say market researchers, is that they provide only a superficial picture of public attitudes. Nor do they explain why such opinions are held.

It was to answer such questions that the second, 'qualitative' method of polling has been developed. Qualitative researchers gather together small 'focus groups' of about ten people and get them into a discussion about, say, BBC programming or a new make of car. Each group can be drawn from a different sector of the population. One group might therefore comprise only women under 30; another might be made up of affluent professionals. The discussion is led by a moderator from the research company and the views of the participants are recorded, analysed and then submitted in a report to the client. The appeal of this method is that it provides a deeper understanding of public attitudes beyond bald statistics. Mike Imms, a leading practitioner in the field, explains: 'Qualitative research developed in Britain in the Sixties because marketing organisations found that conventional polling methods were giving them inadequate answers.' About 13 per cent of market research is now carried out in this way.

There are a number of methodological drawbacks to focus groups. Because the samples are so small, they can never be representative. Groups can be dominated by a

'You say "Boo", she wets herself.'

few confident individuals. Some participants may be fearful of expressing their views, especially politically incorrect ones on subjects such as homosexuality or race. Nor does extensive market research always guarantee success in the commercial world. Before the launch of its 'New Coke', Coca-Cola tested the brand on 190,000 people. It flopped dismally. The corporate re-branding of British Airways, including the replacement of the Union flag with ethnic graffiti on its planes, involved an expensive programme of polls and focus groups, yet has proved unpopular with staff and the public.

The BBC's reliance on focus groups has been bitterly attacked by programme makers, who complain that their findings now carry more weight than the instincts of drama bosses. Michael Wearing, the man responsible for major successes such as *Boys from the Blackstuff* and *Pride and Prejudice*, recently resigned as head of drama, after his proposed new serial was shelved because focus-group research suggested that viewers might find the plot boring. On this basis, TV producer Kenith Trodd has pointed out, *The Singing Detective*, a story about a man with hideous scars lying in hospital, would probably never have been made.

Allowing focus groups to determine our television watching may be bad enough, but even worse is the way market research now drives the thinking of our political parties, especially Labour. It was under Neil Kinnock in the 1980s that Labour first began to use focus groups to influence policy, but now, under Blair, they have become all-powerful. In fact, the focus group has been institutionalised as one of the estates of the realm. Last July, ministers announced the creation of a 5,000-strong 'People's Panel' to test public reaction to new and existing policies. Costing tens of thousands of pounds, the initiative includes telephone surveys, 'citizens' juries' and smaller focus groups made up of the correct gender and ethnic mix. Amidst this frenzy of political marketing, the question arises: why should public policy be dictated by those selected at random rather than those chosen democratically by the electorate? Focus groups might be fine for testing a new brand of lager but they are no substitute for government. **Leo McKinstry**

'The characters are great but it won't last,' I said to my wife, 'so we'd better make hay while the sun shines.' It was Christmas 1960, and I'd just been commissioned to write episode 24 of *Coronation Street*. Before this I had spent 15 years trying to prove that contemporary drama didn't need French windows.

The money bought us our first washing machine, the fee being £100 and the washing machine costing £99. I squandered the remaining £1 on a bottle of something to celebrate. We spent the next eight years wrapped in the *Street*'s warm embrace, the memory of our early money-strapped years fading to a bad dream as we paid off a large slice of our mortgage, bought a car and felt we could at last afford to extend the family.

After Tony Warren and Harry Kershaw I was the first writer to stay the course and become a permanent member of the team, later becoming script editor and, eventually, producer. There was a period, during the first few months, when writers were particularly thin on the ground: Harry and I would meet and knock out storylines for a couple of episodes and then toss a coin to see which of us got to write the best of the two. The first was always the setting-up episode leading to a cliff-hanger, and the second episode the most interesting to write. I used to think that maybe Harry had a double-headed penny, because the coin always fell in his favour.

Soon after this came the death of Ida Barlow, Ken Barlow's mother. This time I got the prize episode, the funeral. I became a dab hand at funerals, and was eventually christened the Undertaker.

Harry then invented the story conference, one of a number of innovations he introduced when it became apparent that we were in for the long term. I haven't been near the place for years, but from what I hear the system is very much as he introduced it. Writers now began to get interested, and there was increasing rivalry to be in the team. New writers were given what the late Jim Allen called 'the hard stare' by some of those who had their feet too firmly under the table. They needn't have worried as some of us were ony too anxious to be released from what Kenith Trodd has described as 'Granada's suffocating paternalistic bear hug', though we weren't ungrateful for the fact that it had paid the rent while we looked around for what we really wanted to do. Harry Kershaw's loyalty to the programme, however, was total, and to say he devoted the rest of his life to it would be no exaggeration.

Actors had the same problem as we did, and probably more, though at least they were eating, as could be seen from the weight problems some of them had, which were visible on screen. Jack Howarth, the actor who played Albert Tatlock, used to complain of his small part in scripts I wrote. If I met him in the foyer he'd shout, 'I'm just going home to learn my line.' There was a good relationship among members of the team, however, as producers came and went. This became somewhat strained when one producer decided to chop Martha Longhurst, one of the three in the snug. I didn't agree with this decision, but Violet Carson, outraged, decided I was

Street talking man

Ida Barlow's funeral helped pay off my mortgage, says **John Finch**

John Finch, above and, left, with Pat Phoenix, Harry Kershaw and Doris Speed at the programme's eighth birthday celebration.

Coronation Street 8th Birthday Dec 1968

tarred with the same brush and stopped speaking to me. Two years later, trapped in the lift, she suddenly said, 'Nice to see the sunshine again,' and I knew I'd been forgiven.

In the early years, despite Harry Kershaw's steady guiding hand, we seemed to move from crisis to crisis. An actor's strike, round about (I think) episode 90, lasted for some time and, as actors' contracts ran out, they were obliged to leave the programme. As the cast shrank it became increasingly difficult to find stories. Harry Driver, who was almost totally paralysed, worked with Vince Powell as storyline writer. I was editor, and we would have story meetings that went on into the early hours of the morning. As the weeks went by the silences became longer and longer. Eventually we were down to half a dozen or so actors with no one to serve behind the bar in the *Rover's Return*. If a pint was called for it was slid in from the wings by a technician.

A major worry was removed when the series ceased to go out live. We were on a learning curve and one improvement followed another. Directors like Mike Newell (*Four Weddings and a Funeral*) and Michael Apted (*Seven Up*) cut their directorial teeth on early episodes of *Coronation Street*. A major step forward was the building of an actual street outside, something I had advocated from very early on.

After serving my time I was released to write and edit a series called *A Family at War*, which took four years of my life, and was followed by a series called *Sam*, which took another three. We worked on the principle that you didn't have to grossly distort reality to create popular television.

The so-called Golden Years sped by, until eventually I found myself needing a sabbatical with some work to come back to. I discovered that Granada's paternalism had become reserved for series like *Brideshead Revisited* and *Jewel in the Crown*, and I was left with a frosty landscape but no bear and no hug.

I was asked by the BBC if I would be interested in working on a new soap called *EastEnders* and would I like to visit the metropolis to talk about this. I said I would watch a couple first. I did.

'Not much point in me going,' I said to my wife. 'Nice characters but it won't last.'

What was... the Northover Projector?

SIXTY YEARS and one day after the launch of World War II, we had the police, the fire and rescue service and an army ammunition disposal team in our village. Half of Church Street was cordoned off, old folks were evacuated from the old folks' bungalows and no one could get to the jumble sale in the Reading Room.

What had happened was that builders digging down to lay the footings for a house extension had unearthed a crate of glass bottles containing a yellowish fluid. They pulled one out. It was about three inches in diameter, sealed with a metal cap, unlabelled. They tossed it into the skip and it shattered with a lot of smoke and foul-smelling fumes. The lad standing closest coughed and choked.

Tear gas? Poison gas? Nerve gas? Germ warfare? Ambulances were sent for, too, just to be on the safe side. But there was a smell of petrol mixed up with all the other smells. Might these things be Molotov cocktails, the improvised anti-tank petrol bombs first used by Republicans in the Spanish Civil War? That was more like it, a police inspector was eventually able to tell displaced householders who had sat themselves in folding chairs on the village green to await developments. The bottles did contain petrol, plus something like latex to make it stick to the target, and phosphorus to ignite the mixture on contact with the air, only the phosphorus had, luckily, long since degenerated.

The penny dropped. I was whisked back to those giddy days of 1940–41 when invasion threatened, the Home Guard was

'Let's get married'

formed and the regular army was upstaged by left-wing Spanish War veterans who reckoned they knew more about real warfare. Tom Wintringham ran a battle school at Osterley Park, while a Canadian, Yank Levy, toured Home Guard units trying to teach them to fight dirty. The Molotov cocktail was their dream weapon, ideologically as well as practically. The only snag was that while athletic young Spaniards brought up in the bull-ring might have danced up to an enemy tank to deliver their cocktails by hand, it was unrealistic to expect the same from respectable, not to say arthritic, members of Dad's Army. They needed a weapon to whizz the bottle some hundreds of feet to the target. Thus was born the Northover Projector, dreamed up – it was said – by a colonel of that name.

The barrel was a length of three-inch steel tubing, roughly the diameter of prewar milk bottles and beer bottles. This was mounted on a tripod made of angle-iron. There was a crude open sight and a breech-block like a saucepan lid with a double clamp to hold it shut. You slid the bottle into the barrel, followed by a bit of wadding, then the gunpowder propellant charge, and clamped the lid shut. There was also a sort of pistol-grip connected to the back end, and when you pulled the trigger it fired the charge. If the bottle proved to be a tight fit and got stuck, the important thing was *not* to open the breech, as the whole grisly mixture could whoof back over you.

To make sure our glass bottles really were Northover projectiles I rang my friend Dan Raschen, who wound up a versatile army career as weapons expert at the Royal Military College of Science. What's more, he had been a 16-year-old Home Guard in 1941 and had actually fired a Northover. 'Yes,' he confirmed breezily, 'the metal caps prove it. They were crown corks really, the same as beer bottles had, except they never seemed to last very long. The stuff usually deteriorated after a year or two.'

Our village Home Guard had evidently been issued with a Northover, if luckily never having to use it. When the war was over and they didn't know what to do with the bottles, they must simply have buried them. The army of today carried them away. The jumble sale at the Reading Room was rescheduled. **PHILIP PURSER**

Theatre
Beryl Bainbridge

AT THE AGE of 14, owing to a misunderstanding, I was sent from my native Liverpool to a ballet school in Hertfordshire housed in a huge mansion originally built for Nell Gwyn and later owned by the Rothschilds. The misunderstanding was my mother's, who, after I had appeared, aged seven, on the stage of the Garrick Theatre, Southport, tap-dancing and bawling my way through that well-known ballad, 'Kiss Me Goodnight, Sergeant Major', was convinced my future lay on the boards.

Thus, I found myself, six years later, standing at the bar in leotard and pink tights, being trained for the corps de ballet. To say I was unsuited to the task is an understatement: be that as it may, in pursuit of this goal the school regularly went up to London to watch the great ones perform. I saw Massine's successor, Lifar, leap his way through *The Three-Cornered Hat* and Robert Helpmann looking very pale in *Miracle in the Gorbals*.

I never saw *Swan Lake*, which is why two weeks ago I booked five tickets for a matinee performance at the Royal Albert Hall. Three of us – my grandchildren – were very young, no more than five, four and three years old. Myself and gallant friend by the name of Pussy were slightly more advanced in years and had some difficulty persuading August, aged three, from climbing up the pillars outside the Hall.

The stage was circular for the occasion, similar to an ice-rink, and we had ringside seats, which was advantageous from a viewing point but not so suitable when the dancers came too near and actually sat down in front of Angie. He had to be restrained from poking them with his finger and twice he asked, loudly, why they weren't wearing trousers.

Swan Lake, first danced in 1877 at the Bolshoi theatre, concerns the everyday story of courtly folk. Princess Odette is turned into a swan by the dastardly magician Rotbart and is wooed by Prince Siegfried only after midnight when the magic

wears off and the swan maidens all turn back into girls. Only love can break the spell but Rotbart tricks the Prince by substituting his own daughter Odile in Odette's likeness.

It seemed to me that love won in the end, but Inigo, aged five, confused both Pussy and me by insisting that there'd be a stabbing. In the interval he wouldn't budge in case he missed anything, so he was left in the care of a nice family sitting a row behind. When we returned the mother said they'd been very entertained by his recounting how his grandfather had been shot by gangsters and how he himself had lost half his leg from being bitten by an Alsatian. Esmé, aged four, liked the music. She said it made her feel sleepy: to prove it she lay down in the aisle.

Daria Klimentova danced the role of Odette and Odile, and Dimitri Gruzdyev that of the Prince. They were both wonderful and received hugely deserved ovations, and not just because they were replacements. Paul Lewis as the magician was sufficiently scary to send all three children scrambling for the comfort of grown-up legs. To be a dancer must be hell. No wonder Nijinsky went mad. When the swan-maidens folded their wings and lay down at the coming of the dawn, you could see them struggling to draw air into their lungs. There was a stain of blood on the shoe of the third swan to the left.

Ballet is a strange art-form, verging on the comic and just swerving away through a combination of athletic grace and swooning sound.

'We're a little concerned about your attitude, Stevens'

Out of this world

Was Jesus an alien? former BBC producer **Hugh Burnett** *travels to the outer reaches of credulity. Illustrations by* **Geoff Waterhouse**

I saw my first unidentified flying object over Albania one evening last summer, from a balcony in Corfu. Like the Greek wine in my glass, it was there one minute – and vanished the next.

Some years earlier, I had filmed two enthusiastic UFO-spotters. One was a mortician, the other an electricity company employee. They scanned the skies over Box Hill with a converted portable electric fire, powered by batteries. 'Try over there towards Dorking. They hide behind the clouds – the crafty little so-and-sos!' One had seen a craft over Parsons Green Underground station. 'But if I'd have rung the Air Ministry, would they have believed me? No way!' When a lady reported her car being brought to a screaming halt by beams from a huge machine in a field near Winchester, they offered to check the car for radiation. Result negative, despite her reports of a spaceman gazing at her through

the window and the car's engine revving wildly with the ignition switched off. She had been instructed to keep quiet about the matter, but this was a free country and she was going to report what she had seen. Officials from London were due to visit her, she said.

To his colleagues, Lord Clancarty was a more worrying UFO expert. He had obtained an evening's debate in the House of Lords concerning the UFO cover-up being conducted by the government. When we arrived to film he offered me his card. It read: 'My card'. He had published a book with photographs of what, he explained, were two huge holes at the earth's poles. The holes were about 200 miles wide, said his Lordship, the southern one usually obscured by cloud. It was from these, he believed, that the UFOs were coming and going. He had also met a spaceman in Sloane Square. When asked how he knew that the being was genuine, he said the alien

had told him so. All biblical phenomena, explained Lord Clancarty, were UFO manifestations. Jacob's ladder was an obvious example. Elijah's flying chariot was another. The white figures at the empty tomb were obviously spacemen. Jesus had ascended to Heaven in a craft. His Lordship added that it was not generally known that a flotilla of German submarines had secretly headed north at the end of the last war, probably taking Hitler to a safe haven inside the northern hole. There were implications that the UFOs and those polar holes had evil connections.

George King, a former taxi driver, reported being visited by an Indian fakir who had suddenly materialised in his London flat. Mr King was instructed to go to a hill in Devon where 'something of import' would be revealed. It was. Jesus appeared, having arrived from Venus in a UFO. This event resulted in the formation of the Aetherius Society – and the creation of their Prayer Box. Each year thereafter coachloads of followers arrived at the hill to chant mantras into the box, which would then be beamed towards world disasters to alleviate suffering. We filmed the faithful, gathered in a V formation behind Mr King, intoning into the box. A lady on a stool with a stopwatch recorded the amount of prayer power being gathered. Only Mr King could tell when the box was full – he could feel the tingle.

George King, when I last heard of him, had become His Eminence, Archbishop Metropolitan of the Aetherius Churches, Count de Florina, Doctor, Sir, Shri, Yogoriji, PhD, and had just been awarded the Christian Chivalry International Union Prize of Peace and Justice.

In the course of making the documentary I received several interesting phone calls. The first was an anonymous warning that there was a mole in the BBC, put there by the government to prevent the truth about UFOs emerging. I said if the mole's name could be revealed I would blow his cover. There was a pause and the caller explained that he would have to put it in a letter. But no letter arrived. Perhaps it was intercepted by the mole. The second was from a UFO Group Leader asking me if I would like to film an alien being from another world. I said I would, very much, and arranged to meet him in Leeds. The day

before I left I was called again and asked to bear in mind that he might not be an *actual* alien, but someone under alien control. When we met he looked quite normal in jeans and T-shirt, clutching files and a copy of Nostradamus. To complicate matters, the UFO Group Leader was having a sex-change. The alien was unable to reveal very much, having received orders to be reticent in dealing with the media. He said there were many aliens like himself, disguised in human form. His wife had laughed when he told her he had come from a distant planet. His mother, looking like John Cleese in drag, strode in at the end of our conversation and said: 'I don't know what's wrong with my son. He thinks he's an alien being from another world. Would you like a cup

of tea?' He did not make it into the final film.

Then an ex-diplomat who was due to appear in the documentary phoned to say that he was definitely *not* going to appear with a transvestite. I assured him that the person having a sex-change was a) not a transvestite, and b) not appearing in the film. 'Oh,' he said, 'one has to be very careful. These aliens are on collecting missions. Sperm, bits of animals, plants – you name it.' He rang off, leaving me wondering if they had collected Lord Lucan.

The editor of the *Flying Saucer Review* showed me piles of pictures and drawings of UFOs, mostly saucer-shaped. And there was a multitude of sketches – humanoids with arms, legs, ears and eyes seen by various night-watchmen and people in cars in America. A Brazilian peasant had been abducted while ploughing a field and taken into the craft, where, to his surprise, he had encountered a naked space lady. On meeting her, 'the inevitable' had happened, and when released, he had come out in spots.

Another witness was quite certain what she had experienced. When her

> '**I don't know what's wrong with my son. He thinks he's an alien being from another world. Would you like a cup of tea?**'

husband arrived home from work he found her hiding under the kitchen table with the children. She had gone into the garden and seen a huge UFO 'blocking out part of the roof and the chimney pots'. In the cockpit, looking down at her, were two figures 'with long golden hair, like the old kings'. Then the craft had taken off at enormous speed and disappeared.

The film was duly completed and transmitted. But it was not regarded as a success by the ex-diplomat. I had, he thought, deliberately left out a reference by a French minister on the subject of visitations – proving that I too was part of the BBC conspiracy suppressing vital facts.

It had all been very interesting. That unidentified flying object over Albania had certainly disappeared as fast as my wine. Perhaps it had been St Spiridion, Corfu's Greek Orthodox saint, returning to look at his embroidered slippered self, lying in his tomb in the Cathedral. With UFOs, perhaps anything.

Evening clashes

John Bowen *is kneed in the groin, poked in the nostril and slung onto a thin blue mat. Illustrations by* **Bob Geary**

W riters persuade them-
selves into various
forms of idiotic
behaviour in the cause
of research. Last sum-
mer I signed up for some evening classes in
self defence, run by a local College of
Further Education. I could have studied
Origami, New Ways With Lemon Grass or
Dorothy Wordsworth and Her Circle, but I
wanted to know about self-defence.

The course consisted of six two-hour
classes, given on Wednesdays by a sergeant
of police in the sports hall of a local com-

prehensive school. I had missed two
classes, but was told I would soon catch up.
No special standard was required; the
course was for people of any age. I imagined my classmates. They would be vulner-
able and fearful, many of them pensioners
like myself, scared of being mugged or
raped in ill-lit alleys by disturbed persons in
woolly hats. Even in the agricultural
Midlands there would be a lot of them these
days.

I wore a track-suit and trainers, and
arrived early. A plump young man in a
sweatshirt with 'New York giants' on the

front had arrived before me. He was pulling
blue rubber mats from a corner and placing
them in groups of three and four. The mats
were old and thin and did not appear to
offer much protection to anyone with brittle
bones.

I said, 'Good evening. I'm joining the
class from today. Are you the instructor?'

'Do I look like a policeman? Want to
help with the mats?' I helped with the mats.
'I'm Les. Dave's the instructor. He'll be in
soon. You done this kind of thing before?' I
said I hadn't. 'You'll soon get used to it.
What it's mostly been so far, since I'm the

only man, is them throwing me about.'

He would no longer be the only man. I too would have to get used to being thrown about. 'Must be painful.'

'Boring. It's how you're supposed to deal with different sorts of attacks. I'm usually the attacker. I come at them, one at a time like, and Dave tells them what to do and then it all goes into slow motion.'

'Surely it must get quicker as they get used to it?'

'Not really. They don't want to hurt me, y'see. And they have to do it slowly to make sure they get the sequence right. It's very important, that, the order you do things. Like right or left hand. Which fingers they jab into your nostrils. Right or left knee in the groin.'

'They knee you in the groin?'

'Very gently. So far. Drives Dave wild.'

'But what do you learn in all this?'

'Not a lot. I try to remember what they're supposed to be doing so's I could do it myself if the need arose. And sometimes I get to throw Dave about, but he doesn't really like it.'

'Doesn't like being hurt?'

'Oh, he doesn't mind being hurt. He's very tough, all muscle. He's always trying to get the women to hurt him, but they won't. No, he doesn't like being beaten. So if I do force him to the ground, first he doesn't go easy, then he'll do a back flip to show I'm not really forcing him at all. Does nothing for my confidence, that.'

I promised that if I had to put my fingers in his nostrils or knee him in the groin, I would try to strike a balance between gentleness and aggression, and hoped he would do the same for me. Then the rest of the class arrived with Dave, who surveyed his kingdom like a stag, head up, sniffing the air, and welcomed me to the class.

I looked at my classmates. I had been told at the FE College that there had to be ten or the class did not cover its overheads. Perhaps there had been ten for the first lesson. There were now five women and Les. Sue and Sandra, Nicola and Rachel, and Mrs Placket.

Dave started a warm-up and we jogged round the room, first one way, then another. Mrs Placket dropped out for a while to get her breath, and remained out for the rest of the two hours, watching from the side. I had been wrong. There was no demand among the pensioners of the agricultural Midlands for evening classes in self-defence. Those who live in fear of muggers and rapists deal with their fear by not going out at night.

Three of Dave's former students had been written up in the local paper for fighting off attackers. 'They had the element of surprise going for them: that's important. Most of these attackers, they don't expect confrontation. Show a bit of fight and they run away.' Sue and Sandra, Nicola and Rachel, even Les, we didn't believe it.

'Most' is not 'all'. What about those attackers who prefer a bit of fighting back, find it a sauce to appetite? But we did not speak our thoughts.

'Trouble with you ladies, you think you're weak.' The women nodded. 'Don't know your own capacities. A lady's handbag is full of bits and pieces, mostly weapons if you think of

'Most of these attackers, they don't expect confrontation. Show a bit of fight and they run away.' We didn't believe it

it. Nicola, what do you carry in your handbag when you go out?' He was in full flood and did not wait for her to answer. 'Nail scissors.'

My mouth opened. No woman I know carries nail scissors in her handbag. But the first rule of research is not to contradict. My mouth closed. Dave said, 'You don't need a CS canister if you've got a bottle of hairspray. Aim for the eyes.' Hairspray! Was Dave married? (Yes, I discovered later. He had a wife and two daughters but did not root about in their handbags.) 'Even a Biro, it's got a sharp end. I know one lady let a man into the house and he turned nasty. She took a Biro from the sideboard and jabbed the point into the side of his neck. Went in two inches. You've got to become wild animals if necessary.'

But we were not wild animals. Even Les was not.

The class developed into a series of exercises, each with its ordained sequence of action and reaction. It was what I imagined choreography to be like – movements to be learned by heart and performed meticulously on cue – but they all seemed to involve two people, and could one rely on one's attacker to know his part? 'Let your body-weight do the work. Offer him your weak side. He grabs it – grab her arm, Les – then you can use your strong side. Now, there's a nerve on the inside of that leg, exquisitely painful if you can find it with a well-placed heel

R.G

or toe. Don't *look* where you're about to kick, Rachel. Never look. First because it takes time and second because it tells him what you're going to do.'

Rachel looked away from the direction she was about to kick and missed Les's leg altogether, to his relief. 'We'll assume the kick, Rachel. We'll do it again in a minute and get it right. Now sweep his feet from under him.' With some co-operation from Les, Rachel swept his feet from under him and he fell slowly, like an ancient building toppling after detonation. She stood above him, having already forgotten what she was meant to do next. 'Get your full weight on his arm once he's down.' She knelt gingerly on Les's arm. 'Your *full* weight, Rachel.' Her knees were bony. I could see that Les was actually being hurt, but Dave didn't seem to notice. 'Now order him to look the other way.' Les, trying to quicken the process, was already looking the other way. 'That's how you exert mastery. Tell him what you want him to do and see that he does it. Then jump away and run like hell.'

Rachel jumped away and ran to the other side of the sports hall. Sandra said, 'Run like hell. I can remember that bit.' Les got to his feet and rubbed his arm.

It was all like that. Dave knew nerves in almost every part of an attacker's body which could cause pain if correctly jabbed. We offered our weak sides; we countered with our strong sides. We went through the motion of kneeing, the motion of kicking, the motion of sticking outstretched fingers into nostrils. Dave paid particular attention to me because I had missed a couple of

weeks. 'That's right, John,' he said. 'Fold his arm back. Starts like a handshake. Right! Further! Dislocate his shoulder.' Les looked into my eyes, imploring me not to dislocate his shoulder. 'You should be able to rip that arm off. Hopefully.'

The theory seemed to be that all this knowledge would come back to us in an emergency; it would become instinctive. Even in Mrs Placket, watching from the side of the room, this instinct would somehow be implanted. I did not believe it. I did not believe that, even if we could learn the choreography, what Les called 'the sequence', so that the moves flowed easily one from the other, attacker and counter-attacker becoming partners in a dance, that this would work in reality either. The desire to hurt had to be there and was not. Not in Sandra, or Les… not even in me.

At the end of the two-hour class each of us took a turn at standing in the middle while the rest came running from the edge of the mats, one after the other in varied ways of attack. It should have been a clip from a James Bond movie, a saloon fight in a cowboy movie; it should have been like Chinese acrobats. It was none of these. It was a shambles of stop-and-start. So it went. Wednesday followed Wednesday. We lost Mrs Placket, lost Sandra and Sue; even Les dropped away. At the end only Rachel and I were left. Dave was not defeated. 'We'll carry on,' he said. 'I owe it to myself, I owe it to you. I won't say you've improved, because you haven't, but you've stuck it out. So get into opposite corners of the room, if you please, and try to come at each other like tigers.'

What do a bottom-spanking colonel, a businessman accused of murdering his third wife and a 'mad genius' art forger have in common? They all achieved their peculiar brand of notoriety as a result of placing or answering an advertisement in *Private Eye* magazine. Like characters from a Ruth Rendell novel, their misdemeanours spanning almost 30 years are inextricably linked.

In 1972 London solicitor, ex-mayor and hunting squire Lieutenant-Colonel John Elliott Brooks, 64, placed an advertisement in *Private Eye* asking for 'good-natured young ladies' to crew his motor yacht on the Thames. Miss Sue Carr, a 19-year-old student, answered. During her interview, the Colonel gave her an enormous measure of gin and Campari ('It is not my practice to offer small drinks') and told her she could either earn £5 for domestic duties, which included leaping on and off the boat with ropes at the locks, or £15 if she would allow him to spank

> GOOD NATURED young ladies required as crew for Motor Yacht on Thames. Week-ends Easter to October. All found + good pay. No technical knowledge required. Phone 262 0591 mornings or BOX NO 563.

her. Sue Carr opted for the spanking. She later sold her story to the *Sunday People*, alleging that he had forced her to undress in his cabin cruiser before beating her bottom severely. The Colonel sued the paper for libel, protesting that he only ever spanked women with their consent and was not 'a menace to young girls' as the paper had suggested.

During the trial, he cheerfully admitted spanking Sue Carr's naked bottom 30 times, but denied ever beating her. He was even more affronted that the article had got his weight wrong. 'I am not 17 stone, but in fact 14-and-a-half stone. If I had beaten her she would have felt more than, as she herself says, "a little sore".' After the spanking session, the Colonel thoughtfully poured whisky over her bottom – 'It takes away the sting, you know' – before whisking her off to London in his Rolls-Royce. On the way, Sue Carr told the chauffeur to stop so that she could watch a wedding. That pleasant little interlude

Small ad, not many dead

People answering Private Eye's *personal advertisements have done so at their peril, reveals* **Alice Pitman**

The small ad that started it all

Bottom People read The Eye!

Large Scotch on the bum

Drinks on the arse

Cheeky!

over, she and the Colonel repaired to the King's Head at Shepperton for drinks, where they chatted away merrily.

The Colonel agreed that he got enormous pleasure out of spanking. He had spanked his way through half a dozen girls' bottoms at his London flat, another half a dozen on his boat, and 'one or two after hunting'. Spanking, he said, was rather like walking on a pebbly beach: 'It's painful at first, but pleasurable when you get used to it.'

Summing up on behalf of the Colonel, Roger Gray QC suggested that 'every full-blooded, healthy, normal, vigorous male is a bottom-slapper in mind if not in deed', adding that his client 'did something which will horrify Scotsmen – he poured whisky over her'.

He eventually won his case, and was awarded damages of a halfpenny. The unrepentant Colonel – an ex-Japanese prisoner of war – said: 'In order to prove the truth, one sometimes has to go into battle. In the war, the generals didn't count the cost when they had to fight for what was right.'

Spike Milligan once placed an advertisement in the *Eye* which read: 'Spike Milligan seeks rich, well insured widow. Intention: murder.' (He got 12 replies.) It would have seemed bizarre for anything as macabre to happen in real life, but in 1996 Kevin Sweeney, a 45-year-

> **BASED MANCHESTER**, male, slim, 30 years, looking for solvent lady for fun days, nights ..... Box 4640
>
> **INCOMPLETE SINGLE** Dad, widower with two splendid young children, seeks Single Mum (with young children) for friendship, mutual support and perhaps a chance to recapture a complete loving family. I am a British businessman living in Brussels (also a home in the UK), educated, cosmopolitan, confident, solvent, cheerful, witty, tender and fantastic with kids — and mums. Box 4740.
>
> **CAPTIVATING** green-eyed brun..e, 31, seeks amusing and erudite male Valentine. Box 4840.

old British businessman, was tried for the murder of his third wife, 32-year-old Suzanne Davies, whom he had met through 'Eye Love'. Sweeney's wording was a little more subtle: 'Incomplete single dad with

two splendid young children… seeks single mum… I am a British businessman living in Brussels, educated, cosmopolitan, witty, tender and fantastic with kids and mums.'

Intrigued divorcee Suzanne Davies responded straight away. Within weeks, she had left her job as a sales director, moved to Belgium with her young daughter and married Sweeney.

Nine months later, she was lying dead in a house fire. Although it was a hot night, all the windows and doors were closed and traces of white spirit and inflammable liquid were found on the carpet. The additional fact that her husband stood to receive around £300,000 as a result of her death made the police suspicious.

During the investigation, it transpired that Suzanne was not the only wife of Sweeney's to die unexpectedly: 33-year-old Beverly Flint, his second wife and mother to his two young daughters, died suddenly in 1993. She dropped dead while feeding her two startled Siamese cats, just

137

two days after being given a clean bill of health by her GP.

Beverly Flint was cremated without a post-mortem and Sweeney later received $500,000 in insurance money. Within 24 hours of her death, he gave away all her clothes, telling friends: 'These will make the best-dressed Bosnians you are ever likely to see.' He later refused to attend her funeral. Nor was he at the funeral of wife No. 3. He was eventually tried for the murder of Suzanne Davies in the Netherlands in 1996, but – despite the judge's assertion that her death was 'highly suspicious' – got off due to lack of evidence.

Sweeney was said to have had a number of odd fixations. He insisted all his wives and lovers wore Nina Ricci perfume; he was obsessive about hygiene and always wore zip-up black boots, perhaps to match his black driving gloves, which he also wore whenever possible. He had up to 12 different identities, once styling himself Kevin Alexander Edouard Oban d'Xivry Sweeney, the Paris-born son of a French countess and British university lecturer. In reality, he was plain Kevin Sweeney from Bishop's Stortford. He ran several dubious companies which sold business information, and in March 1990 *What to Buy for Business* magazine condemned his reports as 'page after page of old cobblers'.

Zip-up boots and driving gloves apart, Sweeney seemed strangely irresistible to women. Three weeks after the death of

Beverly Flint, he hired an Australian nanny, 23-year-old Christine Rowley.

She arrived on the Friday; by Sunday she was in bed with him (doubtless reeking of Nina Ricci perfume) and on Monday he proposed to her. Rowley was suitably elated. However, her delight rapidly turned to astonishment when only six months later a sombre-faced Sweeney, air ticket poised in black glove, calmly informed her that the engagement was off and that she was to fly back to Australia immediately. When she asked him why, he told her he had a brain tumour and was about to die.

Eighteen months later, the police tracked her down and told her Sweeney had been charged with the murder of his third wife. Christine Rowley was amazed to discover that he was not dead himself.

His first wife, Lis Larsen, appears to have been the only wife to have escaped the curse of Sweeney. She remains one of his closest friends, describing him as 'a good man' and 'a good father'. A chilling echo of the words in his original *Private Eye* advertisement.

The small ad tucked away in the 2 May 1986 edition of *Private Eye* read simply: 'Genuine fakes – commission your own renaissance impressionist modern painting from £120. Phone…' Little did impoverished artist John Myatt realise that his ploy to earn himself a bit of cash would spark the biggest contemporary art fraud of the century.

When unscrupulous but brilliant conman John Drewe scanned the back pages of *Private Eye* that month, his eyes must have lit up when they fell upon Myatt's advert. Drewe contacted him and told him he wanted a modern master pastiche (they were easier to fake than the old masters). It

'Mad genius' art faker John Myatt ended up in jail for forgery after falling victim to a conman

seemed a reasonable request and Myatt was happy to oblige, thinking Drewe wanted something to hang on his wall. By the time he learnt the truth – that Drewe was using his paintings to hoodwink top galleries (notably the Tate), leading auction houses, eminent experts and private buyers – Myatt was too deeply involved to be able to stop. Drewe continually encouraged his accomplice to 'practise and perfect the style of famous artists' while he concentrated on producing highly plausible false documents to add authority to the forgeries.

For ten years, Myatt beavered away in his attic, churning out one master after another. He perfected the fakes with a combination of lubricating jelly, household emulsion, hoover dust and a little sprinkling of garden mud. Together the dynamic duo flooded an unsuspecting market with up to 200 fake modern masters, satisfying John Drewe's quest for intellectual superiority as well as his greed.

Drewe became a lavish-living millionaire, while Myatt received a more modest £100,000 (£250 per painting). When Myatt – who was getting cold feet – meekly suggested that it might not be such a bad idea if they called it a day, Drewe got into a rage and threatened him with a gun.

However, it was an ex-lover of Drewe's who was to finally end the pair's decade-long partnership. Following an acrimonious parting from Drewe, she rifled through one of his properties, where she found a host of incriminating documents. She informed the police, and the two men were eventually arrested. Sixty fakes were recovered, leaving up to 140 still undetected. At their trial, a 'deeply ashamed' John Myatt turned Queen's evidence. Cross-examined in court by John Drewe – who led his own defence – Myatt said: 'I was very much your creature. I found you hypnotising, charming, challenging.'

Myatt, 53, was sentenced to 12 months' imprisonment in February this year, while an unrepentant Drewe, 50, who always maintained he was the victim of a stitch-up, was jailed for six years.

Celia Boggis, doyenne of the advertising department at *Private Eye*, is not surprised when Eye small ads such as these lead to highly publicised court cases. 'I expect it, and I'd be very disappointed if they didn't.'

Danny Kaye

IT WAS IN 1955 or 1956, in Nigeria. Unicef, the children's agency which had been set up after the war, was planning to make a film to draw attention to the plight of sick children in Africa, and had brought in Danny Kaye to take part. Presumably Nigeria was chosen because amenities such as hotels and phones were available, yet Africa in the raw was easily accessible. I was on the staff of the World Health Organisation in Kano, which was to be the film-maker's first stop, and was asked to liaise with the local authorities.

An ancient walled city, Kano lies not in the tropical south of the country but almost on the edge of the Sahara, and is a thoroughly Muslim town. I remember it as a spread of small, white-washed, one-storey houses thickly scattered along a confusion of narrow dirt lanes, with the twin minarets of the mosque towering over all.

I don't suppose that the Kano scene, though picturesque enough, was what the director had in mind for a film about suffering African children. The local medical people dearly wanted to oblige, but they had little to suggest except their hospital. They were proud of it and only too keen to show it off. The matron was particularly proud of the nurses. They were missionary-educated girls from the south, Christians, capable and dedicated, and with a cheerfulness that enabled them to survive in this alien, anti-female society.

It's unlikely that any of them had even heard of Danny Kaye, let alone seen him on film, but everybody agreed that they deserved the reward of seeing the great film star, perhaps even of appearing in a film. It was suggested that the film team, and Danny, might first visit the local hospital and take a look in the children's ward. It was not a filming session, just a preliminary look round to get the feel of things.

The ward had been tidied up, the grannies who usually slept on the floor under the beds had been shooed out, and the nurses were all lined up in their best uniforms, their shining black faces wreathed in shy grins. The long rows of beds and cots were full of sick children, many of them very ill indeed. Everyone knew that a VIP was going to visit the ward and there was an air of silent expectancy. Even the babies stopped crying, for once.

On or off screen, Danny Kaye believed that his mission in life was to make children laugh and, as an old trouper, was determined to make his entrance as dramatic as possible. The doors were flung open and he pranced in, waving his hands, 'Da-de-da, da-de-da', a big smile on his face, an overgrown Pan or Puck. The words faltered, half-out of his mouth, as he took in the scene and realised that his levity was not really appropriate. Trying hard to smile, he looked around. Sitting up in the bed at his side was a little girl, perhaps three or four years old, wondering what was going on. Slowly she turned and looked up at him with big sad eyes. One side of her face was perfectly normal, even pretty, but on the other side, where her cheek had been, was a dark, cavernous hole. The lips had gone and a string of glistening white teeth stretched conspicuously across the black hole that was her mouth, surrounded by ulcerous, rotting flesh. Known as *gangosa* or *chancrum oris*, her condition was common in those days and perhaps is still, where malnutrition and neglect prevail. It was a disturbing enough sight for anyone.

Danny Kaye froze in his tracks, the words jammed in his mouth as he tried hard to retain his agonised grin. His complexion went white, then green. He slumped and turned, gasping for support. 'My God! Take me out of here!' We complied. That was the last I saw of Danny Kaye. I don't know whether they ever made the film.

Bill Norman-Taylor

139

I'm dying, but what the hell

Caroline Richmond *wishes people would stop pretending death doesn't exist*

In the old days it was still possible to have a good death. You know the sort of thing – a heart attack or a sudden stroke, 'the apoplexy' while walking home from the pub. Failing that, there's the good-death-in-bed scenario: family gathered, a bottle of port, will sorted out, the doctor administering cheer all round. A touch of pneumonia usually put the finishing touches. Three days earlier, the deceased had been out hunting.

Nowadays 65 per cent of us die in hospital, 10 per cent in public places, on the street or in hospices, and only 25 per cent at home. Of the home deaths, over half will be sudden. Most of us will end up in a hospital ward, quite the most unsuitable place – not to mention the expense, much of which is avoidable. We will suffer loneliness without privacy, surrounded by ill strangers but separated from families and friends. Even when the curtains are drawn, our conversations and medical consultations can be overheard by the strangers in adjoining beds. Other people will make the rules about what and when to eat, and who shall visit. We won't be able to offer hospitality to visitors, share food or drink with them, live according to our own timetable. We will lie in sheets and perhaps even night-clothes that aren't our own. Simple medicines, such as aspirin, indigestion mixtures and laxatives, may be forbidden or, if prescribed by a doctor, you may have to go without them until the nurses do the next drug round.

My friend Fay is in hospital in Portsmouth, having had a stroke while visiting relatives. She was disabled by her first stroke ten years ago, and now she cannot speak. She has tubing going into her nose and arm, and a few days ago she was given four pints of blood because of internal bleeding. I don't know if she can hear, but sometimes she opens her eyes when people speak to her. I wish she had been allowed to die happily, graciously and in familiar surroundings. My widowed father died in hospital while being coerced into drinking lemon squash, something he would never normally have touched, from a spill-proof plastic baby cup. When I brought him a gin and tonic, the nurses were so fussy that he gave up drinking it. I later learnt that the doctor had restricted visiting to family only, so he was denied the company of his cronies and his girlfriend. I wish I'd taken the old boy back to the small hotel

Caroline Richmond: friends will rally round

where he lived. He didn't need much in the way of nursing, and he could have had all the G&Ts and visitors he wanted.

I have promised an oldie neighbour that if he collapses, I won't call an ambulance. I'll put him to bed and call his family and the doctor. But dying, and talking about death, is made difficult as the D-word is almost taboo. People talk of 'if anything happens to me...' as if they are probably immortal but must make contingency plans in case they are not. Talking of death becomes even more taboo on the deathbed, forcing the dying and the soon-to-be-bereaved into ludicrous mutual deceit.

I've felt this way about death for a long time, before I got my own calling card from the Grim Reaper. A couple of years ago a lump in my cheek turned out to be an immune-system cancer called a lymphoma (does this make me a lymphomaniac?). A quick visit to the library told me that low-grade non-Hodgkin's lymphoma is incurable, but that the survival period is five to ten years. I just have to accept it. I'm not brave about it. It would probably be fun to stay longer, but there again it might not be. The party might be very pooped by the time the stagecoach comes for me. But I find that people get embarrassed about my cancer, either suggesting that a cure might be found in time (unlikely) or that we might all be run over by a bus in five years' time (more unlikely).

I'll resist any attempts to coerce me into hospital when the Reaper gets close. I'll make a will, arrange my funeral (I'll have the 'Ying Tong Song', please, while they slide my cardboard coffin into the family plot in Highgate cemetery). I want such a bloody good wake that I'm feeling piqued not to be present. In my dying days I intend having friends around my bed and staying in the house – if they can stand the idea – bringing me good food and drink. If needs be, the NHS is rather good at arranging nursing round the clock. The absence of hospital facilities will, I hope, prevent my life from being dragged out for a few more days by expensive horrors such as tube-feeding and intensive care.

I will have my favourite books by my side, including Don Marquis's *Archy and Mehitabel*. As Mehitabel would have said, 'What the hell, Archy, what the hell.' And as Ambrose Bierce remarked, 'We all fear death, but once we're dead we don't mind.'

Not so golden rule days

A Montreal education, by **Mordecai Richler**

In high school, we were introduced to poetry as a punishment. Caught swearing, we were obliged to memorise 12 lines of Tennyson. Failing to deliver a composition on time (' "A thing of beauty is a joy forever": Explain'), we were ordered to memorise 15 lines of Scott. Nineteen forty-four that was, and after all these years fragments are still lodged in my head:

The stag at eve had drunk its fill,
As danced the moon on Monan's Rill.
In tenth grade, we finally connected with an admirable Scottish class master who was a passionate poetry lover. A veteran of the Great War, Mr McLetchie told us that when he was confined to a rat-infested trench during the nightly bombardments on the Somme, he fixed a candle to his steel helmet, which enabled him to read Milton, Donne, Marvell, Blake. Marvell, it seemed to me, was just the ticket when I tried to get under Molly Herscovitch's cashmere sweater late one night on a park bench. 'The grave's a fine and private place,' I recited, 'But none, I think, do there embrace.'

Slapping my hand away, she squealed, 'Cut it out.'

The only Blake we knew at the time was Hector 'Toe' Blake, who skated on the fabled Montreal Canadiens Punch Line with Elmer Lach and Maurice 'The Rocket' Richard. So we were not impressed with Mr McLetchie. No wonder, said Bercovitch – who would go on to found Regal Ready-to-Wear and turn up at our 1988 class reunion in a Rolls Royce, his name homogenised to Burke – that McLetchie ended up no better than a high school teacher, driving an ancient Austin.

In our defence, however shaky, I must protest that our poetry reader was a non-starter. We were not yet ready for the pretty stanzas of Keats, Shelley and Wordsworth. I mean 'A host, of golden daffodils'? Forget it. We dismissed such lines as sissy stuff, remote from the experience of our own city streets, where Greenbaum, of Herky's Best Fruit, suffered from a heavy thumb, and gave only 14 ounces to the pound. What we needed as an introduction to the canon was an anthology that featured poets who addressed us directly in our own idiom: say, W H Auden or e e cummings.

My education, such as it was, began in a Jewish parochial school, the Talmud Torah. Striving mothers registered us for kindergarten when we were still under age.

'Birth certificate, please?'

'Lost in a fire.'

'You too?'

'He's short for his age. Do me something.'

As far as our mothers were concerned, we were already in pre-med school. However, just in case we failed to get the point, we were force-fed Paul de Kruif's *Microbe Hunters* and were summoned in from games of run-sheep-run, or tic-tac-toe, to dig into *The Books of Knowledge*.

At the Talmud Torah, we breezed through the English-language curriculum required by the Montreal Protestant School Board in the mornings and concentrated on Hebrew studies in the afternoons. The Pentateuch: '*Braishis boroh elohim ha'sho-mayim ve ha'eretz*'. Years later I dined out on that in the homes of Gentile friends. 'You ought to read the original,' I'd say.

The war in Europe intruded, inadvertently leading me into a taste for what was scorned as 'classical' music. When I was an ignorant 12-year-old, back in 1943, wartime propaganda radio broadcasts were unfailingly preceded by four emphatic musical notes. These notes replicated the Morse code's three dots and a dash for the letter 'V', and were conscripted as a symbol for 'V for Victory', the slogan we lived with in those troubled days. 'Who wrote that?' I asked an aunt, whose literacy was certified by her membership in The Literary Guild. 'Beethoven,' she said. Such was my introduction to genius. For, of course, those were the rousing opening notes to Beethoven's Fifth Symphony, which my aunt was good enough to play for me on scratchy 78 records. So, at a tender age, I learned there was more to music than 'Gertie From Bizerte' and 'Bésame Mucho', two of 1943's hit parade ditties. Beethoven was nifty, I conceded at the time, but you couldn't dance close to his stuff with Bessie Goldfarb in her family's furnished basement when her parents were out for the evening.

The Hebrew teachers who instructed us in the Old Testament were a sour lot. 'Obviously,' I said, 'Adam and Eve's sons had to marry their sisters. Was that allowed in those days?' 'Idiot. Big mouth. You will stay in for an hour after school and wash the blackboards in every classroom.' Twice a week, after school, I was obliged to attend Talmud classes with Mr Yalofsky in a stuffy back room of the Young Israel synagogue. If a man tumbles off the roof of a five-storey building, Mr Yalofsky intoned, and two storeys down another man sticks a sword out of the window and stabs him, is the second man guilty of murder or not? Rabbi Menasha asks, Was the man already dead of heart failure before he was stabbed? Rabbi Yehuda asks, Did he fall or was he pushed off the roof? Were the two men related? Enemies? Friends? Was the sword already sticking out of the window or was it thrust into the falling body? Would the man have died from the fall in any event?

Saturdays we used to wander downtown, puffing on Turret cigarettes, then on sale in packs of five for five cents, and whistling at girls older than us, unavailingly. Our destination was Eaton's department store, our mission to shoplift. Assembling again on Fletcher's Field, we would compare our booty and trade. Once I came away with one of the first of the Pocket Books, which I acquired in exchange for a pair of socks: *The Good Earth*, by Pearl S Buck. I started to read. Going on from there to the Perry Mason books, *The Three Musketeers*, *The Count of*

Monte Cristo, some G A Henty and Kipling. This led me into my first attempt at a short story, set in London clubland. Sir Marmaduke Tingley-Winterbot-tom, remembering to pass the port to the left, says to Lord Beauchamp, pronounced Beecham, 'I say, did I ever tell you about the time our thin red line confronted the Fuzzy Wuzzies on the African plain…'

From the Talmud Torah, I graduated to a high school that was a legend in our neighbourhood: Baron Byng High School on St Urbain Street. Under the aegis of the Protestant School Board, its student body was, nevertheless, about 99 per cent Jewish. We were the progeny of taxi-drivers, clothing factory cutters, junk dealers, peddlers and sewing-machine operators, enjoined to do better *or else*, and so we did. Baron Byng had already churned out more doctors and lawyers than I could count, a few rabbis, as well as a notorious stock swindler and a couple of writers. Assembled in the gym on our first day at school, we were forewarned that if we intended to go on to McGill, we would, because of the Jewish quota, have to earn a 75 per cent mark in our matriculation exams. Our mechanical drawing master, a dour Swede who couldn't hack it as an architect, stepped up to the backboard on our first day in his class and said, 'I'll show you how the Jews make an "S".' He drew an 'S', paused, smirked, and then ran two slashes through it, making a dollar sign.

Sex had begun to drive us crazy. The boys were taught on one side of the school building and the girls, who had to wear black tunics, on the other. Dashing Gordy Birenbaum, sporting a brilliantined pompadour and a multi-crested sharkskin windbreaker, claimed to have gone the limit with Birdy Hoffer, who was to die for. Not only that, he boasted, 'But, you know, like she admitted to me that she masturbates once a week after *Lux Radio Theatre*.' Especially if it featured Ronald Colman or Tyrone Power. Me, I wasn't born yesterday. 'How could she?' I protested. 'She's a girl, for Christ's sake.'

Each of our schoolmasters was honoured with a Yiddish nickname. Yossel, who taught us physics, was

deaf and wore a many-dialled apparatus on his chest the size of a chocolate box. We would speak softer and softer in class, ultimately simply moving our lips, obliging him to adjust his dials higher and higher, and then we would all shout out at once, forcing Yossel to flee the physics lab, his hands cupped to his throbbing ears. I earned my epaulettes by being strapped for insolence more than once, rubbing my palms with candle wax first, the traditional precaution before my appointment in the medical room. The first time I was dealt 'ten of the best' on each hand, I cried. 'I had hoped you'd take it like a man,' Mr Patterson said.

Trigonometry, a subject I abhorred, was the last class of the day on Tuesdays. I made a habit of fleeing the building before that class began, a ruse that enabled me to get to the Rachel Pool Room, claiming the prized first snooker table, before any of my chums turned up. Other afternoons, slouching home from school, I had to survive a gauntlet of temptations: the Rachel Pool Room, the Mount Royal Billiards Academy, the Laurier. I seldom made it.

A Christian mission to the Jews opened on Laurier. We enjoyed dropping in, chatting up the pale young missionary, assuring him we thought Jesus was one hell of a swell guy, misunderstood by our parents, and leaving with a stack of goodies.

'Run, run, as fast as you can, you can't catch me, I'm on performance-enhancing drugs.'

Unfortunately the New Testament had no trading value in our neighbourhood.

Our prose reader was not much better than our poetry book, most of its short stories set in unfamiliar England. I made another attempt at a short story, also set in clubland. Viscount Leatherbottom said to Sir Peregrine, 'I jolly well didn't believe in ghosts until, by happenstance, I spent a weekend at Lord Corby's country estate, where a beautiful virgin had been the victim of a murder most foul in my very boudoir. At the stroke of three am her spirit appeared to me, attired in the flimsiest of negligées, her breasts very, very nice…'

Our music master, a Welshman, also formed a school choir, and once a year he led us in a concert in the gym. An annual standard was 'British Grenadiers'.

Some talk of Alexander,
And some of Hercules;
Of Hector and Lysander,
And such great names as these!
But of all the world's great heroes
There's none that can compare,
With a row-row-row-row-row,
To the British Grenadier.

Fanning themselves with the programme in the overheated gym, our girdled mothers sat bolt upright, and our fathers, in their three-piece suits from A Gold & Sons, managed to stay awake. Beaming. Joy unconfined. Only once removed from the shtetls in the Pale of Settlement, terrified of rampaging Cossacks, they were thrilled that their children were acceptable enough to celebrate British Grenadiers.

My matriculation results went badly. Boning up on trig the night before the exam, I did manage a 35 per cent mark. Not bad, considering. But my total average was .645, not good enough to get me into McGill, even had I been born a Gentile. So I enrolled in Sir George Williams College, dropping out after two years to sail for Paris. One day a letter from Sir George Williams was forwarded to my Left Bank hotel. For a fee of $10 I was entitled to an Associate of Arts degree. I declined for fear that if I wrote 'AA' after my name, strangers would conclude I was a member of Alcoholics Anonymous.

Pictures of you

drawings by **Rick Tulka**

New York Sketchbook

After years of visiting the Impressionist wing of the Metropolitan Museum of Art, I tired of Renoir's saccharine subjects and Van Gogh's insanities. So I turned my attention to New York's 'connoisseurs of art'.

Armed with my pencil I would follow them around the galleries, peering at them as they peered at the paintings. It only took a few minutes to capture my prey.

They were always oblivious to my presence. The only other people who knew what I was up to were the museum guards. It brightened up their time in the museum almost as much as it brightened up mine.

Bleeped out

It was her big moment – but **Zenga Longmore** could only watch helpless
opportunity went down the Tube

as her star acting

Those of you who are suffering from over-stressful jobs will glean comfort from reading about my recent work experience. The job was an acting one, advertising a local paper, which I shall refer to as the Daily Bleep. At last! Fame, money, invitations to the Jerry Springer show (is it Jerry Springer who interviews pompous actors? Or is it Melvyn Bragg? I always confuse the two). Anyway, as it turned out, the advert was not to be filmed, but to be performed on the Tube train. The advertising company preened itself on having devised so innovative a coup. Has any other product been advertised live on the Tube before?

I was paired up with a fellow thespian by name of William, who was required to don a bowler hat and a pin-striped suit, and carry a quality newspaper under his arm. Our script went somewhat as follows:

William: (standing at the end of the carriage) Sorry to break the unwritten law of silence on the British Tube, but I just have to say that I have bought my newspaper in good faith, but it is not giving me the interesting news I want!

Me: (from the other end of the carriage, waving my newspaper) I have all the news I want in my paper, because I read the Daily Bleep!

The script then became rather technical, describing the latest political shenanigans, business news and travel updates overflowing in the Daily Bleep, but lacking in William's newspaper. The whole scene was to last but one stop. We were asked to work for seven hours, thus performing hundreds of scenes with which to thoroughly hammer the virtues of the Daily Bleep into the receptive heads of thousands of commuters. The rates of pay soared to the heights only advertising companies can scale, and we were assured of a full house and a captive audience. It was satisfying to know that, for the first time in my acting career, I would be able to complete a speech without anyone walking out in the middle. And if the train stopped in a tunnel, all the better; my performance would have a chance to be brilliantly embellished. The Daily Bleep could be extolled in loud, ringing tones, contrasting so well with the voice over the Tannoy, announcing that 'due to the umble jumble on the ungle, the train will not be moving until further notice'. I could imply that the Daily Bleep knew exactly when the train would move, and the precise time we were all to arrive home. The possibilities for stretching my acting skills were limited only by my imagination, and the length of each stop.

I was passionately looking forward to starring in my new career in advertising, and as William and I stepped onto the Tube for our first performance, I experienced that heady rush of adrenalin so familiar to all great divas. Sarah Bernhardt, I have been told, sensed a similar feeling each night before every performance of Hamlet.

The train rattled out of the station, and I sat, with quivering fingers gripping my Daily Bleep in delicious anticipation. William stood stock still, bowler-hatted and grim. Our audience consisted of three teenage punks with nuts and bolts through every spare inch of visible flesh, five American tourists, who instantly whipped out cameras and camcorders to point at William ('Holy Shamoley! A gen-u-ine Briddish guy in a bowler!'), and a dishevelled Eastern European man with a long-suffering expression. Not what you might call a full house, but for all I knew one of the Americans was an in-law of some great Hollywood mogul. Perhaps I was about to be discovered. I closed my eyes and waited for my partner's opening lines.

Two seconds later, a rich voice rose over the clanking din. 'Pleeease! I have wife and three children and no home! You must help! Just few coins!'

What on earth had happened? This must have been one of the worst fluffs in the history of Tube theatre!

Turning my head I saw that William was gazing speechlessly at the dishevelled man, who stood before the passengers waving his arms with far more charisma than any mere actor could summon. This man had star quality! 'Just give few pence.' The Americans tucked their cameras out of sight, and the punks stared at him in terror. Well, that put the kibosh on our opening night. Just as well the critics had stayed away.

The beggar got off at the next stop, and the train proceeded to rattle along. I took a deep breath. Now, at last, my big moment had arrived.

We boggled off into the tunnel. Silence,

147

except for a loud 'dig-a-de-dig' sound. I tried to catch William's eye, but he stubbornly refused to meet my gaze. We continued to travel in silence, me with my Daily Bleep loyally held aloft, and William with his bowler hat the object of veiled titters from the other passengers. After half an hour I subtly approached him and signalled to him to get off at the next station.

'William! What's wrong? Why aren't you speaking your lines?'

'Speaking my lines? How can I speak my lines with such an audience? Where's the tension? The drive? I can't possibly begin my speech in an artistic vacuum. When I get an audience with a fuller poetic awareness, then I shall begin my performance.'

'All right then, but we've already done one lap round the Circle Line, and we are being paid to advertise the Daily Bleep! And with better money than we'd get at the RSC, I might add!'

William gave me a withering look as if to say, 'Have you no soul?' and we climbed onto the next train.

The next lap around the Circle Line proved equally unfruitful. William gazed into space, lips pursed. Just as we pulled out of Liverpool Street for the third time, I became unbearably frustrated at having my big moment wrenched from my grasp, and boldly took matters into my own hands. The fact that I had a terrible feeling we were being tailed by one of the advertising executives who were paying us to advertise their product, had, of course, nothing to do with my next course of action. Shouting clearly above the train's clatter, I fed William his lines.

'What newspaper are you reading, my good man? I am sure it could not be nearly as interesting as the Daily Bleep! Do you have the latest political moves, transport news and fashion update like what the Daily Bleep has got?'

All eyes of the passengers fell upon me. All, that is, except William's, who stared into the middle distance, then turned his back in a marked manner. Sizzling with humiliation I picked up my Daily Bleep and continued to ride round and round the

'MIND THE GAP!' His big speech so cruelly interrupted, William threw his arms in the air

Circle Line until lunchtime.

'No! I just can't do it, the feel of the audience just isn't right,' lamented William over his tagliatelle and salad. 'When I was at the Half Moon Theatre in the Mile End Road, it was all so, so different. I was able to engage a dramatic essentialness with my public, but this! Impossible! Can't be done!'

'So you've chickened out completely?'

'Oh no! Of course I will perform, and when I do I shall give of my all, but only when the feel of the audience is right.'

After lunch, we boarded the next Farringdon-bound train with freshly fired verve and energy.

Just as we approached the Barbican, the train pulled to an inexplicable halt. William and I exchanged significant glances. The 'feel' of the audience was undoubtedly right. The carriage was filled with learned commuters frowning into airport novels. William cleared his throat, and miraculously his resonant tones filled the carriage, a voice to make the eyes of Laurence Olivier's drama coach moist with admiration.

'I have bought a newspaper, my good people!' he began. All eyes turned upon him. Enquiring eyes. Who is this charis-matic man in the bowler hat, the eyes asked, and what does he have to tell us?

'Within this newspaper, what do I find? Do I find informative news? Methinks not! I find –'

'MIND THE GAP!'

His big speech so cruelly interrupted, William threw his arms in the air, showering his audience with pages of that day's quality newspaper, and staggered blindly through the door of the train. His public carried on gaping at this lone figure on the platform until our train chugged eastwards. I bid him goodbye through the window with a feeble wave of my Daily Bleep.

The next day, we were supposed to collect our pay cheques. I did not turn up. After all, even actresses have a conscience, and mine would not allow me to accept money for merely sitting all day long on a Tube train, reading the Daily Bleep, even though advertising companies love nothing better than to throw as much money about as possible.

As for William, I am not sure whether he felt his non-performance was worth payment. When next I saw him, a few weeks later, he was on the other side of the footlights treading the boards in an Islington pub theatre. When I went backstage to congratulate him on a 'dramatically essential' performance, he pretended to have forgotten who I was.

'Pull over and let me drive - you're too drunk to hit anyone.'

Illustrated by John O'Connor

Berkshire flora

IN FARNBOROUGH village church there is a beautiful stained-glass window by John Piper in memory of his great friend, and my father, John Betjeman. To see it on a summer evening with the lowering sun shining through makes your spirits soar. In richest blues and greens, it is set with butterflies and flowers as the downs around once were. It is hard to find any unwrecked patches of wild flowers now. The agri-farming chemicals have drifted everywhere.

From the south door into the churchyard the view from this, the highest village in Berkshire, 720 feet up into the downs, falls away across undulating country in one breathtaking sweep to the blue distance of Watership Down above Highclere on the edge of Hampshire. I head out towards it. The hedges have long gone along the lane which leads down from Farnborough to the small farmhouse called California. There are prairie-like acres of cereals stretching away on either side. You notice every change of hedgerow and verge vegetation if you are walking, bicycling or, lazy like me, travelling in a horse-drawn cart. Here along the verge only the toughest weeds survive the sprays and seem to thrive on the fertiliser. The hogweed grows as tall as apple trees above the head-high legions of nettles,

and the tough old docks rocket up between. Sometimes there may be a patch of the wonderfully dull mugwort. The monotony, if you are travelling all day, is relentless. Perhaps the answer is to learn about the dock (Rumex) family – there are 20-odd kinds, after all. I could be differentiating between Sharp Dock, Red-veined, Fiddle, Curled or Broad-leaved.

Further on, past Brightwalton Church with its stained-glass window above the font by Ford Maddox Brown (which John Piper particularly loved), past the Wesleyan chapel converted into a home and the thatched cottage with imitation butterflies settled on its walls, past Oakash Farm, suddenly an island of well-husbanded shooting country begins. Towards Leckhampstead thicket hedges edge the road and shield you from the wind. Where there are gaps, new hedges have been planted and there are small woods on the sides of mild valleys, and here in the lee of a roadside spinney is a bank of the wild flowers which used to be everywhere: bladder campion, lady's bedstraw, knapweed, agrimony, rock roses, bird's-foot trefoil, lady's-slipper, scabious and St John's wort.

Then as suddenly as the vision of flowers appeared it ends and the sprayed wilderness

begins again after Nodmoor Corner. Near Court Oak Farm and the tunnel under the thundering M4 the verges are mown to earth revealing hundreds of old foil crisp packets tossed out of car windows months ago. There are lush gardens in brick-and-thatched Boxford and Hoe Benham and willowy meadows beside the Kennet on a beautiful little lane to Marsh Benham. Here the river, canal and railway run beside each other in the valley bottom and the long hill up passes the grandest gate piers in England leading to a long-lost great house at Hampstead Marshall. On the lane leading towards Holtwood there is normal-sized hogweed on the banks and cranesbill, rosebay willow herb, pearlwort, hedgewoundwort, woody nightshade and purple vetch and honeysuckle in the nut-filled hedges, and high oak trees and briony and white dog rose.

Beyond Burghclere, where the Primitive Methodist chapel is for sale, a sweet disorder begins again below the lines of Downs. Nettle-leaved bellflower spills out of coppiced woodland, and just before Echinswell there is a bank thick with pyramid orchids and dotted with the strange primaeval-looking broomrape. Like John Piper's window, the sight of it is enough to make the spirits soar.

J K Galbraith

William Keegan *caught up with the famous economist and former*

Presidential adviser at the Ritz Hotel in London

Professor Galbraith receiving his honorary degree at the London School of Economics in June this year

Many years ago, en route to economics at Cambridge, I was introduced to J K Galbraith's The Affluent Society. It was such a joy to read that one was rather misled about the ability of economists in general to express themselves in English.

The success of Galbraith's 30-odd books has caused a certain amount of envy in a profession best known these days for mathematical equations. Having admired Galbraith for many years, I finally made contact with him in the early 1980s, when the Observer asked him to take part in a debate, through our columns, with Milton Friedman about the then fashionable doctrine of monetarism.

The great man – Galbraith, that is – told us Friedman was unlikely to agree to a written debate, because the two were agreed that he was better in print and Friedman on his feet. But if we were to commission Galbraith to write a major article, and give Friedman the right to reply...

The episode increased my own personal debt to Galbraith. The article was a great success, and Friedman, while not writing specifically for the Observer, sent us an advance copy of evidence he had submitted to a Parliamentary Committee: it turned out to be a world scoop – the first time that Friedman, her hero, had criticised Mrs Thatcher's economic policies for being too strict on public sector borrowing.

Galbraith in turn claimed that his article, attacking the British economic policies of the time, which was syndicated around the world, had put him 'back on the map'. This was characteristically generous of him, but we did not believe it for a second. It is impossible to conceive of the six foot eight-and-a-half Galbraith ever having been off the map. But the result was that I got to know him a little, and often see him on his annual visits to England.

Not long ago his secretary rang to say that he would be over here to receive an honorary degree from the London School of Economics and deliver a public lecture there; would I telephone him at the Ritz on a certain Saturday morning?

The Ritz? Yes, Galbraith always stays at the Ritz. Years ago his friend John Strachey, who served very much on the left-hand side of Attlee's 1945–51 governments, told him it was ridiculous to stay in poky little hotels near the BBC. 'Men of the Left, men of your stature, should stay at the Ritz.'

Galbraith is 90, your correspondent a mere 60 or so. I was not sure whether this was to be a social call, but took my notebook just in case. Galbraith was waiting at the entrance, led me into the lobby for coffee, and proceeded to fire away. 'When you hear it being said that we've entered a new era of prosperity with prices of financial instruments reflecting that happy fact, you should take cover,' he drawled.

Alan Greenspan, the much

> **It is impossible to conceive of the six-foot eight-and-a-half Galbraith ever having been off the map**

ROBERT THOMPSON

fêted chairman of the US Federal Reserve? 'He's wonderfully avoided any action that might seem to make him responsible for a slump, but that does not rule out the possibility.'

The so-called 'new paradigm' that financial analysts talk so much about? 'In the late Twenties it was impossible to read any discussion of the economy without encountering the new paradigm, namely radio and electronic communications. One should
read about that before putting too much emphasis on the computer world as the new paradigm.'

A great professional, Galbraith knows exactly what economic journalists want for their columns. But on this trip he was also in reminiscent mood, brought on no doubt by publication in the United States of his latest book, Name-Dropping, From FDR On. At a lunch in his honour held by Lord Eatwell, President of Queen's College, Cambridge, a few days later, he recalled how East Coast liberals were desperate that the US should not disengage from Europe during the second world war. When Japan attacked Pearl Harbor in December 1941 there was widespread concern that this would affect the US commitment here. 'Then within hours came Hitler's declaration of war on the United States,' said Galbraith. 'It is impossible to describe our sense of relief.'

Galbraith was in Europe after the war, assessing the effectiveness of the Allied bombing campaign. He points out in his book how, at the interrogation of von

Ribbentrop, the former Nazi foreign minister was asked why Hitler had declared war on the United States. He replied that Germany had been bound by the terms of its treaty with Japan and Italy. At which point one of the translators could not resist asking, 'Why was that particular treaty the first one you decided to keep?' As Galbraith adds, 'No American ever solved so grave a problem for FDR as Hitler did in December 1941.'

Galbraith worked for and advised a

whole series of Democratic Presidents and candidates. When he was not in Washington, or on duty abroad, there was a constant stream of important visitors to his house in Cambridge, Mass. He recalled the other day that there were mixed views about the impact on the neighbourhood of the strict security the night that Henry Kissinger came to dinner when Secretary of State. This prompted someone to ask him why it was that, by contrast to Henry Kissinger's thick Middle-European accent, his younger brother spoke 'perfect American English'.

'The answer', said Galbraith, 'is that Henry never listens.'

Galbraith is one of the more famous Canadians, although, given his prominence in American public life (among other things he was Kennedy's ambassador to India), most people think of him as American. The subject of another prominent Canadian came up at the lunch: Conrad Black, and the question why some obscure law of the state of Ontario was being blamed for the delay in granting a peerage to the Telegraph's proprietor.

'Oh, I can help you there,' said Galbraith with a delighted chuckle. 'My father was responsible for the legislation.'

DUNGARDNIN

The many stages
of development

*A stint in local rep was **John Bowen**'s introduction to the trials and
tribulations of a life on the boards. Illustrations by **Peter Bailey***

Who now remembers weekly rep? Does it still exist? It used to be thought, at least by old-stagers, to be a better training for actors than any drama school. 'It's not to do with the fact that you've played Hamlet, Benedict and the Hunchback of Notre Dame, all before the age of 23,' the late Leonard Rossiter once told me. 'That teaches you how to paraphrase, I suppose, in a fairly elegant way, but mostly you've been playing leads in Dodie Smith. No, the real point is you're seasoned. Everything that can happen has happened. Doors won't open or the handles come off, flats tear or fall round your ears like a collar, traps stick or open when they shouldn't. Rain through the ceiling, mice in the piano. You dry or someone else does and you don't know which. Missed entrances ("If only little Kevin were here he'd tell us what to do," will buy time, but not much, and somehow you've got to stop the other bugger saying, "I'll go and find him," which would leave you alone on stage), drunks in the audience, heart attacks, fights, people in the last stages of tuberculosis, parties of ten who've come on the wrong night. It's all happened to you and you've survived. Does wonders for your confidence, and that's what it's all about. Confidence – you won't get that from Stanislavski.'

True words. Years later I was at a performance of Hamlet in Birmingham when Peter Howell as Polonius dried, of all unlikely places, in the middle of the 'Neither a borrower nor a lender be' speech. A moment of bewilderment, then, 'By the Mass, what was I about to say?'

The young Tyler Butterworth as Laertes gulped, and replied, 'I think, my Lord, it may have been about not getting into debt.'

'You're right. It was.' A moment's search for some way to complete the pentameter. 'Hardly a venial fault.' And they were back on track. None of the audience near me seemed to have noticed. Confidence.

Et in Arcadia ego. It was a long time ago. I was still an undergraduate, but already 25 years old: we were the post-war generation, determined to make our marks. I had done some university acting and made no mark whatever, but intended to turn professional. I answered an advertisement in *The Stage* for the Royal Players, who were to present a summer season in the Assembly Rooms at Barmouth on the Welsh coast. I was engaged at a wage of £6 a week.

I'm not sure what was royal about the Royal Players. Mr Brian Plunket Greene, who hired us, may have had royal connections, but I can't remember that we ever saw him at Barmouth. I can't even remember an interview, far less an audition: he may have engaged me by letter. We were cheap: that was the point. Two of us were middle-aged: a Character Gentleman, who was also the Director, and a Character Lady, who should have played all the mothers and marchionesses but turned out not to be able to remember her lines so that she was always given the smallest part in the play, irrespective of age. All the rest except myself had just graduated from the Webber

Rain came through the roof, flats fell on us, doors stuck, we forgot our lines and missed our entrances

Douglas Drama School.

The front of the programme read, 'For the Society for the Promotion of Drama in the Provinces', but none of us had ever heard of the Society: it may have been invented for the season. We did not attempt Shakespeare or Strindberg: our repertoire was what Mr Plunket Greene believed would appeal to holiday-makers on a wet night in North Wales (which most nights were): it included *George and Margaret* and *The Chiltern Hundreds*. Our one 'working-class' play was *Easy Money* by Arnold Ridley, author of *The Ghost Train* who was later to play Private Godfrey in *Dad's Army:* it was about winning the football pools. None of the plays required more than one set, and the bill changed mid-week so as to catch the tourists twice, but we were not rubbish; we played the full six days.

Four days a week, we rehearsed in the mornings, learned lines in the afternoons and performed in the evenings (tickets from Jose, the hairdresser in the High Street, next to the theatre). On Wednesday there was a matinée at 5.30, then the evening performance, then the cast dismantled the set, laid out the flats on the floor, repainted them so that the next night's audience would notice an immediate difference, and went back to their digs at 3 am to a cold collation, mostly Spam, left out by the landlady. By next morning the flats would be dry and could be reassembled in a different order. Doors which had been upstage were moved downstage, the French window shifted either left or right: there always was a French window, even in the pools play, since we had one and there would be a gap if it were not used. The new set would be up and refurbished with furniture and flow-

There always was a French window...

ers, ready for a dress rehearsal in the afternoon and for the First Night that evening.

I have to admit that there was a certain sameness about the flats, even repainted and repositioned. The real difference was made by the furniture, all of which had to be borrowed; we had none of our own. Since so many of our plays were set in the living-rooms of the upper or professional classes, most of the furniture came from a local antique dealer, a Mr Barton, a man of extraordinary kindness and tolerance with a genuine devotion to the theatre which I cannot believe we entirely satisfied. Every Thursday morning, once the set was up, last week's antiques, often scratched or even slightly chipped, lightly speckled with paint and marked with the rings made by mugs or glasses, were returned to his shop by barrow, and fresh furniture, shining with wax polish, would be borrowed to promote another week of drama in the provinces. Mr Barton's commitment was total. Sometimes he stood us cream teas at the Golden Lantern Café.

And the rain did come through the roof, flats fell on us, doors stuck, we forgot our lines and missed our entrances; it all happened to us too. What did I learn? That I could make an audience laugh by removing my shoes and socks and twiddling my toes. I forget why or in which play I had to take my socks off. The twiddling just seemed natural at the time, and I was astonished by the laughter, but it was not a discovery I have been able to put to much use since. And I discovered that I was not an actor. I moved like a camel and developed a habit of sucking air through my front teeth when under pressure, which I was for most of the time; it is a habit I still have.

The coup de grâce came from Mrs Wynn Parry, landlady to one of the cast, who gave us an end-of-season report. 'You're always well spoken, John,' she said to me, 'I'll grant you that, always the gentleman no matter what, and natural with it. But Winkie,' – Winkie was the pet-name of the young actress who usually played opposite me – 'when she's on that stage you can tell right off she's acting. Winkie's acting all the time, and that's what the people pay for.'

So I went back to Oxford and decided to become an academic. That didn't work out either.

Bottoms up!

Jonathan Routh's *piles operation was a right pain in the backside. Illustration by* **Larry**

They told me back in January in Jamaica what the matter was, why I had all this pain in my behind. But rather foolishly, and most painfully, I opted not to put myself at the mercy of the Jamaican hospital services – nothing wrong with the skills of their doctors or the good looks of their nurses, maybe some tiny reservations concerning availability of equipment – but to wait until I returned to Europe in June.

So, Italy, early June. Initial consultation and cursory examination by doctors at the hospital in Poggibonsi (Florence about 20 kilometres, us some 10), resulting in very immediate dates fixed for proper examination and operation 24 hours later.

To the hospital on the designated morning. The first hour filling in forms – father's middle names and all that sort of vitally pertinent information. Finally allotted a bed, Number 49 in a six-bed all-male ward.

My wife Shelagh, with her fluent Italian, helps subdue the curiosities of inmates 44 to 47 (no one in bed 48) as I get undressed, and then she goes off into the unknown to solicit another pillow (tasks the like of which I am unable to undertake with my 35-word Italian vocabulary).

Now before I can settle down with my new colleagues and determine what common friends and interests we might have, a nurse summons me to follow her to the Examination Room. Operating tables surrounded by electric cables, TV screens, two doctors, two nurses. I'm told to lie on the table on my back and then I hear the ominous words, 'Relax, this isn't going to hurt,' as they place some long tube up my bottom, which is, of course, my cue to tense up and make pathetic little noises.

On the TV screens in front of me and which the doctors are studying there now begins to appear a multitude of moving shapes and colours not unlike animated

Paul Klee or Schwitters paintings – the insides of that part of my body in which the doctors are interested and which is shown to them here care of the TV camera which is the long tube they've stuck up me. It goes on for at least ten minutes while the doctors study it and presumably draw up a plan of action for their attack on it the following day, and I meantime continue to provide my curiously morbid sound-track.

I feel really groggy when they turn off their screens and pull their camera out of me. So, back to my ward then. The old men are talking to each other very loudly from bed to bed, all except one who has a permanently open mouth out of which come – I'm sure unbeknownst to him – the sounds, 'Oy, oy.' Our next visitor is a well-dressed priest – surely not Last Rites already? No, thank goodness, just general greetings and the information that his name is St Agnese if we require his services. Then, after him, there comes to me, beckoning with one

hand, the other clutching numerous razors, this man – no medical costume – who gets right up to my chest before he takes my hand and tells me to follow him. Well, I suppose it's safe. He gets me into a room with the usual operating table in it, tells me to strip my lower half and get up on the table on all fours.

Oh God, what now? Quite simple, anyone else would understand, he wants to shave my bottom. The tricky part of the operation is when he wants me to change my position for some reason. I try to understand him, encourage him to use a more extensive vocabulary. Eventually he drops down to the ground and himself assumes the position he now wants me to adopt. At least, I assume that's what he's up to. But next, and this is really quite a little surprise, he clutches me by the balls – and starts shaving off the back of each, humming some gentle Italian air the while. Well, I have to hand it to him. It's a pretty difficult

155

thing to have to explain to anyone who speaks only a foreign language that you want to shave the back of their balls. Not the sort of Common Every-day Experience ('At Home', 'In the Street', 'At the Office') that gets into the phrasebooks. We part with my having more trust and understanding in him than I did at our initial encounter.

Back to the ward again. Shelagh is there to tell me that the old men have been discussing for the last half-hour how breast of wild pigeon should be properly cooked. For them, when dinner comes, there is Colourless Broth with Semolina. Lucky fellows, because for Routh, nothing – he's the first to be dealt with the following morning.

After this great feasting the room fills up with wives and womenfolk looking suspiciously at the empty semolina bowls, and another excitement for me when a nurse tells me to get up and follow her. What part of my anatomy is she allowed to shave or touch, I wonder. But it's nothing like that. She drops me off at the office of the anaesthetist. His first question certainly baffles me. Am I allergic to my dentist? Well, of course I am, I tell him. Everyone is allergic to their dentist. So, are they suddenly going to produce mine from Jamaica and ask him to do something on me? Take out some teeth while they're working on the other end of me? No, it's not that, they're just trying to find out whether there's any particular anaesthetic that they shouldn't use on me on the morrow. A jab in the gums for what they're planning to do to me elsewhere? Surely not? Not at all, in fact. The man placates me by telling me I'll be having an injection in the spine which will eliminate all feeling in the lower half of my body. Let's hope he's telling the truth.

The night is comparatively without incident. The 'Oy, oy' man reduces his output – but increases its volume – to some two every hour. Number 45 manages to find fault with the terrace doors being imperfectly shut and so every now and then gets up to bang them. And we still have no one in bed number 48 – it's obviously going to be ambulance men bringing in some headless victim of a motor accident at 3.30 am – but no, it isn't, bed number 48 is still empty when it turns light.

Still waiting for a late breakfast when they come in to wheel me away at 11.30. Transfer to the operating table in the operat-ing theatre. Nurse finds the right bit of backbone into which her injection can be put, then I just wait while the doctors busy themselves doing I don't know what. My legs have been strapped up to poles going ceilingwards and a great panorama of green sheets hung over them, so I still haven't got a clue what the doctors are doing. And no helpful TV screens this time. I'd have liked to know what a laser beam looked like, which is what I've been told they're using in lieu of any knives.

It's most curious – I was going to say 'a most curious feeling', but feeling is what there is none of. It's like having your legs set in concrete. You want to wiggle your toes, but because of the concrete you can't. And yet I can move my hand and feel something which must be a warm leg – mine – which cannot reciprocate, which has no idea a friendly hand is making overtures to it. (If there was a pill you could obtain which had the same numbing effect just think what you could do to guests at a dinner table.)

But how wonderful to be being operated on and not know a thing – at least I hope that's what they're doing down beyond the green sheets. No one pays any attention to me, leastwise not to my upper half, until, after I think not much more than an hour, the chief doctor appears and addresses me. 'Finito,' he says. 'Finito bene.'

How quite incredible. It takes another couple of hours, though – I'm back in my ward by then – before I can wiggle my toes again, before the numbness disappears. And what they haven't told me is that the lack of numbness is going to be accompanied by the most awful pain. I want to scream and am only constrained from doing so by the presence of Shelagh and my fellow warders. It's a far worse pain than that which, and because of which, I entered the hospital. I am wondering whether Shelagh shouldn't now be looking around for another group of doctors, perhaps in some other hospital, who could take away this pain. But are those doctors going to believe her when she explains it's because I no longer have any haemorrhoids? No, it's getting far too complicated. And anyway, very soon a doctor arrives to give me injections in my lower regions, and a nurse comes to put a drip in my arm. The pain lessens. But not all that much.

It's probably a little less on the following day, and a further little less on the day after that when they let me go home. Since when some 153 people have very sagely told me, 'But you can't expect it to completely vanish until 15 or so days after the op.' Oh no? Can't you? Can't I? I'm just waiting for the 15 days to be up before finishing this piece, just in case anything really new and upsetting happens.

Modern Life

What is...
A call centre?

DO YOU REMEMBER what it used to be like using a telephone – before answering machines and voice mail, before listening to hold music and 'press the star button twice' and banging your head against the receiver whimpering that you 'just want to talk to a human being?' You used to dial the number (say, your local bank), and a bank clerk would answer, and they would help you with your query and you would thank them and go away happy.

Well, businesses have finally cottoned on to the fact that things were, unsurprisingly, better in the good old days, when you got to talk to a real person and didn't have to listen to 40 minutes of 'Greensleeves' played on a stylophone. So if you call your local bank these days you do indeed get to speak to a real person almost immediately, and they are very polite. But something doesn't feel right. Perhaps it's because they ask, '*Who* are you calling?' Perhaps it's because they inform you, 'Your call may be monitored for staff training purposes.' Or perhaps it's the way that the simplest queries about opening hours are met by long pauses and the furious tapping of keys.

This is because you have not really called your local bank at all. You have dialled a Call Centre. You may have innocently rung the number for Bloggs Bank, 23 High Street, thinking you may get to speak to Mabel on the far counter who always asks after your dodgy elbow. But in fact your call has been rerouted to a massive tin shed on the outskirts of Glasgow to be answered first by a computer, then for-

warded to one of Bloggs's 600 'Customer Care Agents' who have been demographically selected for their pleasing telephone voices, who will communicate with you in line with approved protocol and will process your request in accordance with an hourly call quota. If you are phoning a non-specialist organisation (such as a credit card booking line) your call may even be answered by a 'freelance' call centre, whose operators will have no knowledge of what you are calling about, but whose computers will recognise the telephone number that you have dialled and supply the agent, via a computer screen, with the relevant questions to ask you.

Press 1 now if you feel dehumanised…

Call centres are the UK's largest growth industry, expanding at 40 per cent a year. By the year 2000 two per cent of the work-force will be sitting in vast shopping-mall-like offices and writing on their CVs that they work in 'Customer Processing Operations'. Most call centres are to be found around Glasgow (self-proclaimed 'Call Centre Capital'), due in no small part to the fact that the Scottish accent is deemed by the purveyors of psychobabble to convey just the right amount of friendliness, clarity and efficiency necessary for the most effective telephone transaction. (A mild Geordie accent is also seen as telephone-friendly, as is just a touch of

Brummie. If, however, you harbour ambitions to work in the call centre business and you speak with a pronounced Welsh or West Country accent, you would do well to seek the help of a good speech therapist…)

This creation of a whole new industry has arisen from the two chief aims of modern business. Firstly, the relentless pursuit of the holy grail of 'consumer choice' ('Anything you want, whenever you want it, from this limitless range of worthless shiny baubles') – you roll in drunk from the pub at midnight and see an ad on the telly for a holiday, a sofa, an all-in-one-body-toner-and-vegetable-slicer, and there is somebody on the end of a phone line waiting to take your credit card details.

Secondly, Call Centres have facilitated the replacement of expensive skilled staff with the worthless veneer of 'Customer Care', because thanks to the Call Centre it is now cheaper to fill tin sheds with thousands of unskilled workers (with nice accents) to read platitudes about how much 'your custom is valued' off a computer screen than to actually provide any genuine service.

I called the Call Centre Association to ask them to respond to the charge that Call Centres were set to become the sweat shops of the next Millenium, but my call was taken by an electronic woman who put me in a queuing system, so I hung up.

NICK PARKER

Miles Kington

The folk that lived on the hill

The main effect of the Hugh Grant film *Notting Hill*, as far as I can see, has been to give the green light to every journalist who ever lived in Notting Hill to jump into print with an article which remembers W11 their way, whether it was the hippy W11, or the black W11, or the Carnival W11, or the celebrity W11, or the media W11…Well, the way I remember W11 (yes, I lived there for 20-odd years, and this is my article on how I remember the old place) is as an odd transitional place between the boring respectable W11 of olden days and the boring trendy, glitzy Notting Hill of today. I first moved to Kensington Park Road (No 76) in the mid-Sixties, when the initial wave of hippiedom had already invaded but the old guard were still holding firm. I can well remember meeting old ladies who reminisced about World War Two in W11. 'There were barrage balloons moored in Ladbroke Square, you know…'

No, I didn't know, but I could well imagine. Ladbroke Square was and I hope still is the largest wooded private square in the whole of London, all six or seven acres of it, and there was a time when I knew every inch of every one of those blasted acres, as I was the assistant gardener in Ladbroke Square for several years and did more digging, raking, chopping, weeding and bonfire-making than I have in all my life since. I wasn't a vocational gardener. I was merely a freelance writer starving in a first-floor flat. So one day I went and asked if they needed any part-time help, and Mr Pyke, the permanent gardener, said he did, and Ladbroke Square Garden Committee hired me as a part-time underling, and I did three mornings a week for him for half a dozen years. David Pyke (though I only ever called him Mr Pyke) was about the squarest person I ever met, in the old sense of decent and honest. He was a north Norfolk man, who had learnt his trade in the old days of big country estates and large gardening staffs. He worked as a young man on several of them and gave the impression that he had started so long ago, they were still cutting the lawns with scythes. 'One thing – always clean spades and forks before you put them away,' he would say to me. 'You can't put a spade away dirty. My old head gardener taught me that. Indeed, he used to tell me to clean a spade every time I came off a flowerbed. The earth on the spade might contain little seeds which could spread where they weren't wanted. I've never forgotten that.'

And nor have I, and a fat lot of good it has done me. I can't remember much else that he taught me, except, oddly, that if you wanted really big onions you should dig in horse hoof clippings at the roots, which I have never had the chance to try out, but I can see now that the presence of Mr Pyke, a survivor from the grand old days of pre-war county aristocracy, may have coloured my view of Notting Hill.

But there really were genuine relics of those days. The ladies and gents who wandered round the Square by day, as I dug and raked, were mostly retired diplomats and army people – one splendid old man who often stopped to chat to me was called Sir Herbert Marchant, and was our retired ambassador to Cuba – and even Mr Pyke himself lived in a tiny cottage actually inside the square gardens, like a country mansion lost in a Brobdingnagian world.

And we had our celebrities knocking around Notting Hill even in those days. John Cleese came to live round the corner. Antonia Fraser was up the hill, and Patrick Lichfield somewhere beyond, and Michael Moorcock and Anthony Sampson were down the Grove and George Melly way down the other end – yes, real celebs, mates, not TV trash like nowadays. And just the other side of the fence from my digging was the residence of Roy Jenkins, with the Gambian Consulate next door. I mention that because when Jenkins was Home Secretary there were for a long while small angry crowds outside his house, chanting at him to release the Price Sisters (that season's Irish martyrs). Jenkins must have become impervious to it after a while, but when a new Gambian consul came to take up residence next door he heard the chanting outside and optimistically assumed it was a welcoming crowd for him, so he got dressed up in his full rig and took his family out on the balcony to take the salute, only to retire, mystified, under a volley of Irish oaths.

In fact, looking back, I viewed Notting Hill as a bit of history rather than as glittering modernity. This was partly because when you are a gardener you keep digging up the past. 'This might be a relic from the days of the racecourse,' said Mr Pyke, holding up some misshapen metal one day. And there had been a racecourse there, too, long before Notting Hill had had any houses. Where St John's Church now stands at the top point of Ladbroke Grove was the grandstand looking out over Notting Hill Hippodrome, designed to be the London replacement for Ascot or Epsom. It failed, partly because the going was too sticky and partly because the gypsies who lived in the potteries resented their right of way across the racecourse being taken away and kept taking the fences down.

The potteries… the gypsies… the race course…I didn't mean to talk about any of this. When I sat down to write about the unlikelihood of Hugh Grant meeting a world-famous actress in W11, I was actually going to tell you how, when I lived there, I really and truly met Julie Christie. Some other time, perhaps.

THE OLDIE EMPORIUM

...so how about subscribing then?

More of *The Oldie*'s wit and wisdom can be delivered to your door every month by becoming a subscriber. Please call our subscription department on **0171 734 3311**, or write to the following FREEPOST address for further details:

The Oldie

Freepost 39 (LON 5202)

London W1E 3HU

no stamp needed!